In Combat in Korea

In Combat in Korea
*Eighteen Veterans
Remember the War*

RYAN WALKOWSKI *and*
ED GRUBER

McFarland & Company, Inc., Publishers
Jefferson, North Carolina

Unless otherwise noted, all photographs were provided
by the interviewees and/or their families.

Library of Congress Cataloging-in-Publication Data

Names: Walkowski, Ryan, 1993– author | Gruber, Ed, 1928– author
Title: In combat in Korea : eighteen veterans remember the war / Ryan Walkowski and Ed Gruber.
Other titles: Eighteen veterans remember the war
Description: Jefferson, North Carolina : McFarland & Company, Inc., Publishers, 2026 | Includes index.
Identifiers: LCCN 2025039265 | ISBN 9781476698526 print ∞
ISBN 9781476657349 ebook
Subjects: LCSH: Korean War, 1950–1953—Personal narratives | Korean War, 1950–1953—Veterans—United States | BISAC: HISTORY / Wars & Conflicts / Korean War
Classification: LCC DS921.6 .W286 2025
LC record available at https://lccn.loc.gov/2025039265

ISBN (print) 978-1-4766-9852-6
ISBN (ebook) 978-1-4766-5734-9

© 2026 Ryan Walkowski and Ed Gruber. All rights reserved

*No part of this book may be reproduced or transmitted in any form
or by any means, electronic or mechanical, including photocopying
or recording, or by any information storage and retrieval system,
without permission in writing from the publisher.*

Front cover images: *inset* a photograph of Marines saddling up for a
nighttime combat patrol, photograph taken by interviewee and co-author Ed Gruber
near Munsan-ni Korea, 1952. *Background* untitled drawing, gift of the artist
to the National Museum of the Marine Corps, Triangle, Virginia (used with permission).

Printed in the United States of America

*McFarland & Company, Inc., Publishers
Box 611, Jefferson, North Carolina 28640
www.mcfarlandpub.com*

To all who served under the UN banner to bring freedom
to South Korea, particularly to the veterans who courageously
volunteered to share their Korean War experiences in their own words
so that their surviving and lost comrades are not forgotten.

Table of Contents

Acknowledgments ix

Preface by Ed Gruber 1

1. Stewart Sizemore, U.S. Army: The Orphan 5
2. Charles R. Ross, U.S. Army: No One Left Behind 21
3. Glenn Galtere, USMC: Thou Shall Not Kill 36
4. Bob O'Keefe, USMC: Battling Bob O'Keefe 50
5. Jim Hostetler, USMC: Marines Don't Cry 59
6. Elroy "Sonny" Roeder, U.S. Army: My Pal Sonny 68
7. George Sousa, U.S. Army: The Survivor 79
8. Ed Gruber, U.S. Navy: The Navy Combat Correspondent 84
9. William "Willie" Cybula, U.S. Army: The Polish Kid 100
10. Vincent Salceto, U.S. Army: The "F" Word 113
11. Joseph Barna, USMC: Navy Corpsmen Are Angels 126
12. Cecil Love, U.S. Army: The Old Bootlegger 135
13. Bert Ruechel, USMC: The Widow Maker 143
14. Salvatore Scarlato, USMC: Now I Know Why I'm Here 152
15. Paul Marsa, USMC: Box Me In 165
16. Forrest Mullins, U.S. Army: Pork Chop Hill 174
17. Frank English, USMC: No Racism in a Foxhole 181
18. John Breske, USMC: The Hall of Famer 194

Conclusion: The End of One Journey ... the Beginning of the Next (by Ryan Walkowski) 206

War Statistics: The Korean War June 25, 1950–July 27, 1953 208

Index 209

Acknowledgments

Ryan Walkowski—Deepest appreciation and thanks to these Korean War veterans who shared with me memories of the grimmest times of their lives. Thank you all for your trust and hospitality. To those who couldn't or wouldn't agree to be interviewed, I understand. For some, some things are best kept hidden. Thank you for your service. I salute you all. I want to thank Collin Wilson; his contributions and help went a long way. I am also immensely grateful that my supervisor, Dan Peterson, worked with me on my vacation schedules and even let me go into the negative so I could capture these stories. I would also like to thank everyone who helped keep me on the road with generous donations; the list is almost endless. Most notable, though, have been the O'Keefe and Openshaw families, along with James Neitzke and River Valley Express Trucking, for contributions that helped me complete my mission. A big thanks to Jack and Justine Stika for their generous donation. Also, to everyone who donated to my many GoFundMe campaigns, you know who you are—I will forever be in debt to you all. I would like to thank Tori-Jo Photography for taking on a last-minute photoshoot so I would have a portrait of myself for the book; I was quite nervous because I am usually behind the camera, not in front of it. I would especially like to thank featured veteran Ed Gruber. Ed took me under his wing almost immediately after our interview and took on the crazy task of mentoring me all along this incredible journey. He believed in me and in my mission, enough to help put these forgotten stories from a forgotten victory to paper. What he must have thought when I sent him my first draft of Chapter 1! And a big shout-out to Grandpa Sonny and Great-Uncle Smokey for piquing my interest in the Korean War and inspiring me to help keep it "unforgotten." Finally, my gratitude to everyone I met along the way; you all helped make it a journey I will forever hold close to my heart.

Ed Gruber—First and foremost, a special hoorah to co-author Ryan, the electrician/valve technician who calls himself a blue-collar kind of guy. I call him a true American for originating this much-needed book and for his outstanding dedication to this amazing journey of helping to remember a meaningful moment in history that has been regrettably unremembered: an anxious time when young men fought and died in the cause of liberty for a nation about which few had then heard. Also, I

Ryan Walkowski's Grandpa Kasmer "Sonny" Walkowski (left) and Great-Uncle Vincent "Smokey" Walkowski.

am especially grateful to the New York City Public Library System for sparking what would become a most challenging and fulfilling lifetime career. The more I read, the more I wanted to write. Deepest thanks, too, to the U.S. Navy and U.S. Marine Corps, where I learned my trade, honed my literary skills, and proudly served alongside heroes who taught me about brotherhood, honor, and getting the mission done. Thanks, too, to Bob Babcock, who, when I was in my eighties, published my first two novels. We have our differences, Bob, but you made a big difference in my life. To every one of my copy chiefs and clients in the mad, mad world of advertising, thank you for teaching me not only how to accept criticism, but also how to accept praise if and when it comes. And I can't forget my Atlanta Writing Club Critique Group—seriously talented friends and authors who made weighty and witty contributions to my Tuesday-evening submissions. Of course, to my devoted brother Jordy and dearest daughter Alison, thanks for watching over me in these senior days like I watched over both of you so many years ago. Finally, to beautiful Shirley and dearest Seth, who helped make me the man I am today—you both live on in my heart.

Preface

ED GRUBER

Washington bureaucrats ingloriously and outrageously called the 1950–1953 Korean hostilities—where they were sending young men to fight and die—a police action. Only five years past the horrors and hardships of World War II, they didn't believe the American public would support another war.

Over time, this police action, which also involved United Nations forces, became the Forgotten War. Forgotten because it received less media attention than two significantly historic conflicts that were appropriately and extensively immortalized—World War II with its global scope and dramatic victory for the free world and Vietnam with its massive antiwar protests and inglorious conclusion. Forgotten also because it was overshadowed by the Cold War that followed World War II. And because nobody gave a damn—except those who were there. Eventually the name stuck: Korea, the Forgotten War.

Those who were there? Bewildered yet courageous young men who left their homes, schools, jobs, and loved ones for a foreign land that some had no idea even existed. Engaging in ferocious battles under the grimmest and grisliest weather and topographic conditions. Fighting hand to hand—sometimes with sharpened trench shovels. Killing or being killed. Seeing brothers-in-arms wounded and slain. Being maimed physically ... and psychologically.

American Korean War survivors, along with those from twenty other United Nations forces, have not forgotten that their sacrifices had some meaning, this being the first battle against the advance of Communism. What these warriors have also not forgotten is that their heroic efforts helped save a nation which grew into an economic powerhouse: a highly developed democracy ranked in the top ten on the Human Development Index in Asia and Oceania. Neither could they forget what they saw and experienced.

They were young men, Army, Navy, Marine, and Air Force combatants, who so valiantly fought against well-trained and well-equipped North Korean aggressors, against hundreds of Soviet Air Force pilots secretly flying combat missions, and against hordes of the Chinese People's Volunteer Army and civilian workers that entered the fray—three million have been estimated. These on-the-ground, seafaring, and airborne combatants—they remember.

Some fought through minus-forty-degree temperatures on low ammo and rations; many survivors still suffer the ravages of debilitating frostbite. There were foot soldiers who day and night patrolled hazardous hills, rugged mountains, and soggy rice paddies in the torrid heat and dust of Korean summers and through the miring mud that came after torrential Asian rains. Against some of the most accurate antiaircraft fire in history, daring Air Force, Navy, and Marine aviators flew just above ground level, supporting allied combatants with withering gunfire and napalm bombs. They won dogfight after dogfight against famed MIG jets—and against some of the most accurate antiaircraft fire in history. And there were those who sailed on naval warships along both Korean coastlines, through storms and calm, aiding their land-based comrades with on-target shelling, delivering ammunition and much-needed supplies: corpsmen, nurses, and doctors. They all remember.

In the words of U.S. Secretary of State Dean Atcheson, "If the best minds in the world had set out to find us the worst possible location in the world to fight this damnable war, the unanimous choice would have been Korea."

But all of that was long, long ago. Now the time for these grizzled warriors to share their accounts is winding down. Those who remain are in their nineties, with stories that must be told, so that a war which saw almost 1,300,000 American and United Nations combatants dead and wounded, plus millions of civilian casualties, is not forgotten. Their time to speak is here and now.

Enter young Ryan Walkowski, from a small town in Wisconsin. An electrician and valve technician who works in factories, power plants, and mills around the Midwest. A blue-collar kind of guy on a mission, who when only a sixteen-year-old high school sophomore heard a teacher preach that the Korean War was the first war America had lost. Recalling his Great-Uncle Smokey's and his Grandfather Sonny's rare and sparse words about their Korean War experiences, Ryan rebuffed his teacher, who laughed and challenged the student to get the facts from his relatives.

Ryan Walkowski.

Ryan's father warned him, "Don't get your grandpa started with something said by a liberal teacher. He'll be off on a rant and never stop."

But Ryan had to know the truth. The old-timers in his family had never gone into detail about their days in battle. When Grandpa Sonny heard what the teacher said, he pointed a finger at Ryan and snapped, "You tell that goddamned liberal pinko communist teacher they don't know what the fuck they're talking about. Ask them if they teach you that our machine gun barrels would melt."

These were the old man's exact words. Ryan has never forgotten them. From then on, this long-haired teenager, in torn jeans and T-shirts emblazoned with the names of popular rock bands, became a different person—a determined young man on a unique and incredible journey, devouring as much information about Korea as he could. But first, Ryan had to learn how it all started.

After World War II, the United States was supporting the anti–Communist southern administration out of Seoul. The Russians were backing the northern administration based in Pyongyang. Two unstable regimes, each considering itself Korea's rightful authority and each rejecting the legitimacy of the other.

After many border skirmishes, on June 25, 1950, North Korean troops unexpectedly invaded South Korea. The few U.S. troops based in Korea immediately joined the battle. Army and Marine occupation forces in Japan were scrambled and hastily shipped to the Korean mainland. The U.S. Navy steamed up, raised anchors, and sailed into action. Through the United Nations, Australia, Great Britain, France, Greece, Thailand, the Philippines, and other countries contributed troops, warships, and air and medical support, though the Americans were the major participants.

On the opposing side, even Communist China got involved, becoming North Korea's most important ally by sending swarms of battle-hardened Chinese soldiers across the border. It was a devastating war. What war isn't? Millions of civilian casualties. Cities crumbled. Villages burned to the ground. Rice fields destroyed. Children left homeless, hungry, without parents.

The irony is that technically the Korean War did not end. Oh, there was no more fighting when North Korea, China, and the United States reached an armistice in 1953. Only South Korea objected to the armistice. But there was no formal treaty. There is still no formal treaty. Thus, the Korean War became the Forgotten War.

Armed with this knowledge, in 2022 Ryan embarked on a determined journey, leading him to videotape in-depth interviews with Korean War veterans all over the country—wherever he could find this dying breed. "I had to reach them and get their stories before it was too late." He met veterans from the first U.S. combat team to enter Korea on July 2, 1950. He sat across from Marines who survived the nightmare that was the battle of Chosin Reservoir. He listened to GIs who manned remote and embattled outposts. He heard from those who went on dangerous nighttime combat patrols. And those who battled at Taejon, the Pusan Perimeter, the Frozen Chosin Reservoir, Heartbreak Ridge, Pork Chop Hill, and so many other nameless hills and battles. Some of these veterans were ambling along with walkers and canes. Some were in senior care facilities. A few were still at home—surprisingly spry and active. But each had a story to tell that honored his gallant brothers who also served. Stories bringing tears to their eyes as they recalled and related terrible times in battle. Stories which puffed their chests with pride when they talked about the unique comradeship—that special brotherhood and the heroics of their buddies. Stories which may have been told and retold over a beer or two at local VFW and American Legion clubs, stories that have been repressed for more than seventy years because of horrific memories that when recalled cause a visceral pain. Ryan gently and mindfully interviewed these old-timers, letting each speak in his own way, at his own pace, and in his own words.

Ed Gruber.

Ryan interviewed me, as well, and I was profoundly impressed with his sensitivity, listening skills, and deep regard and respect for all my brothers and sisters who served in Korea. So I volunteered to perform what became a labor of love. Ryan had done the hard part—spending a couple of years on the road meeting and talking with dozens of campaigners and culling them down to the eighteen represented here. My role was to create an interesting format and help turn Ryan's stirring one-on-ones into a smooth-reading piece of literature. It was a team effort all the way that I'm pleased to say has led to a deep friendship.

Now, on the pages that follow, you can meet, along with storyteller Ryan, some of these forgotten heroes and know their stories—stories told by men who were there. And you, too, will remember the unremembered.

Chapter 1

Stewart Sizemore, U.S. Army
The Orphan

Sergeant, U.S. Army, 34th and 19th Infantry Regiment, 24th Infantry Division. Interviewed January 25, 2022, and April 2, 2022, Delavan, Wisconsin. Born 1932. Died 2024.

> *You wouldn't believe it, I'm firing this weapon that fires 550 rounds a minute, and they just kept coming. You think to yourself, oh Lord, the shit hit the fan and I'm not getting out of here. And you know you're going to be overrun, you know that!*

I'll never forget the look on Stewart Sizemore's face as he described his first engagement with the North Koreans. It was as if he was seeing a nightmare come alive.

Stewart contacted me after seeing my Facebook post seeking interviews with Korean War veterans. In his first e-mail, he explained that on July 5, 1950, he was part of the 34th Regiment of the 24th Division sent to support the first 540 American troops facing invading North Korean forces. The regiment's mission was to delay the rapidly advancing enemy that was overtaking the South Koreans with blitzkrieg-style tactics. Stewart went on to write that he'd fought from Osan south through Chonan, as well as at Taejon (where he earned the Bronze Star with Valor), all the way down to the Pusan Perimeter and back north to the Yalu River. At the end of his Army enlistment, Stewart joined the Marines, returning to Korea for a second tour. This was a Korean War veteran I had to meet.

He lived just three hours south, giving me plenty of time while driving to mull over the research I'd done on his units and to think of questions. Me? I'm just a blue-collar kind of guy—no Hemingway or Ernie Pyle, so I knew I had to rely on being a good listener and giving these gentlemen time and attention to open up, and tell their stories in their own words, in their own ways. My GPS took me to the wrong address, so I called Stewart. "Look for the house with a yellow garage door with cats painted on it."

A two-tour Korean War veteran with cats painted on his garage door! I guess he'd earned the right. All verified, with what I found in Stewart's basement den—impressive display of military awards, medals, citations, and commendations. Stewart turned out to be one hundred percent candid and honest. Given our frequent e-mail exchanges and phone conversations prior to meeting, it was as if we already knew each other. I told him how my journey to help make the Korean War—the Forgotten War—unforgotten started after learning that my great-uncle and my grandfather were Korean War veterans. Later, I learned that they had both been members of the same division as Stewart. He applauded my efforts, pointing out that he didn't expect such a young kid to be interviewing all these old-timers. As I was conducting only my third interview, I was still a novice in this venture. However, with him being so willing to tell all, I was able to capture his inspirational, extremely graphic, and well-detailed story.

Stewart began with being orphaned at age five, and often sent to work at local farms with other orphans as free labor. In 1946 he became a hobo, hopping railway cars until he turned sixteen and quit. He and a buddy were running from the railway police (railway bulls, he called them) and his pal fell onto the track and was killed. That moment, Stewart made up his mind—this was not the life for him. He ended up at a military recruiting center where he explained that as an orphan there was no adult to sign for him. He was told that if he enlisted in the Army, they would make an exception. This was the beginning of Stewart's long and storied military career.

After completing half his basic training, he was assigned to the 34th Regiment/24th Infantry Division and sent to Japan for the other half of the training. Stewart commented that things in the Army then were extremely laid back, and that the military was one-tenth of what it was five years prior during World War II. His division only performed squad tactics and not much else. "Snot-nosed kids" was how he described his fellow soldiers, with a company commander who, at twenty-four, was the oldest man in the unit. They were training with weapons

Stewart Sizemore proudly displaying his shadow box of medals earned from his service during the Korean War.

1. Stewart Sizemore, U.S. Army: The Orphan

that were remnants from WWII's South Pacific Theater of Operations—all junk and shot out. As members of an occupation force in Japan, no one thought a war would break out. Most of the soldiers were kids who lied about their ages so they could travel and see the world. On June 25 when North Korea invaded South Korea, the 24th Infantry Division was considered the most combat-ready, and immediately went into high alert. Stewart was deployed to Korea on July 2, 1950, just seven days after the invasion.

We were told we'd be back in a week, as the North Koreans are going to run when they see Americans. Well they had news for us.

It had been a life of luxury for the occupation forces in Japan, with the 24th Division engaged in limited training. Any exercises imposed were not intense. Even so, when the war broke out, everyone—including Stewart—boasted:

Well, wait until they see the Americans, and we'll be back in Japan in three days continuing what we were doing. Unfortunately, that wasn't true. Never happened. We went over on a Japanese fishing boat, from Sasebo, which is about forty miles from Korea.

Stewart Sizemore poses with his division flag from Korea, which he graciously gifted to Ryan Walkowski.

The 34th Regiment entered the port of Pusan and made their way to Osan, where they quickly found the complete opposite of what they'd been told. What isn't talked about was that the 34th came in support of Task Force Smith, which was made up of only 540 men. Stewart's regiment was 1,982 strong when they first engaged the North Koreans just a few miles south of Osan. What remained of Task

Force Smith—which only had only a three-day lead on the 34th regiment—looked like they'd been chewed up and spit out.

They had been to hell and back would be an understatement.

In addition to the horrors of combat, they faced brutal weather conditions. It was monsoon season, everything was flooded, even the foxholes.

The biggest thing I'd ever seen in my life was the North Korean T34 tank. They must have had a few dozen of them, I guess.

After the first few tanks came in range, Stewart and his mates saw what appeared to be the ground moving. To their surprise, it was the North Korean Army headed straight toward them. It's widely speculated who was the first U.S. casualty, but Stewart said he witnessed what he believed to be the first of the 34th Regiment in Korea—a soldier from West Virginia named Kenneth Shadrick, who he'd seen firing multiple bazooka rounds at one of the T34s.

When he popped up to look, he took nine slugs across his chest from a T34 machine gun. I watched it happen and saw when they carried him out.

Stewart and the 34th battled the North Koreans for hours, giving everything they had, only to be overwhelmed. The lines broke and there was absolute chaos. Stewart was manning a 1919 water-cooled Browning machine gun that fired 650 rounds per minute.

You wouldn't believe it, but I'm firing this weapon that fires 550 rounds a minute, and they just kept coming. You think to yourself, oh Lord, the shit hit the fan and I'm not getting out of here. And you know you're going to be overrun. You know that! The North Koreans were phenomenal. They rolled right over us like we weren't even there. We had nothing. Our artillery battery in the rear was just as bad off as we were. All the gear was junk left over from WWII. Half our weapons didn't work, and those that did only carried a minimal amount of ammo, which was about 100 rounds. On top of that, the field radios didn't work because the batteries were corroded.

Despite the hopelessness of the situation, after being orphaned at such a young age, Stewart had grown accustomed to fighting for survival.

I had everything to gain and nothing to lose.

Figures vary from multiple sources, but Stewart recalled that on the fifth of July, elements of three North Korean divisions—five thousand men—confronted them at the Battle Osan. More than once, he described the North Koreans as "ants on a hill—mean and aggressive," as they attacked the 34th wave after wave. Antitank weapons had little effect on the heavily armored Russian-made T34s thundering toward them. The enemy forces were on the brink of surrounding the 34th when the Americans heard a new and unfamiliar term—bug out, meaning it was every man for himself. The rally point was Pyongtaek, about twenty miles south. Stewart elaborated on just how unprepared for combat he and his fellow GIs were. During their training in Japan, they had executed only squad tactics; they couldn't do battalion, regimental, or divisional, because they didn't have the manpower. His company was supposed to have eight heavy machine guns—they only had two. They were also only equipped with two 75mm and two 57mm recoilless rifles.

> *I was in a heavy weapons company: we were supposed to have 81mm mortars and all those other heavy weapons, yet we had nothing, just rifles.*

U.S. intelligence also failed to recognize that the North Korean Army was made up of combat veterans from the Chinese 8th Route Army who had fought the Japanese from the mid-1930s to the end of World War II. These were battle-hardened soldiers—not the second-class citizen army the generals wrongly believed. The July 6–8 battles for Pyongtaek, as well as for the village of Chonan further south, were terrifyingly bloody. Stewart chose not to recall the carnage he witnessed. He did say that at those two battles, members of the 34th "dropped like flies." In each engagement, soldiers were either killed or captured, with all the others being pushed further back. One detail Stewart did share about the battle for Chonan was when they first saw American half-tracks with quad-mounted .50-caliber machine guns.

> *They brought these half-tracks up, backed them to the hill, and started firing—flat wiping out hundreds of North Koreans, but they still kept coming. Ever see ants on an ant hill? That's what they were like. After seeing those 50s shred them up, that's where I came up with them being like ants.*

The 34th lost almost half its troops in these fierce battles yet remained in combat for six more days. But these encounters were just the prelude to what was yet to come at Taejon. What was left of the 34th once again bugged out—ordered to rally at Taejon and to hold the city at all costs. Two days at the very least would be needed for reinforcements to land at the port city of Pusan to help create a line of defense. The battle for Taejon and the surrounding area started July 14 and continued for seven days of pure hell. The 34th's sister regiment, the 19th, was finally able to link up at Taejon, adding an additional two thousand or so combatants, bringing their combined manpower to over three thousand. But that was small in comparison to the mass of North Koreans making their way slowly but surely toward Taejon. The U.S. Command in Japan scrambled to figure out how to relieve the decimated 34th and save what was left. Commanding General William Dean, at division headquarters in Taejon. issued orders to hold out for as long as possible—at all costs. Stewart and the rest of his company, at this point not much larger than a platoon, dug in with their machine guns and rifles at an airfield just north of Taejon.

> *Every morning I have to have my coffee. It was misty out there while I was heating up my brew in a C-ration cup when I poked my head out of my foxhole to see nothing but gooks marching to the left of us, gooks marching to the right of us.*

Elements of the 34th Infantry Regiment, 24th Infantry Division engage North Korean forces outside of Taejon, July 15, 1950 (courtesy Jane Sherwood).

The North Korean Army had broken through the defensive line just outside of Taejon. Soon the city itself would be in jeopardy. Stewart raced to the command post to inform the company commander that he believed they were being surrounded. "Don't think they are," the officer snapped. "They've done it. We are surrounded." Stewart and what was left of his company retreated from the airfield to set up a new defensive perimeter on the edge of Taejon, only to see big trouble ahead—T34s rumbling down the road. Previous attempts with the 2.4 bazookas had proven ineffective, so newer 3.5 bazookas were air-dropped into Taejon, but with only four rounds of ammunition. Trapped and surrounded, Stewart made the decision to expose himself with his M1 to draw the attention of the oncoming tanks in the hopes of knocking them out and bottlenecking their entry into Taejon. His plan proved successful as he drew the fire of the third tank, enabling the bazooka team to take out one of the T34s. Exposing himself again, this time he drew the attention of the first tank and the trick worked a second time. The bazooka team scored a direct hit, with Stewart firing his M1 at the crews fleeing both damaged tanks. The result: The main road to Taejon was blocked, with the middle tank unable to drive off due to rice paddies on both sides of the road. For these actions, Stewart Sizemore earned our nation's fourth highest honor for an enlisted man—the Bronze Star with Valor. His bravery threw the North Koreans into a moment of confusion, providing time for the Americans to take up better defensive positions.

I'm no hero, I don't deserve that medal. I have seen guys do things far more heroic and never got nothing for it. Some of them should have received the Medal of Honor too. When I die, all I want with me is my Combat Infantry Badge and my jump wings, you can have the rest.

After knocking out the T-34s, Stewart fell back with a fellow soldier and entered the city of Taejon, where they found a horrific mess. MPs (Military Police), posted on the bridge, were found in their Jeeps—dead. The North Koreans had gotten into Taejon before anyone knew, and there was nothing but chaos. Stewart and his buddy constantly ran into North Korean soldiers, dispatching them with single shots, and finally reached the division clearing where they discovered even more comrades shot and bayoneted. Eventually, they came across a convoy that was preparing to move out.

Columbus Yank and M-1 Rifle Spell Doom for Two Red Tanks

An 18-year-old Columbus infantryman, member of a rocket launcher team, tangled with two Russian-made T34 tanks and, armed only with his M-1 rifle, came out the winner.

The score: Two smashed and burned tanks and 10 dead Chinese commies.

Cpl. Stewart Sizemore, 419 S. Champion Av, son of Mrs. L. G. Tanner, 1590 S. 3rd St, and brother of Mrs. Natalie Carter of the Champion Av address was the "David" credited with killing the two "Goliaths."

A member of the 24th Division, Cpl. Sizemore and the other members of his rocket team saw an enemy tank approaching.

The young Columbus soldier moved a few yards away from his buddies and opened fire with his M-1.

Then the unsuspecting tank gunner fired back at Sizemore and the bazooka man with Sizemore scored a direct hit on the tank.

Cpl. Sizemore then calmly shot the tank crew as they fled from the burning vehicle.

The bazooka team then spotted another tank coming down the road and the same trick worked again.

Commenting on Cpl. Sizemore's exploit, Stars & Stripes, official Army GI paper said:

"The Reds are short two tanks and 10 men all because they were so anxious to knock out a lone rifleman."

Hometown paper clipping explains Stewart Sizemore's actions at Taejon that earned him the Bronze Star (courtesy Jane Sherwood).

What are you guys waiting on? We gotta get outta here. And they said, well, we can't. I told them we gotta get out of here. The engineers are going to blow the roadblock. But the engineers didn't blow the roadblocks, the North Koreans were swarming everywhere.

Pandemonium continued as fierce fighting took place around the city. Stewart tried to locate his closest comrades, only to find they'd either been killed or captured. Coming upon a medical post, he made yet another horrific discovery. The North Koreans had bayoneted and shot the wounded. There were no survivors. Ultimately, he was able to connect with a squad led by General Dean, who gave the order to fight their way out of Taejon and retreat through the mountains and hills to Pusan. The 24th was given orders to hold Taejon for two days so reinforcements could arrive to fortify what later would become the Pusan Perimeter. For three long days the 24th valiantly held on. The Battle of Taejon was a hard victory for the North Koreans who took the city and continued south, outgunned, tired, and running low on supplies, and at a significant cost. Hearing Stewart tell me this, I couldn't help but think it must have been like Custer's Last Stand, except for Stewart and a few other survivors managing to escape. Unfortunately, General Dean was captured, becoming a prisoner of war until the 1953 armistice. Upon his release, he received the Congressional Medal of Honor for his courageous leadership actions during the Battle of Taejon.

Trekking through the stark hills and mountains of South, stragglers spent the next two weeks dodging North Korean patrols and evading capture.

I had one round left for my M1, and it was for me.

These survivors were in a race against time. As darkness set in, they bugged out of Taejon and made their way up the mountains just outside town. At about midnight they reached a high point where they rested and watched the carnage below, as Taejon was being taken by the North Koreans.

We got up high in the mountains and you could see down below Taejon, just burning. Just on fire with flames all over the place. It was myself and two other men with me, we had no idea where anyone else was. We walked for three days until we came to an apple orchard and met up with more members of the 24th who also got out in time.

Describing meeting up with these other stragglers—what was left of their regiment—made Stewart remember his company was down to only twelve men. Twelve men out of 206. Little by little, more soldiers joined up, eventually making up a small force that began moving towards Pusan. Making matters worse, they had nothing to eat or drink, so they stole and foraged what they could from fields and rice paddies and drank muddy water to quench their thirst. Some survivors were so out of shape (only a few weeks earlier, they had been part of the relaxed occupation force in Japan) that they were unable to climb the steep hills and mountains. These weary soldiers told Stewart and the others to leave them with grenades and ammo to slow down the North Koreans, while the rest kept moving toward Pusan. Stewart described that he was so fatigued he fell asleep while walking, only to be awakened when he fell face-first into a rice paddy. Finally, they reached the Naktong River, where they linked up with friendly forces—what was left of the 24th Infantry Division. He did not remember the exact day or time but did recall never being happier. Even the Marines who saw them commended them for surviving the hell they'd been through. The 1st Cavalry however, according to Stewart, wasn't as welcoming as the Marines, telling everyone to step aside and unwittingly boasting, "The Cavalry is here, and we'll get the job done."

A day later, what was left of that 1st Cavalry detachment fell back across the Naktong River.

The North Koreans chewed them up and spit them out—just like they did to us. We had a saying for them—a horse you never rode and a line you never crossed.

From August 4 to September 18, the stage was set for the final stand of Republic of Korea (ROK) and U.S. forces on the Korean Peninsula—the Pusan Perimeter. General Walton Walker issued the following statement: "A retreat to Pusan would be

1. Stewart Sizemore, U.S. Army: The Orphan   13

August 1950, Pusan Perimeter. The 78th Tank Battalion, 24th Infantry Division advances to the front of the Naktong Bulge (courtesy Jane Sherwood).

one of the greatest bloodbaths in American history. We must fight until the end … if some of us die, we die fighting together. Any man who gives ground may be personally responsible for the deaths of hundreds of thousands of his comrades. I want everybody to understand that we are going to hold this line. We are going to win."

Stewart's next combat experience occurred during the battle of the Naktong Bulge. He didn't recall the exact date, but said he'd spent multiple weeks fighting without rest. Fatigue, combined with lack of food and clean water, was taking a nasty toll.

We were drinking water out of this well on the Naktong for a week or so, when one day they sent a bucket down and pulled up a dead gook, followed by three more corpses. The North Koreans poisoned the water with dead bodies to kill us. I don't drink plain water to this day. It had a sweet taste, like a death taste, and that's why.

From drinking the poisoned water, in addition to everything else he'd endured, Stewart contracted dysentery and his weight dropped to less than one hundred pounds. An Army medic warned him of the serious consequences of not curing the dysentery. If Stewart wanted to ever leave Korea alive, the medics needed to act swiftly.

"You know, Sarge," the medic told me, "if we don't cure this dysentery, you don't have to worry about them killing you. It will."

Stewart went on to say that if they killed an enemy soldier in the morning, by noon the body would blow up like a fifty-five-gallon drum and turn black from being exposed to the extreme heat of the Korean summer.

Talk about stink. That smell is still with me today.

To stop the spread of disease, the U.S. Corps of Engineers dug massive pits in which to bury the North Koreans. Despite his weakened condition, Stewart sometimes had to help drag bodies to these makeshift burial sites. He recalled that the arms of the corpses would rip out of their sockets due to exposure to the 115-degree heat. Hearing these stories in such graphic detail, I couldn't help but think, God, this man has literally been to hell and back and lived to talk about it. Mercifully, the first round of replacements began arriving, providing much-needed relief to the exhausted troops. From an initial complement of 1,982 men when they first landed in Korea, the 34th Regiment of the 24th Infantry Division was down to only 182, one of whom was my Great Uncle Smokey.

Deemed ineffective, the 34th was merged with the arriving replacements and made part of the 19th Regiment. The Pusan Perimeter was just what General Walker predicted—another Dunkirk. However, U.S. and ROK forces held their own, fighting the North Koreans for six weeks, eventually forcing them further north. Stewart and what was left of the 24th were positioned on high ground, killing any North Koreans attempting to cross the Naktong River. On numerous occasions, counterattack missions designed to throw the enemy off surrounding hills came at high costs. Stewart carried a .38-caliber Combat Masterpiece pistol, as he (in his words) "couldn't hit the broadside of a barn with a standard issue 45." The company fought uphill to throw off the North Koreans, but the massive counterattack resulted in savage hand-to-hand combat, with Stewart stating that "We beat the enemy to death." (Author's note: I thought I had an image of modern warfare, but never imagined I would hear a veteran recall beating an enemy to death with his bare hands.) Hand-to-hand combat occurred frequently, as the North Koreans did all they could to push American and ROK soldiers out to sea. (The details of these battles, fought around the Pusan Perimeter, would later be published by the Army and taught at West Point as valuable tactical strategies. The Leavenworth Papers described these engagements in greater detail, and they would later change the course of warfare.)

The North Koreans built rafts they used in nightly attempts to cross the Naktong River. Contact ended quickly as Stewart's company attacked viciously, using quad .50-caliber half-tracks perched on the high ground—completely overwhelming the enemy. Stewart had previously mentioned how .50-caliber machine guns ripped attackers in half, flat-out leveling them. This armament continued to be a potent weapon.

At the tail end of one fight, Stewart and most of L Company withdrew a few miles, only to be cut off by the North Koreans. They linked up with another company, bringing their combined total to about ninety men to set up defensive positions,

Stewart Sizemore (left) and fellow GI camped out at the Naktong Bulge after fifty consecutive days of combat, circa August 1950, Pusan Perimeter.

dig in, and take on the attackers. Once again, Stewart found himself in bloody hand-to-hand combat, with the GIs eventually defeating the enemy. The mountainous terrain gave the Americans and ROK units a distinctive advantage. Additionally, North Korean numbers were dwindling, with those that remained held at bay. In all, the 24th Infantry Division, along with other units, launched at least sixty counterattacks. On September 15, 1950, Stewart and his worn-out comrades breathed collective sighs of relief when word came that General Douglas MacArthur had landed the 1st Marine Division and Army 7th Infantry Division at Inchon—bringing a total of 40,000 fresh troops into the fray.

> *We had them on the run now. They knew they'd be cut off. The fighting stopped as quick as it began.*

Including action at the successful Pusan breakout, Stewart had seen an unbelievable fifty consecutive days of brutal combat. The 24th and accompanying units soon discovered even more atrocities committed by the North Koreans.

> *We found men in ditches with their hands tied and shot in the back of their heads. All of them were members of the 24th infantry Division who got left behind in the madness.*

While retaking the ruined and smoldering city of Taejon, even more grisly horrors were discovered in a military barracks where GIs had been murdered. Stewart showed me photos of battle scenes from Taejon and the retreat to Pusan, as well as more pictures of soldiers heading north to the Yalu River.

Members of the 19th Infantry Regiment, 24th Infantry Division with a captured portrait of Joseph Stalin (courtesy Jane Sherwood).

After crossing the 38th Parallel, and reaching the North Korean capital of Pyongyang, the 24th was relieved by the 1st Cavalry Division. Moving further north, Stewart and the 24th were a mere fourteen miles from China's border—the calm before the storm. The storm? A surprise attack when the Chinese Army crossed the border, significantly altering the entire Korean War scenario.

When the Chinese came in, they really kicked our asses. They attacked in massive waves of what looked like thousands. A common tactic used by Communists, which looked like a sea of people, knocking each of our machine gun nests out one at a time. That's the whole Communist way to fight a war: they surround you and murder everyone regardless of their own casualties.

One of the most incredible things I'd ever heard from a veteran was when Stewarts said that when he and his fellow GIs ran low or out of ammunition, they'd routinely use their trench shovels to attack enemy soldiers, a totally unconventional tactic he said started as early as the battle of Taejon.

They would break our lines. So, we used sharpened shovels for close-in fighting. They were deadly afraid when they found out we were using those as weapons. We could decapitate more than one man when we swung that thing. They were terrified of it, and this happened regularly, because how do you stop what looks like a million men coming for you? Those shovels were used just as much as our rifles and machine guns.

It was clear to me, hearing all this, that our soldiers were reverting to ancient battle tactics—man-to-man/hand-to-hand combat, fighting like savages to live to see another day.

War is like anything else in life—kill or be killed, you or him; the sooner you realized that, the longer it is you are going to live. You fight with everything in you, using everything you can—rocks, clubs, rifles, your fists.

Stewart next talked about his foxhole buddy, Native American Mitchell Red Cloud, Jr., a member of Wisconsin's Ho-Chunk tribe, describing him as one of the bravest and toughest men he'd ever met. In one fierce battle, Mitchell suffered severe chest wounds. Refusing medical aid, he volunteered to stay behind and tied himself to a tree, arming himself with a BAR (Browning automatic rifle).

We gave him as much ammo as we could. Next morning, after the Chinese had withdrawn, we returned to the hill where Mitchell was last seen fighting the Chinese. We found his body still tied to the tree, with over two hundred Chinese lying dead around him. The Medal of Honor he received posthumously still doesn't do enough justice for what that brave man did saving all of us. Now that's a hero!

During another Chinese attack, a concussion grenade lobbed into Stewart's machine gun emplacement rendered him unconscious. His teeth were knocked out by a Chinese soldier's rifle butt, and his assistant was sliced with a bayonet.

They rolled right over us and kept going.

Regaining consciousness, Stewart dragged two dead Chinese soldiers into the hole, ripped off their quilted uniforms, and used those to disguise himself and his assistant. When things quieted down, they made their way back.

But crossing into friendly lines dressed like that was even more dangerous than walking with the Chinese.

Stewart and his buddy, finally reaching friendly lines, were rushed to a M.A.S.H. (Mobile Army Surgical Hospital) station to have their wounds treated. Stewart remembered lying in a roofless church. Although groggy from his injuries, he recalled a doctor coming in and out of the room carrying a basket. He wondered what was inside. What he'd seen was a surgeon carrying amputated body parts from the adjoining operating room—arms and legs.

I gotta get outta here. So, I got up. There was a pile of weapons in the courtyard. Any weapon you wanted. I found a BAR, then headed back to the front.

Stewart made it clear that, though he'd gone AWOL (absent without official leave), he did return to his company on the front lines.

It seemed like better odds on the front line of surviving in one piece than being stuck at that field hospital.

With his face swollen, and what seemed like everything in his mouth abscessed, he remained at the front for about two days until MPs came to take him back to get proper medication for his wounds, after which they let him return to his unit.

> *I went back to my unit, yeah. War is hell. I felt that was where I had to be because I was single at the time. I could say, being raised the way I was, I didn't really care one way or the other. Because after a while you see all these dead people, you might not believe it, but after a while you begin to envy the dead. They got eternal rest and you're gonna keep right on and think when am I going to get it? And if I do, Lord please make it fast as I don't want to suffer.*

Later reports revealed that the Chinese had brought in over 750,000 troops, drastically changing the tide of the war by forcing UN forces back across the 38th parallel where the outpost war would later be fought.

After his discharge from the Army, Stewart enlisted in the Marine Corps and would see his second Korea tour during the last three months of the war, along with patrolling the DMZ (Demilitarized Zone).

> *A Marine private told me, "I understand you were here once before, Sarge." Yes, I said, and we didn't have flak jackets then. All we had were our shirts.*

For Stewart Sizemore, it had become a different kind of war; a stalemate had been reached, though flareups did occur along the MLR (main line of resistance). When it was over in 1953, Stewart participated in amphibious landing maneuvers with the Marines on various South Pacific islands, including Iwo Jima. In the late 1950s, when this enlistment expired, he rejoined the Army and was shipped to Germany.

> *In fact, I was sent over with Elvis. He was in the 3rd Armored while I was in the 4th. You know, I had a lot of respect for him for one reason. As a celebrity he didn't ask for no favors. You know what his job was? He was an armored scout watching the Russians and would be among the first to get it if they invaded through the Fulda Gap. I also went to basic training with him at Fort Hood in Texas. Elvis was just a nobody to us in the Army and I think he liked that. We talked a few times, and he even performed for us on occasion. In fact, one day, all the recreational halls had new televisions, radios, and pool tables. Elvis was a kind man, and his generosity proved it.*

Stewart often attributed his survival to growing up as an orphan and being constantly placed on work farms with his four brothers and sisters where they worked twelve- to fourteen-hour days. He recalled the nearest school being seven miles away. Never being allowed by the orphanage to do anything more than work and go to school, he and his siblings learned early on how hard life can be. After dropping out of high school, Stewart lived in a hobo jungle, and then joined the Army. All these hardships turned him into a rough and tough individual. Upon his return to the United States from Korea, Stewart was required by the Army to attend therapy sessions with psychiatrists: reliving the horrors he'd witnessed and taken part in.

Stewart Sizemore on his second tour of Korea as a U.S. Marine, 1953.

Stewart went on to explain how much a human body can really take and all the punishment and abuse an individual can endure, explaining that you're not only beaten down physically, but also mentally and emotionally. Yet you still carry on because you'd rather feel like that than die.

> *When we were moving back from those early battles like Osan and Taejon, more than one guy would give up and say he can't go any further and just give up and sit down on the side of the road. And there's no way you can stop and help this guy. And you know he's gonna die. But they just literally give up. But you wonder, and then you're amazed, at how much punishment the human body can actually take. Doing this day after day after day, you're beat every way possible. That's why so many of those men just gave up and—especially the heavier, overweight people. They just couldn't go on. Korea's all mountains. You'd spend half a day climbing a mountain. And they'd just sit down and say, "I give up." I saw more than one soldier do this.*

Lastly, Stewart mentioned that for so many guys in his company, to this day he doesn't know what happened to them. When I started these interviews in 2022, the remains of many of the Korean War deceased were being identified and returned home: almost all 34th and 19th Regiment members of the 24th Infantry Division.

Some names Stewart recognized—finally answering his questions as to what happened to them.

> *I saw so much death and killing that it's just a natural thing. That's why when I came back, I went in front of a board of psychiatrists and shrinks and they told me that you kill with no remorse whatsoever. But you're conditioned for it. It's either you or him. A lot of people might not understand that, but that's the way it is. They also told me it's a good thing I don't drink, because if I did and had a flashback, I could wipe a whole town out before even knowing what happened.*

This statement reminded me of Argentine author José Narosky's poignant words, "There are no unwounded soldiers."

As you've read, Stewart Sizemore's stories are extremely compelling and emotional. From the early days of the Korean War to Chinese intervention, to meeting the King of Rock and Roll, it's safe to say this orphan turned soldier and Marine had one hell of a military career. Becoming his friend was more than an unexpected bonus gained to this mission. With all my grandparents now gone, we even joked about him being my adopted grandfather, which I proudly share when talking to others about him. I treasure this unique friendship with Stewart Sizemore and think of him as one of the best of the best. Although he will tell you that he isn't a hero, to me he's that and a lot more. He's also my friend. Each ensuing visit was a special joy where I learned even more about Korea, about the horrors and wastes of war, life in general, and so much about Stewart Sizemore—a man's man, a soldier's soldier.

> *It's my humble opinion, the Korean War was fought and won in the first six months. We went from being beaten and almost pushed out to the sea, to annihilating the North Korean army and taking their capital.*

Author's note: My dear friend Stewart Sizemore's final mission was on January 28, 2024, when he passed away. During our last phone call I told him that I loved him and was thinking about him every day, and that I will never forget what he told a reporter who was interviewing him about his involvement in my project:

> *Ryan just has a knack for getting things out. I'll tell you something, we need him. He's showing the country what we did.*

Losing friends like Stewart is the saddest part of my journey.

CHAPTER 2

Charles R. Ross, U.S. Army
No One Left Behind

Sergeant, U.S. Army, 3rd Battalion, 8th Regiment, 1st Cavalry Division. Prisoner of War: November 1950 to September 1953. Interviewed April 19, 2022, Cave City, Kentucky. Born 1928.

These Koreans came out firing at the Marines who hit the ground firing back. As we were driving away, we were stopped by a lieutenant who ordered us to get in the ditch and give them some of our ammunition so they could go back for the wounded men. We told him we don't have any, and that was the oh shit moment where the Lieutenant said, "Really? Get your asses back on the truck and get the hell out of here."

After Charles Ross responded to my Facebook posting, he agreed to meet when my travels brought me to Kentucky. I let him know I had no intention of passing up the opportunity to speak with any Korean War campaigner. While planning interviews in South Carolina, Florida, and Tennessee, I arranged for Charles to be my last stop before returning home to Wisconsin. It dawned on me that I had yet to ask him about his unit, which I learned later was the 3rd Battalion, 8th Regiment of the 1st Cavalry Division. So far, my trip had been unbelievable: hearing priceless stories from the various men I interviewed. But I had no idea how emotionally charged this session was about to be.

When we finally met, as I was setting up my recording equipment, I mentioned to Charles that I'd recently interviewed another member of the 1st Cavalry, 8th Regiment. Charles asked a question that almost knocked me off my feet.

Was he also a POW?

This was how I learned that Charles had been a prisoner of war. The stories that followed over the next three hours—one of my longest and most moving sessions—were extremely detailed and unforgettable.

Charles's Army enlistment began in 1947. Sent to Fort Jackson for his physical, he remained for about two weeks until he was shipped to Anniston, Alabama, for basic training. He was next transferred to Germany, where his original eighteen-months enlistment was extended for another eighteen months. Charles then signed up for an indefinite hitch that lasted until 1956 in Hawaii, where he was given the option to end his enlistment and then re-enlist for three-year periods, which he did. Charles retired from the Army October 31, 1970, after twenty-three years, eight months, and twenty days of continuous service.

He sailed into New York Harbor June 13, 1950, and was on leave when the Korean War broke out June 25. He reported to Fort Devens, Massachusetts, on July 3, and was assigned to a company in the 7th Infantry Division. Three days later he and twenty-five others were sent to West Point on a two-week assignment to teach cadets how to perform nighttime attacks. One day at lunch in the mess hall, some officers ordered the team to rejoin the 7th Infantry at Fort Devens, where they learned they had been reassigned to the newly created First Provisional Battalion. Laughing, Charles said:

We were referred to as FNGs (fucking new guys).

Upon arrival, they discovered that the company commander, first sergeant, and platoon leaders had already been appointed. While being interviewed by the leading officer, he was informed that he would lead the third squad of the first platoon. (After World War II, the Army had been so decimated, they promoted any qualified, able-bodied man.) Encouraged to move up in the ranks, Charles took an NCO (noncommissioned officer) leadership course, finishing first in his class, and was promoted to corporal. In 1950, while stationed in Germany, he was promoted to the rank of sergeant. In his new detail, he discovered that he didn't have a squad; however, the battalion was filled within a few days, and the men were told they'd be going to Korea—likely seeing action soon after arrival. They boarded a train headed west.

Charles Ross in the closest military photograph to the Korean War–era part of his military career. Unfortunately, Charles did not have any more military photos, as he was a POW in Korea for 34 months.

We had people come right out of basic training. Cooks, military police, men from ordnance companies—all put together and issued rifles. The entire battalion was sent by train from Massachusetts to California. Different companies would pass through our car to the mess car, and this would happen three times a day.

It wasn't until reaching Colorado that they were allowed to detrain and stretch their legs. Upon arrival in California, they were ordered to perform a road march—their only training before Korea. Then the new battalion boarded the USNS *John Pope* for a six-day ocean trip, with the ship breaking down in the middle of the Pacific—floating in the water like a sitting duck. With repairs made, the troopship cruised on, bypassed Japan, and sailed directly into the port of Pusan, Korea, where powerful tugboats nudged the huge transport into its docking.

> *I can remember the morning when we came up on deck to see the sky was as red as could be in the east. We were lined up alphabetically and told to carry only what was essential, so to be combat light. Personal items were supposed to be held until we were ready to leave the country. We were on the dock for about four hours until they brought us back on the boat for lunch.*

One disturbing event Charles remembered of his time in Pusan was when he and three other GIs heard screams coming from nearby. When they investigated, they saw a group of Koreans beating other Koreans.

> *They had sticks. They had what looked like pipes and used their fists. Nearly killed 'em.*

Told these were captured North Koreans, they left without intervening, and were soon loaded up on two-and-a-half-ton trucks. That's when Charles noticed the 1st Cavalry patch on the hood of the rig.

> *That was the first indication on what unit we might be going to, but we still had no idea. I was now a member of Company C, First Provisional Battalion.*

During this period, Charles was promoted to sergeant first class. The battalion was moved to the town of Taegu, where the men left the train and pitched tents. Ammunition was issued to each man the next morning—a basic load of eighty-eight rounds for the M1 rifle. But that didn't last long.

> *It wasn't more than four or five minutes after they started distributing ammo that someone fired and hit the tire of a two-and-a-half-ton truck. Everyone was ordered to turn in their ammo.*

Next, they were loaded on trucks, traveling four or five miles north where they unloaded to watch a Marine unit perform an actual hill attack.

> *They told us we should dig fox holes, cause we're going to dig in every time we stop, so get used to it. We were instructed to look to our left front where we saw Marines going up a hill. They were so far away they looked like little worms going up that hill.*

The Marines got one-third of the way up when North Koreans surrounded them by moving into flanking positions. What Charles witnessed was in-combat training—observing and learning from a live assault happening about a thousand yards away.

These Koreans came out firing at them and the Marines hit the ground and fired back. As we were driving away, we were stopped by a Marine lieutenant who ordered us to get in the ditch and give them some of our ammo so they could go back for the wounded men. We told him we don't have any, and that was the oh shit moment where the lieutenant said "Really? Get your asses back on the trucks and get the hell out of here."

The following morning the unit marched until they were told to dig in and set up a perimeter on a hill. After dark, Charles and his mates came under their first fire from North Korean troops, whom they were able to fight off.

It was a strange feeling knowing you were the target. They were firing flares that looked like little candles. Very eerie with shadows moving everywhere and gunshots ringing out. It scared the devil out of younger guys who were never in combat like that. Someone said it was a Banzai attack—whatever that is.

What Charles and the battalion witnessed were the wave tactics the North Koreans used repeatedly throughout the war—unprotected frontal assaults by offensive infantry against enemy lines with densely concentrated formations intended to overrun and overwhelm. (The battle cry from Japanese soldiers in the Pacific during similar suicidal charges during World War II was "Banzai," short for "Tennoheika Banzai'i"—long live the emperor.)

They were coming at us—yelling, screaming, firing rifles. We fired into them with our rifles and mortars, and they just disappeared. The next morning we were ordered to move down the road and get on trucks to take another hill. We hadn't been there very long when we received small-arms and indirect fire. When I think back, I don't believe it was very accurate because most went over us or landed in front of us, and this went on for a week or so, maybe ten to twelve days.

The battalion fought and retreated hill after hill, battle after battle, until they received the bone-chilling order to stand or die—there will be no more retreating.

I thought well, this is it ... first time we got direct tank fire with what were ID'd as Russian tanks.

The battalion got word that on September 15 an assault was planned on the Korean west coast that would take pressure off everyone fighting in the Pusan Perimeter.

We didn't know then, but later we were told it was (at) Inchon, designed to cut off the North Koreans, deplete their supplies, and force them north. When the assault happened, the pressure just ended, it was like someone flipped the light switch, and they went away. Those who got past us couldn't get out, and that's when I captured my first prisoners. One of my squad members told me he saw two guys coming up the hill. We drew our weapons, raced down and took them.

On a date he's unable to recall exactly—either September 16 or 17—Charles and his group boarded trucks to head north. Any North Koreans they encountered just put up their hands and surrendered.

We went all the way to the 38th Parallel where we sat and waited for the United Nations to give us permission to cross. Once given the go-ahead, the convoy loaded up to cross into North Korea, and off we went.

Once over the border, the battalion marched to a field where, after posting up, small arms fire came in from an enemy tank hidden in the bushes on a hill just ahead.

Was a soldier named Hernandez who took out the tank with a 3.5 bazooka—that became a really powerful weapon for us.

While he didn't witness it right away, Charles added that he'd heard of UN planes dropping napalm up ahead. Although used toward the end of World War II, napalm had not been heavily employed there, but eventually became a lifesaver for UN ground troops. I asked Charles what it was like seeing napalm being dropped.

Well, you see it, and it was a big tank that came out of a plane, and it wasn't long, and you see flame and black smoke shoot up.

Meeting no further resistance until they reached the North Korean capital of Pyongyang, UN forces stepped aside after the first fighting began, allowing the ROK Army to take the capital, for political reasons.

While in Pyongyang this was also the first and only time I've seen a woman give birth. Was a pregnant woman the North Koreans threw in a ditch, and I saw the steam of the newborn rising.

Later, they were bivouacked in a building—a makeshift hospital, where the entire battalion hunkered down for three or four days. One platoon sergeant, cleaning the magazine of a pistol he'd retrieved from a dead North Korean officer, had failed to clear the chamber and shot himself in the knee. Charles volunteered to replace the sergeant and lead the platoon and squad. For the rest of their time in Pyongyang, all they did was perform house searches for weapons and ammo.

We were told at that time the war is all but over; the North Korean Army is kaput. Our battalion was to lead a parade in Tokyo for General MacArthur on Armistice Day. Little did we know, because of the coming Chinese intervention. the entire course of the war would change.

On October 13, the battalion was at evening mess when a lieutenant made an announcement: "Can I have your attention, please? The moment you finish your meal, pack up and get ready to move out." The men slept in ditches and trucks until the next morning, when they crossed a bridge into the city of Unsan. They'd been there for a day when the platoon was sent to the southern part of the city to establish a listening outpost. On October 31, Charles got a call at 10 p.m. telling him that the lieutenant had ordered the platoon to report back to the command post. The regiment would be withdrawing at 2400 hours, a mere two hours later. Charles sent word to all the outpost listeners to also move out. With Charles at the platoon's rear, they started down the hill—marching in a tactical formation with at least five yards of space around each man so if they came under artillery or mortar fire, one round wouldn't take everyone out. Then they heard: "Sergeant Ross, report to the front. Sergeant Ross, report to the front. The lieutenant wants you." Charles told his assistant to move the platoon into a ditch off the road, take a seat, and hold until he returned. While waiting to see the officer, Charles was talking to Sergeant Luther Wise when they heard some unusual sounds.

> *Whistles, bugles, bells, screaming and hollering from the hill we'd just come off. They started firing and the crack of bullets was everywhere. I ran under a bridge where I yelled as loud as I could, "First Platoon under the bridge! First Platoon under the bridge!" Rounds began hitting the water, then the bridge—that sounded like bricks being thrown against it.*

Accompanied by ten men, he stayed for a while before moving out in search of the command post.

> *Three of them followed me and we went up the ditch to see our trucks in the convoy on fire, still with the engines running ready to move out. At the edge of the ditch was a machine gun firing and rattling so much you could see the smoke rise off the barrel. You could feel it in the air, and I told myself this is it; I'm not getting out of here, there's too much going on. We tossed grenades toward the ditch across the road. Suddenly there was a loud BOOM, and all we could hear were yells and screams.*

The first phase of the battle continued for about five hours. Finally, he heard someone yelling "Are you GI?" To which Charles called out, "I'm GI! I'm GI." Next, he heard "Stay low and come across the road." Charles heaved a sigh of relief since he was by himself at this point and had no idea what happened to the rest of his squad. He did as he was told and made it to a crater hole where there was a wounded KATUSA (South Korean soldier on loan to the U.S. government).

> *The poor guy was calling out what sounded like a mule, and I told him there's no mules here. I don't know what you're talking about.*

The KATUSA was asking for water, but Charles didn't quite understand. The bleeding Korean kept nodding his head … until he died.

> *He had on a field jacket like I had, but instead of a cartridge belt he had a pistol belt and a carbine.*

Charles stayed until the morning light, when he heard yelling and saw people motioning for him to come over. He raced to a large crater harboring about thirty to forty GIs, most of them wounded.

> *We were so disorganized we didn't know who was who, what unit anyone was in, or what rank anyone was. A lieutenant, whose last name was Mayo, finally took charge and began telling us what to do and how to do it. So, we set up a perimeter.*

Finally connecting with two of his squad members who had left him to return to the bridge, Charles and the two others dug a waist-deep three-man foxhole.

We were on the low ground, so they had the advantage. If we got out of our hole, they would take a potshot at you. But we kept firing as they popped into view. I remember three tanks being there with a Sergeant Miller—commander of the closest tank, ordering his gunner to fire on the hill to keep the enemy at bay. That was the only communication we had from air to tank to us.

Radio equipment in those days had at best a two-mile range, but the tanks with more powerful radios were able to contact air units. Charles was close enough to the tank that when its hatch was open, he could hear messages being exchanged.

I could hear this radio, and I heard them say the Fifth Cavalry has an attachment coming towards you to relieve you. I thought okay, this is good. At least someone is thinking about us. But the last message I heard was that the Fifth Cavalry has run into a roadblock and resistance is too stiff. They're going to abandon the attempt, you're on your own. Godspeed. I think if my heart could have, it would have dropped to my feet. but for reasons unknown, I didn't panic, I just told myself if I can see them, I'm going to shoot them. We fought there for three days and three nights. At the time we didn't know who these people were who were shooting at us. Later we found they were Chinese.

Sections of two battle-experienced divisions of the Chinese People's Volunteer Army had unexpectedly crossed the border and attacked Charles's battalion.

They would come at us in droves you wouldn't believe. They would come at us like three deep, right across that open field, and we would fire as hard as we could at them. When we pulled out, I think I had only had three rounds left. I remember a sergeant telling us that the supply trucks were destroyed the first night, is why we ran out of ammo. The Chinese just kept on coming and we kept on firing.

One afternoon Charles was in a foxhole when he heard a strange sound like a thump, followed by screaming.

I raised up just enough to see white smoke and fire particles falling down like an umbrella, and I realized they were dropping white phosphorus on us now, which ended up working in our favor as it added a smoke-screen effect.

That's when Charles, after hearing a rumble and seeing a wall of people running across a field, yelled to his comrades to follow him. Along with two others, they emerged from their foxholes, getting to the road where the convoy of trucks were still burning. The group made their way to a road about seventy-five yards away from a river. Charles recalled the river being waist high at its deepest point, but fortunately it was not running rapidly.

We took our helmets off and dipped them in the river to drink, we were so thirsty.

They remained in the river for a while before wading out to cross a field, continuing another four or five miles until they came across what was assumed to be the same river. Meeting another group and uncertain of its identity, they came close to firing on that group, but it turned out to be friendlies who had organized into a unit.

The entire group marched through a valley, down the side of a hill, coming to a small village. As nighttime approached, Charles and the others moved into a few of the houses for refuge.

It was about five or six houses, and we slept in them at night. It was warm in there and we just slept on the floor.

The lieutenant gave his wristwatch to an old Korean he'd guessed to be head honcho, as thanks for the hospitality. Morning came and the unit moved out, walking all day long, staying in the hills. They came upon another column marching north. Again, not sure whether the column was friend or foe, they smartly decided not to risk giving their position away.

We didn't know who they were. All we knew was they were carrying rifles.

The following morning, about an hour into their trek, they encountered small-arms fire. Charles and squad member PFC Donald Vaughn ran and hid under a large rock ledge until the coast was clear. After things settled, they made their way down, wandering around for about six days, mainly looking for food and water.

We would drink out of a hillside stream and wipe the leaves away to drink the water. We eventually found an empty house to sleep in, but our sleep was interrupted when an older Korean man came and knocked at the door. He stepped inside and started talking, but neither one of us knew what he was saying. But one word he said sounded like enemy and he kept pointing. He motioned for us to follow him and after some deliberation we decided it was okay. We went halfway up a hill when the old man instructed us to stay. He came back with a bottle of water along with a thermos with soup in it. Donald asked me if we could trust him, to which I said we have no choice. Once again, we followed him as the old man led us into a valley with rocks and washed-out terrain and a waterfall. He then pulled a straw mat back and told us to go in.

Charles and Donald cautiously entered. To their surprise and good fortune, the Korean presented them with another bottle of water. Donald got claustrophobic and left. Charles followed close behind. They were low on ammo; Charles had only three rounds and Donald eleven. Approaching another small house, they heard what sounded like running engines. Feeling uncomfortable, Charles suggested they leave. They tried to find a route to head south toward a river, since rivers typically run north and south. After hiding their rifles under some brush and lying low, they heard a whistle. The two of them got up and continued to walk, when they heard someone yelling.

This guy was looking directly at us, yelling for the others. They were short and brown-skinned, wearing quilted uniforms with a red star on their hats. Donald asked me what we should do. I realized the gravity of our situation and told him to put his hands up. The Chinese soldiers rubbed our faces, laughing at us while asking where our rifles were. I motioned to them as if to say we tossed them away. Of course, the rifles were only feet away under some brush, still there for all I know.

When the Chinese searched their field jackets and pants, they failed to find two hand grenades on the back of Charles's belt.

I leaned back and felt those grenades and said oh my God, and whispered to Donald that I was going to turn around to him so he could slip them off and toss them under the deck. They had a guy who figured he knew English, and he would say, "chop chop okay?" And I would just say yes, and smile and they seemed to like that. They would keep saying the same thing and I kept giving them the same answer.

The next morning Charles and Donald were fed.

It looked like some sort of cereal or something that was boiled, with very little taste, but at least it kept you alive.

The two prisoners, brought to a field unit where the Chinese had set up a defensive perimeter, were forced to squat there for almost the entire day. Charles and Donald were fed two more times.

One was boiled corn, just shelled corn and boiled, and was tasteless. If we had to relieve ourselves, we would just motion to them, and they would take us to do our business.

Some Chinese soldiers motioned to Charles and Donald to follow them down the road, where they were joined by another American and about twenty South Koreans.

The American's name was Potter, from New York, and with K Company. I remember him well. We marched all night long and they put us in houses during the day. We later joined up with about fifteen more Yanks. One man was wounded in the leg and lying on an American-made stretcher. On the third day we left him behind and I don't know what ever happened to the poor guy.

Over a hundred prisoners marched with Charles, all closely watched by the Chinese—every twenty feet, armed with rifles.

If anyone had to go to the bathroom, they did it quickly, pulled their clothes up and got back in line. Any prisoner who fell behind, a Chinese soldier would stay with him, with the Chinese soldier returning to the column later—minus the prisoner. We never saw them again. Whether they killed them or not I don't know. I remember one prisoner jumping out of the column to relieve himself while being held at gunpoint by a Chinese soldier, only to return and fall back in line.

Charles lamented that this went on night after night for about ten nights. Early one morning they started walking again, traveling through fields, until they reached a road. Coming to a village situated in a valley, they stayed in houses that had been vacated by the locals—their first encampment. Charles explained that Koreans heated their homes with heat from fireplaces sent out through channels under the floors. The room with the fireplace was always the hottest, so you were unable to sleep on the floor.

We would change who slept where every night. This heating method was primitive, yet a genius way to heat their homes, But you couldn't stand being in the room where the heat was generated. After a few weeks we were moved to what would become known as Camp 5, where I had to switch sleeping locations nightly.

After about four to six weeks, the Chinese began reeducation classes, later known as brainwashing. At the first session, the students were instructed to call the teacher comrade or instructor.

They spoke perfect English, like you and me. After the lectures began, conditions improved. The Chinese would check people out to determine who would conform and, alternatively, who would resist. My goal became, let's fool these jokers and make them think you're accepting, but hating it from the bottom of your soul. I was made squad monitor, which required documenting the opinion of each prisoner and turning in a report to the Chinese. I stopped anyone who sounded too progressive so I could collectively find the proper way to prepare my reports. I was questioned once about a report I turned in: the subject being about Taiwan, with the Chinese having claimed it for centuries. The opinion I turned in regarding the rightful owner of Taiwan was "Who cares, give it to the Indians."

Explaining that statement, Charles asked what to write down, with a fellow prisoner suggesting, "Who cares, give it to the Marines." Charles couldn't submit that, to which the prisoner then replied, "Well, then give it to the Indians." That too, would have meant Charles having to go through a lengthy explanation.

I just told them that's what he said. It's just an old saying for something you don't want. "Give it to the Marines or the Indians."

The lectures continued, with the Chinese going on and on about how Americans are warmongers, and Wall Street being evil.

These types of lectures would happen every day, and each discussion we had was supposed to last as long as the lecture. We had no entertainment, and it did get boring sitting day after day, month after month, year after year, seeing people die by the hundreds.

One of the saddest stories Charles recalled was about being put on burial detail. The prisoners had no way of keeping records, since they weren't allowed pencils and paper, except during the lectures. Charles went on to explain they didn't know the names of the POWs who died, only that they were Americans. He painfully recalled that most of the deaths began around January to February of 1951.

We carried them, though we were not strong enough. We had to slide them and doing it across the river was easy because of the ice. It would take three or four of us to slip and slide and drag them up the hill to the burial grounds. You would pick out a hole sometimes no more than two-and-a-half to three feet deep and put the poor fella in there. If he had a field jacket you covered him up. Even today it makes me emotional just to think about it, but we had to do it to try and control disease the best we could. Seemingly every morning a dead GI was discovered, who you had spoken with just the night before. We'd take the dead soldiers, leaving them outside in the cold until they could be buried. Lay them with their feet propped up in the air, making it easier to slide them once they were completely stiff. There were multiple religions represented in the building where we were confined—Catholic, Methodist, Jewish, Baptist, et cetera. There were twenty-one of us and we actually touched each other when we were lying on the floor when we slept. We came to an agreement that everyone would say the Lord's Prayer before moving anyone out who had passed away.

It became very clear during this interview that Charles is a natural-born survivor. Twenty-one men started out in his hut, but after being moved across the valley there were only eight.

Some would get to the point they wouldn't eat, saying they couldn't eat that slop. But we'd beg and remind them that the Chinese would get mad at you. I remember one man, he was from Connecticut, and he told me, "Get the fuck away from me and leave me alone!" It was painful, but he died shortly after. A new term we came up with was "give up-ite-ist," because it was nearly impossible to live in these conditions. I was twenty-one years old, single, no family. Both my mother and father had passed away. I had a sister, but had no idea where she was, but I had this hope somewhere inside, that someday, somehow, I'd get through this and go back to the United States. I couldn't say "home," because I didn't have a home. My home was the United States Army.

A good friend of Charles, Bobby Shepperd, was in the same POW camp. Dysentery was rampant and people were dying. Bobby told Charles that his mother would add salt to warm water to help with similar conditions. One night Bobby hopped the wall into the Chinese mess hall and stole a pocket full of rock salt to make some warm salt water for Charles.

By golly it worked, it actually worked really well, and I got to doing okay.

Bobby also snuck into the fields to pick an edible weed he called lamb's quarter, something like dandelions. Though it was tasteless, he convinced everyone it was beneficially loaded with vitamin A, so they added it to whatever the Chinese gave them to cook. When I asked Charles how long he was a POW, I was shocked when he responded with "Thirty-four months from November 1950 to September 1953." I couldn't imagine having to endure those kinds of living conditions for nearly three years. Out of seven thousand U.S. prisoners, 2,800 (40 percent) died in captivity.

Eventually, Charles and all the other noncommissioned officers were moved by boat from Camp 5 to Camp 4. They traveled all day before stopping at noon to be fed boiled wild greens, then were put back on the boats. Upon arrival at Camp 4, they were divided into two companies—A and B, with Charles assigned to Company B. Both units were quartered in school buildings. Company A was in the town of Wewan, North Korea. Charles and Company B were posted thirty minutes away. At this camp, the food improved, with servings of meat, fish, and fresh greens. The lecture topics changed, extolling the benefits of Communism, its superiority to capitalism, and that the prisoners would be better off living under the rule of a Communist government.

Not a lot of men believed what we were told, but there were a few. We called them collaborators and rats. The Chinese called them progressors. These men got whatever they wanted, with the Chinese acting almost like pimps for them while trying to persuade the other prisoners to cross over. The majority held our ground. We're Americans and we're going to stay Americans.

The Chinese also interrogated prisoners individually, asking personal questions about their families. On one occasion, they pulled out a map and asked Charles to show where he was from. They didn't believe him when he pointed to South Carolina, since his friend and squad member Donald Vaughn had pointed to North Carolina. The Chinese didn't accept this as truth until Charles stood his ground. I asked Charles if the Chinese spoke fluent English.

Absolutely, as some of the Chinese had attended American colleges and universities, like Berkeley and Yale. It was these educated officers whose mission was to convince us that our ways of thinking were wrong. We lived on rumors, even if there was no concrete basis to the rumor. In July of 1953, the rumor spread that an Armistice had been signed. While a rumor, this was one worth believing. A progressor—or rat, as they called them—told the other prisoners that there were talks with representatives of both sides at Panmunjom, and everything had been agreed upon except the exchange of prisoners. The United Nations wanted the prisoners to be able to choose if they wanted to stay or return home, with the Chinese wanting all prisoners returned from where they came.

At first, they believed the rumors to be true—for a few days, anyway. But they soon began losing hope, until air activity ceased. It seemed UN pilots had identified Camp 5 as a POW encampment and waved their wings on flybys. The jets came so close that the buildings and shacks would shake. This went on for month after month, until the flights came to an abrupt stop.

They marched us one time during the day, which is extremely dangerous during combat. We had on these blue uniforms with blue baseball caps. In March 1953, we were passing through a valley near a destroyed convoy of trucks, only to stop and spend the entire day there, but no one knew why. About two weeks later, what was known as "Operation Little Switch" took place. Any prisoner who was wounded, sick, or had a disease was loaded onto a truck and taken to Panmunjom. The lingering determination as to when the rest of the prisoners would be repatriated was being discussed. But no word from April through July. One day in August, news came that left everyone speechless. They had a tall pole with a loudspeaker for music and announcements. When Stalin died, they played funeral-type music all day long. But it was better than that Chinese music they played, so loud you had to yell at each other to talk. The big news that day came while we were having lunch, with the announcement that everyone would have to get into formation. We were told to bring our seats, so everyone grabbed their pad and marched out the camp gate to what looked like an athletic field. Once there, a Chinese general came out, which was unusual, and started rattling off in Chinese into a microphone, so we all knew something was up. The translator said an armistice agreement had been reached and within sixty days all prisoners must be repatriated. When we heard that you would think you would hear a big yeah or yelling, but there was nothing— just a sigh of relief.

How did Charles feel at that moment?

You just felt weak and lost all your strength. After almost three years, it can't be. We're getting out of here. Maybe we will make it home.

On the morning of August 20, 1953, one of the POWs went to the bathroom, only to immediately race back yelling and hollering that through the window he'd seen American trucks parked outside.

We knew this was the real deal because these were the same trucks as in Operation Little Switch. Chinese nurses came in with red crosses on their arms and handed out bags with gum, toothpaste and a toothbrush, a small Baby Ruth candy bar, and two folded pieces of paper for napkins. I can remember I got spearmint gum. Not long after, it was announced that anyone who wants to be repatriated could step forward and leave. I run in and grab my overcoat and the little bag I had, and all but six of us went. We had six turncoats that stayed behind.

Safely at Panmunjom, Charles was evaluated by medical staff. He remembered beds lined up as far as the eye could see. Each of the released prisoners was offered the opportunity to speak with a general about their experiences. Charles did, finding some relief in being able to speak without recrimination.

After that, he was given a care package, a camouflage scarf, and a King Edwards cigar. Military ambulances transported the prisoners to Inchon, where they were again evaluated by medical personnel. Next, they were shown pictures of other prisoners to confirm whether they were dead or alive. On September 12, 1953, Charles boarded a transport vessel and sailed to San Francisco. Out of an abundance of caution, an attempt was made to keep the former POWs separate from other GIs. The thought was that they might be treated differently if it was assumed that they had surrendered. However, this turned out not to be the case. Nevertheless, there were some meetings.

The mingling with the other troops was helpful, because they told us what they went through, and we told them what we went through. I don't know a single soul who voluntarily surrendered. Remember, we spent almost five days evading capture.

Arriving in San Francisco, the former POWs were hailed as heroes with a welcome home parade. They were given airline tickets and cash, with Charles opting to go to Columbia, South Carolina, where he was met by friends, particularly the Smith family, who had invited him to their home. His new assignment was Fort

Jackson, where he stayed for about eighteen months before being reassigned to the 25th Infantry Division in Hawaii.

I had many years where I wouldn't talk to anyone about it. It affected me emotionally, especially about the seven men I lost in Korea, and I carry their names in my wallet. I don't look back with any regret and hold no ill will against anyone because I volunteered. I was abandoned twice in my life, once by my mother leaving me to be raised by my father, and the second time at Unsan, where we were told we were on our own and had to fend for ourselves.

This last statement was said with tears in his tired eyes. What Charles next shared had me fighting back my own tears.

There's a saying in the Army, "No one left behind." We were left behind—a whole battalion.

Charles estimated that about less than half the battalion made it out of the perimeter during the battle of Unsan. The chaplain assigned to Charles's battalion was Father Emil Kapaun, who escaped the perimeter but went back and surrendered to be with the men.

I met him a few times and he was a kind gentleman. He always seemed happy. I never got to know him well, but he was the kind of guy who would ask if there was anything you fellas need. I often say he was the bravest man I ever knew.

Charles learned, after the war, that Father Kapaun died in Camp 5. In 2013, President Obama awarded a posthumous Medal of Honor to Father Kapaun for his heroism and the sacrifices he made for his fellow men while himself a prisoner of war.

Charles told me he'd seen a Facebook post regarding the 3rd Battalion of the 8th Cavalry, detailing an event where they were going on an eighty-four-mile march. This was the exact distance he and his fellow POWs traveled to Camp 5. Responding to the post, he informed them he had participated in the initial march. The webmaster reached out to Charles to ask what he remembered. Before the end of their conversation, Charles said he'd like to have a Cavalry Stetson hat like those seen in the movies and was instructed to send his hat size. Although he offered to pay for the hat and shipping charges, he was told that wouldn't be necessary as he'd already paid the price. A short time later, to Charles's great pleasure, FedEx delivered the Cavalry Stetson, which Charles added to his extensive collection of military memorabilia. He was also asked if he would like to be inducted into the Cavalry Museum. He graciously and gratefully accepted. Charles contributed to his induction by sending the only picture he took during his Korean War service while stationed in Hawaii. Years later, Charles was encouraged to write memoirs of his Korean War experiences. He often told people "Yes, I was a POW in Korea, but let's leave it at that."

This very special old veteran added that he'd earned two Purple Heart medals—one for being wounded and one for being a POW. Also, he received a Bronze

Star for service in Vietnam. Because of the harsh treatment as a POW, he still suffers foot problems, in addition to other physical and psychological scars that linger to this day.

Charles's interview turned out to be my lengthiest up to this point—three and a half hours. When we finished, we chatted a bit more and took a few pictures. Before I left, he showed me two collectors' rifles, an M1 Garand and an M1 Carbine. Lastly, Charles contributed to my efforts by donating sixty dollars to help fund my travels. To this day I keep in touch with Charles via Facebook. I am proud to say that we have formed a very special and memory-filled friendship.

Postscript: I'd like every reader to know that the expenses for fuel used to get to this powerful interview with Charles Ross were donated by River Valley Express Trucking of Wausau, Wisconsin. Owner Big Jim Neitzke, also a veteran and a long-time friend, was so impressed when he learned about this project, he volunteered to support my mission. Although he was not a Korean War veteran, he believed in what I was doing and wanted to help keep me on the road. I'm truly grateful.

Finally, on behalf of Sergeant Charles Ross, we would like to recognize his fallen comrades whom the sergeant continues to honor and remember by carrying their names in his wallet.

Private Henry Blanton
Private Jose Gonzalez
Corporal James Lee
Private Billy Myers
Corporate Wilbur Pollack
Private John Rinehart
Private Luther Wise

Chapter 3

Glenn Galtere, USMC
Thou Shall Not Kill

Corporal, U.S. Marine Corps, Baker Company, 1st Battalion, 7th Marine Regiment, 1st Marine Division. Interviewed April 25, 2022, and March 13, 2023, Port Saint Lucie, Florida. Born 1930.

You either get rid of all your ethics about killing or you crack up or you die, so the healthy thing to do is adjust and accept it for what it is. If you can't deal with it now, you'll deal with it later. The normal thing is to grieve, but when you lose someone or experience harrowing events, you either deal with it now or deal with it later. I never talked about what I went through at the Chosin Reservoir for forty years until I went to my first reunion.

Glenn Galtere answered an ad I'd placed on Facebook seeking Korean War Veterans. In our e-mail correspondence, I learned he'd be the first member of the historic "Chosin Few"—the Chosin Reservoir campaigners—I'd be meeting. The exploits of Fox Company, 2nd Battalion, 7th Marines, are well documented, especially their final stand during the brutal battle at that historic battleground where their do-or-die mission was to hold open a pass for withdrawing only Marine units, Army was east of the Reservoir. Glenn mentioned in his e-mails that Baker Company was sent up to reinforce Fox Company, and to his knowledge, after the vicious four-day battle, only twenty-seven out of 235 Marines walked off the hill unwounded … after decimating what seemed like an entire Chinese Division. This was a man who could be the last remaining Marine of the "Last Stand of Fox Company." Or so I thought. So I was quick to include Glenn, living in Florida, on my next trip east that was generously sponsored by River Valley Express. This was the same trip that I met Charles Ross on.

After driving into Port Saint Lucie, I grabbed a quick lunch before arriving at Glenn's home, where I was greeted as a long-time buddy. Glenn had mentioned earlier that he'd never talked in full detail about his Korean War experiences, but figured now was the time. This interview proved to be highly emotional, showing the realities of war from the perspective of a warrior who turned to God—becoming a minister years after the war. A minister who is a hardened combat veteran.

Along with some buddies, he'd tried enlisting during World War II when he was fifteen, forging his age and parents' signatures. But his baby-face gave him away, and the recruiter told him, "Kid get out of here and come back when you're

3. Glenn Galtere, USMC: Thou Shall Not Kill

seventeen." Glenn tried hard to convince the recruiter he was of age, pointing to his fraudulent papers, but he was denied and told to come back when he was truly of legal age.

So at the end of World War II, he joined the Marine Corps. After boot camp, with the government decommissioning ships at the time and no need for seagoing Marines, he was shipped to Camp Pendleton.

Glenn Galtere in his Marine Corps portrait circa 1948. Glenn did not have many photographs to share of his time in Korea, due to constant combat.

I never had any family members who ever served in the Marine Corps, but from a young age that's all I ever wanted to be. I knew when I was old enough, I was going to be a Gung-Ho Marine. I can't tell you how many times I went through combat training. I don't know how they do it now, but we were constantly doing combat training, and I think that had a lot to do with saving my life in Korea.

In 1948, after Camp Pendleton, Glenn and Baker Company were sent to Guam, assigned to remove remaining Japanese forces still entrenched in the island's caves. Glenn couldn't figure out if it was because his sergeant liked or hated him, but he was always the first sent in the caves, armed only with a .45 automatic pistol and flashlight. Thinking the Pacific war was still going on, the desperate Japanese diehards would fire at any Marine entering their caves. He crawled in through all sorts of openings, even tiny spider holes—squeezing in to talk these diehards out of their hiding spots. Glenn spent about two years on Gaum on active duty because it qualified for combat training.

I guess getting shot at by Japanese soldiers was a great prelude for what I was going to experience in Korea. The moment I entered a cave opening or hole, I would hear gunshots and ricochets, because they would aim for my flashlight. Not long after, I would enter the caves in the pitch black to lure Japanese soldiers out.

Glenn's enlistment was just about to end when the Korean war broke out in

June 1950, and Uncle Sam gave him what he mockingly described as "the best gift of all," a year's extension to his enlistment.

Word came down that the 1st Marine Division would be making a daring landing at the port of Inchon. The landing itself had the 1st and 5th Marine Regiments in the first assault. Once the beachhead was established, the 7th Marines were sent in as a reserve force but were redirected north to cut off any fleeing North Koreans. This plan of action went into effect when the 1st and 5th Marines captured Kimpo airfield. Aboard the troopship in the staging area, with the rest of the 7th Marines waiting to go over the side, Charles had a front-row seat before the magnificent power of the United States Navy. Glenn recalled "never seeing so many vessels in my life."

The Navy was clearing its throat, which meant the armada was intensely shelling inland. Glenn remembered the blasts of the battleships and surrounding warships being absolutely ear-shattering as they hammered North Korean coastal defenses. He was witnessing and getting involved in a coastal bombardment and amphibious landing operation that matched those of World War II just five years prior.

> *We were on the deck of our troopship and the roar was continually ear-shattering. We were ordered to go over the side, and down the nets we went. This led us to the landing craft below. It was no easy task, although I had done so in practice many times in earlier training. It was a challenge but manageable.*

Their landing craft seemed to circle forever; the sea was choppy, and many of the Marines became seasick. The deck of the Higgins landing craft was filled with seawater and vomit, making the trip toward the landing point even more miserable. At that point, most of the Marines didn't care if the entire North Korean Army was waiting for them, they just wanted to get out of those bouncing, reeking, leaking boats. Hitting the shoreline—more accurately, a seawall—they had to climb ladders from the rocking boat, no easy task. Finally, safely on land, the 7th Marines headed east, just above the advancing 5th and 1st Marine Regiments. The next day they got their first taste of war.

> *I didn't care, I wanted off that landing craft. After landing, we immediately moved through Incheon, and then moved north several miles, meeting slight resistance.*

The plan was to catch and cut off fleeing North Korean forces. One incident Glenn remembers vividly is charging across a rice paddy thigh-deep in water and human fertilizer, to take a small hill. Glenn recalled their commanding officer (CO) yelling at them to get their asses moving or that's where he'd squarely plant his bayonet. They believed him. The CO was Captain Wilcox, a veteran of Iwo Jima during World War II. Iwo Jima is considered the bloodiest battle the United States Marine Corps ever fought, and now he was leading Marines on a new battlefield in a new war. Glenn made it very clear that Captain Wilcox was a no-bullshit kind of Marine, and as gung-ho as they came.

I can recall the sound of bullets whizzing by. They sounded like angry bees. I heard men yell as they were hit, and others would fall dead without a sound. I tried moving faster but it was difficult to do so in those rice paddies, but we took the hill.

Another indelible event occurred in a small town with a name Glenn couldn't remember, where they were receiving fire from the north and south mountain ridges on both flanks.

Glenn and the Marines attempted an assault. But the North Koreans had slyly set a trap for the advancing Americans, who, when they approached the ridge, discovered that the enemy, only fifty yards away, had set up a deadly crossfire which caught the unwary leathernecks from all sides. Glenn, a corporal named Love, and PFC Ament were at the exposed flank under heavy automatic rifle fire. Glenn recalled Ament crying out as he fell to the ground. With their bodies, they protected their fallen buddy from further incoming, and Glenn returned fire with a BAR (Browning automatic rifle) and Corporal Love with his M1. Glenn was sure they killed and wounded some North Koreans as the others retreated over the hill.

Ament was cussing like a Marine, I could tell he was bleeding profusely from his chest wound. He then cried out for his mother. As he got weaker, he started praying the Lord's Prayer, "Our father who art in heaven...." He never got to finish it. He died. I can recall how my heart ached for him. I replayed in my mind several times what we could have done differently. I found no answer.

Not having enough time to evaluate what they'd just seen and done, Glenn and the other Marines moved out, leaving the fallen man where he'd died. This startling revelation would prove to be a constant occurrence during his time in Korea, having to witness the realities of war: This was not chasing Japanese stragglers out of caves like he'd done in 1948.

Glenn thought it was the next day when they ran into a similar situation and another member of their fire team, PFC Reynolds, took a round in his leg. He survived and, after treatment, returned to Baker company just before they boarded a troopship to make a landing at Wonsan, North Korea.

After landing at Wonsan, they were assaulting a hill to the west. A Chinese soldier armed with a "burp gun" (submachine gun) popped out of a spider hole and came straight for Glenn, who was carrying his BAR. Glenn pulled the trigger of his BAR. That's when he heard a clunk, his weapon jammed. A fellow Marine shot the Chinese soldier with his M1, stopping him in his tracks, saving Glenn.

I never wanted to kiss a man in my life, but I wanted to that time. The next time we got into a firefight he was killed as he was shot through the heart and died before he hit the ground. He was a replacement from Minnesota.

Almost every patrol on recon was reporting running into Chinese units. This information, quickly related to high command, was consistently brushed off as being of no major concern. An event, vividly remembered by Glenn as if it happened yesterday, occurred on November 2 at two in the morning: The Chinese hit Glenn's battalion in full force. Grossly outnumbered, roughly ten to one, the Americans heard what seemed like hundreds of bugles followed by enough flares to turn the black sky into daylight. The Chinese had snuck within yards of the Marines when they began their assault.

Glenn, with a stern look, said that there was no front line—the Chinese were right there among them, in front of them, behind them, and on all flanks. Unfortunately, Reynolds was bayoneted to death along with Vaughn, his foxhole buddy. Most of Glenn's squad died that night in the surprise attack by the Chinese, who were determined to annihilate the 1st Marine Division at what would become known as "the battle of the Chosin Reservoir."

They literally snuck up within yards of our foxholes, blew the bugles, and they were on us. And when I say on us, they were literally on top of us. They came in such massive waves, yelling and screaming, "Marines you die!" I was scared. Anyone who was there that says differently, they're a liar. We were never trained to fight an enemy who would attack in massive waves with no regard to their own safety. As near as I can recall, on the night of November second, our position—"B" Company—was near the top of a mountain; now known to me as Sudong. "A" Company was on the mountain to the east. I believe "C" Company and Headquarters Company were on the road and in the valley. The Chinese hit us without warning at two a.m., Platoon Sergeant Archie Van Winkle had decided, when we set up position, he would dig in with the squad on the outpost. The squad I was in was on the line about thirty yards just below that. The Chinese hit them mere seconds before they hit us. I know he was wounded several times while leading his Marines, fighting back until he received a very serious wound in the chest and went unconscious. I do not recall how many with him were hit or killed, but I tend to remember at least all were hit and eventually evacuated.

The fighting was so fierce and swift that the Marines resorted to brutal hand-to-hand combat—using bayonets, swinging their rifles like clubs. "This was no short battle," Glenn stated. From the moment they were hit, Baker Company spent the next six hours savagely fighting off hordes of fanatic attackers. It seemed as if the Chinese had no fear, running straight into .30-caliber machine gun fire, small arms fire, and hand grenades. The Marines didn't even have to aim when they fired, bodies just kept dropping. It was during this battle that Reynolds and Vaughn died.

Glenn, sitting before me as tense as I'd seen him throughout this interview, graphically recalled the darkness, the muzzle flashes, the horrid sounds of battle, and how the enemy would be on top of you before you knew it.

You would be firing in one direction and look to your left or right, and there would be six more Chinese just feet away. Some didn't even have weapons.

Glenn remembered that his position was in the shadows of a small rise on the side of a mountain, when a Chinese soldier, not seeing him, came running up. Glenn said he literally blew the soldier apart with his BAR. Seconds after, three more Chinese, hip-firing their burp guns, soon met the same fate.

3. Glenn Galtere, USMC: Thou Shall Not Kill

Newspaper clipping provided by Glenn Galtere, whose parents kept every clipping while their son fought at the Chosin Reservoir.

I looked right into their eyes. It seemed like when I pulled the trigger of my BAR, I cut them right in half. You either get rid of all your ethics about not killing, or you crack up or you die. So the unhealthy thing to do is adjust and accept it for what it is. If you can't deal with it now, you'll deal with it later. The normal thing is to grieve, but when you lose someone or experience harrowing events, you either deal with it now or deal with it later. I never talked about what I went through at the Chosin Reservoir for forty years until I went to my first reunion.

He went on to tell me about a Chinese American Marine, 1st Lieutenant Kurt C. Lee, who was a machine gun platoon leader. Lieutenant Lee proved invaluable while leading his team from outpost to outpost during this battle, since he spoke fluent Mandarin. When enemy forces were encountered, Lee tricked them into thinking he and his Marines were comrades. Glenn and his buddies would make a safe approach … and kill them. This brave Marine officer would be wounded more than a few times and receive the Navy Cross for his leadership and heroic actions.

When we were first attacked, Lieutenant Lee ran to our outpost and gathered us to go out and hunt Chinese that he continually located by calling out and speaking to them in Mandarin—one hundred percent fooling the enemy in thinking we were friendly. I remained friends with Lieutenant Lee after meeting at our first reunion and was present when he was buried at Arlington National Cemetery. He always told us in the field his goal was to die in combat to honor his family. He was constantly on point, leading us head-on into Chinese. His amazing and absolute great leadership skills encouraged us to follow him, and we did, even if he would have taken us to the gates of hell.

As the morning sun rose, the Chinese withdrew as quickly as they'd appeared.

After what seemed like an eternity to Glenn, he realized Baker Company had repulsed the attack, but had hung on only by a thread. Pausing to reflect on what he'd just gone through, Glenn took a moment to perform a personal inspection, finding twelve bullet holes in his winter parka.

> *How I was missed was, and still is, beyond me. I was turning every which way you could firing my BAR. It was a startling revelation that I didn't even get a scratch. For the first time in my life I thanked God.*

Checking the foxholes, he found eleven dead Marines out of the thirteen in his squad that had gone into battle. Most distressing was that most were his friends who'd fought together since their landing at Inchon, now shot in the head, bayoneted, or filled with bullet holes. The brutal battle waged that cold dark morning had came at a high cost to both the Marines and the Chinese. Glenn recalled Baker Company and the Battalion fighting and wiping out what seemed like an entire Chinese division; dead enemy bodies littered everywhere.

> *So many close friends all dead overwhelmed me. Looking back, I was in shock or a stupor, maybe both, but that helped enable me to cope physically. During the actual combat you are so busy fighting to stay alive that there is no time for emotions. Before and after is a different story.*

Examining bodies around his foxhole, Glenn discovered a Chinese officer—identified by the red stripes on his pant legs. Searching for maps, messages, and anything that would be of value as intel, Glenn found a small wallet inside the officer's tunic. Inside was a photo of the officer in civilian clothes, with his wife and two small children.

> *I had just made this woman a widow, and these two small children orphans. This was proof that he was more than just an enemy. He was someone's husband and father that I killed.*

The only survivors of his squad after the November 2 battle were PFC Jack Gallapo from Chicago, and Glenn. There were two high awards for valor issued, along with what Glenn described as a wheelbarrow full of Purple Hearts.

The Chinese almost seemed to have vanished, a tactic used to lure the advancing United Nations forces further north to the Yalu River, where the Chinese would surround them and cut them off.

> *What I want people to know, in this book, is that the Chinese came in full force in early November and not December. We had captured multiple prisoners from two or three separate Chinese divisions that hit us. This information was relayed to the high command and was brushed off as if it didn't matter. We were told, "Are you going to let a few Chinese laundrymen scare you?" They just didn't believe or want to believe the Chinese posed a threat.*

The days and weeks following the November 2 attack found Baker Company out on continuous combat patrols as the Communist plan went into full swing. The

1st Marine Division and various Army and ROK units, surrounded by twelve Chinese divisions, had only one option—to fight their way out. Numbers vary from multiple sources, but roughly 150,000 to 200,000 Chinese swarmed around the Chosin Reservoir like bees out of a hive. The UN forces were about to be demolished; the mighty victory MacArthur had overpromised was stopped dead in its tracks. Newspapers back home were prematurely predicting the destruction of the 1st Marine Division and suggesting to the American public that if anyone had family fighting there, pray for them. At a press interview, Oliver P. Smith, Commanding General of the 1st Marine Division, after hearing "It's not like Marines to run," snapped back with, "Retreat, Hell! We're not retreating, we're advancing in a different direction." That became a rally cry that motivated all the Marine and Army units near the Reservoir. But the truth was written on the wall: They did face complete annihilation.

> *Our leaders wisely decided the best defense was an aggressive offense, so we were not just repelling attacks, but actively seeking out the Chinese and attacking them. We knew we were on our own, and General Smith made the decision that all units consolidate at Hagaru-ri to form a full division to fight our way out.*

Glenn went on to recall his squad being on combat patrol Thanksgiving Day, so no holiday meal was served. They did hear about the turkey, gravy, mashed potatoes, and trimmings, which they never got. All a disappointed Glenn and his buddies got … were the stories.

The Chinese, he explained, would send a few troops out to lure in the Marines, and that's when the main force would surround them, forcing them to fight their way out. On that Thanksgiving Day, the battle for what the troops later called Turkey Hill was as intense as ever, with the Chinese swarming among and around the Marines before they even knew what happened. The 7th Marines took a tremendous number of casualties; Glenn figured they lost a third of their company.

> *We were constantly falling for their same tricks and would find ourselves surrounded and fighting to get out. November 27th is when the entire Chinese force attacked all units at the reservoir.*

Readers should know that these actions were carefully planned and orchestrated by Communist China's leader, Chairman Mao, who'd issued a warning early in the war that UN forces must not cross the 38th parallel. If they did, he would send in his army to support North Korea. General Douglas MacArthur, commanding general of the UN forces, was rather scornful of this threat and brushed it off. The moment allied forces crossed the 38th, Mao set his battle plan in action, playing off MacArthur's arrogance. Glenn and other Chosin Reservoir veterans would suffer the repercussions of their leader's ego.

> *Even after all the reports of constantly engaging with Chinese forces, it still was just not accepted. They brushed it off like it didn't mean anything.*

Glenn once again mentioned Captain Wilcox, his company commander, "a calm cool combat veteran of Iwo Jima," who shouted to his men to form a defensive perimeter on Turkey Hill. While standing with his hands on his hips barking orders, the captain took a bullet to his mouth but continued directing and encouraging his Marines. Eventually, after losing too much blood, he was evacuated and taken off the front line. But his orders and leadership helped hold Turkey Hill. The battle lasted until the early morning, when the Marines finally broke through, making it back to friendly lines to find their Thanksgiving meal was gone. Having a moment to finally try to get some sustenance, Glenn resorted to a frozen C-ration, and watched the artillery barrage below as both sides continuously bombed each other.

> *I was finally able to stop and pull a C-ration can out, which I had to break out and chisel with my bayonet, because it was forty below zero. I gave up because it was so frozen, so ended up eating a few handfuls of snow.*

While Glenn was enjoying his faux Thanksgiving dinner—"a few handfuls of snow"—he observed a magnificent display of firepower. In the valley below, both sides were firing artillery barrages, which Glenn described as the most shocking fireworks he'd ever witnessed but he sighed with relief that no one was shooting at him.

The Marines and Army units were running out of everything: ammunition, food, supplies, fuel for vehicles and tanks. Most of all they were running out of men, and they knew it. It was a monumental mistake, but one that in turn was a blessing in disguise which helped save the Marines. All day long, air drops ensured the troops had the supplies they needed to fight off the Chinese hordes. A codeword used by the Marines for sixty-millimeter mortars was tootsie rolls. When the order was put in to drop tootsie rolls, it was never translated. Opening the crates that had been parachuted in, to their surprise the Marines found case after case of the hard candy. Authentic chocolate Tootsie Rolls. The blessing in disguise was that they provided food that was quickly thawed in the warmth of the mouth, giving a jolt of energy to the deprived Marines. The candy was also used to plug bullet holes in the radiators of vehicles hit by enemy fire.

> *I did not see the air drops, but a Marine came up to me with what seemed like armfulls of Tootsie Rolls. I couldn't believe what I was seeing. I quickly loaded them inside of my field jacket.*

Glenn and Baker Company were ordered to go behind enemy lines and attack the Chinese from the rear, which would relieve undermanned Charlie and Fox companies—holding on by a thread after three days of fighting off waves of Chinese, yet keeping the Toktong Pass open for the withdrawal. The strategic value of this pass was priceless; if Charlie and Fox were wiped out and the pass had been seized by the enemy, no one would have gotten out. What later became known as the Last Stand of Fox Company proved to be a singular moment in Marine Corps history. Fox Company was an extremely undermanned unit of 234 Marines, whose formidable mission was to hold the that crucial pass for the fleeing 1st Marine Division. Baker

Company was almost successful, flanking the Chinese to attack them from behind to help Fox Company, but were discovered. At first, a Chinese soldier ran toward Glenn, but Glenn stopped the soldier in his tracks with his BAR and that's when all hell broke loose. The next thing they knew, the same old routine began: With bugles blaring, the Chinese were on top of them. The Marines engaged in hand-to-hand combat, using bayonets, clubbing Chinese to death with M1s, stabbing and slashing with knifes, even resorting to hacking enemy soldiers to death with trench shovels and beating them to death with their bare hands—not uncommon tactics in the Korean War. Glenn. being a BAR man, recalled shooting straight ahead, turning around to the sides and behind, to fire his weapon. It almost seemed like a hailstorm of bullets, but instead of digging in, his group pushed forward, fighting through an entire Chinese division to get to Fox Company, finally reaching those who were left. Forming a defensive perimeter, the combined companies took the Chinese head on. During this chaos, Glenn was wounded.

> I took a bullet round to my groin and fell instantly. At this point, I had ditched my BAR and picked up an M1 rifle that I used in combat until I was evacuated. I had no idea where anyone was, and I continued down a mountainside and would cover myself with snow and conceal my location when I heard any sort of noise. Doing this, I would see Chinese soldiers pass just feet away from me and never see me. I prayed to whatever God would listen, to get me out of here and let me see tomorrow.

Glenn crawled through the snow, dragging his acquired M1 by the sling the entire way, not knowing where he was going or in what direction—just knowing he wanted to survive. He recalled being in and out of consciousness the entire time, but still having the will to live, and finally reaching a road where he was picked up by some Marines.

> It reminds me of a biblical story of a shepherd being saved by some bystanders, but in my case, they were Marines. But to me they looked like angels. I had stumbled upon the convoy heading towards Hagaru-ri and I was thrown on a fender of a truck and was in and out of consciousness until I was flown out of Hagaru-ri.

When I asked Glenn what he thought was the strength of the Chinese force during those encounters, he told me that later figures showed at least fifteen thousand, and that a Chinese division is smaller than one of ours. Records show over four thousand Chinese faced the courageous Marines during those nightly attacks at Fox Hill. In terms of the dead Chinese, those numbers were also fudged as to how many were wiped out by those brave Marines. The true numbers are only known to the men who were there and to the sands of time.

Glenn went on to say that only twenty-seven Marines walked off Fox Hill without a scratch, joining with the forces moving to the coast. But the fighting didn't stop there; they were continuously clashing with Chinese the entire way to Hungnam, where he was picked up.

When Glenn was taking off from Hagaru-ri in a Marine Air Wing C47, the transport aircraft attracted enemy ground fire from Communist troops surrounding the airstrip and it ended up with multiple bullet holes in its fuselage. Glenn gathered what strength he could to look out the window and snicker at the enemy before blacking out. He was eventually evacuated to Japan along with thousands of other wounded. Although his time in Korea was done, he still did not feel a sense of safety until getting to Japan, where all the wounded were kept in what looked like a giant gymnasium.

Going from forty degrees below zero to comfortable room temperatures posed another serious problem for the injured Marines. Their frozen wound scabs and frostbite injuries were thawing out, setting off bleeding and infections. Severe frostbite plagued almost every warrior evacuated from Chosin Reservoir. The "Mickey Mouse" boots issued (given that name due to the bulkiness of the rubber winter design) did more harm than good. When walking and staying on the move, the boots were effective. But when stopped, the feet of the Marines and GIs would freeze, causing severe frostbite damage.

> *Staying in the gymnasium, it was like luxury. They couldn't get to all of us right away, so we were separated, and it was like a first come first serve. When they got to me, they told me they were going to cut my feet off because both were black. I begged and pleaded to not do that, and they decided to leave them be. To this day I have zero feeling in my feet. I could cut myself with a toenail clipper and never even feel it.*

Along with all the wounds and startling news of impending amputations, the Americans faced even more problems. In combat, soldiers do not have time to relieve themselves, so more times than not they unabashedly urinated and defecated in their pants. (Yes, war is hell!) The nurses, as Glenn related, had the most disgusted looks on their faces when frozen human waste began thawing. Glenn and I shared a good laugh as he went on to tell me that if you take the time to relieve yourself normally with your pants down, you could be shot in the bare butt by an enemy soldier who'd think it was a joke to hit a Marine in that semi-naked state. Glenn said he wasn't about to get shot with his pants down, so he did what every other Marine did, "Shit in my pants and kept fighting."

> *We all looked at the nurses and waved at them with smiles and told them don't worry honeys, it bothers us too. A moment of laughter and they got to work cleaning us up. Was like luxury to go from fighting Chinese to have pretty girls washing you up.*

Glenn's interview also proved to be the first time I'd hear from a combat veteran about experiencing and dealing with shell shock or what we commonly know now as PTSD (posttraumatic stress disorder). In the first weeks of being in a cozy bed, warm and well on the road to recovery, Glenn, through nightmarish dreams, would revisit the events he'd witnessed just weeks before. He described how much he hated going to sleep, in fear of what awaited him the moment he'd close his eyes. I have never served or been in combat, so it was hard to comprehend what Glenn was telling me, but after listening it became all too clear.

> When I would fall asleep, I would see the faces of the men—Chinese and North Koreans, whom I had shot at close range. I would clearly see fear in their eyes turn to deadness. Their mouths opened in a scream that never came out. When those events occurred, there was no time to feel or process all that was going on. It was a time to stay alive, dead to feelings of all kinds, (with) responses to training, and an insane desire to stay alive and kill the enemy. I dreaded going to sleep when I was in the hospital and often didn't.

Saying that his nightmares were not only of the enemy he'd slain but also of his fellow Marines he'd seen killed, Glenn reiterated that you simply don't have time to process what's going on in battle, even when it's your friend who's killed right before your eyes. Seeing his fellow Marines being killed—some of them especially good buddies since basic training—was just as haunting as seeing the face of the enemy he'd taken down.

> I would relive, often, the times when fellow Marines around me, some my good friends, would be killed and some of their brains or shattered flesh would fly in my direction. We were in almost daily combat for three months. Most of the original company had died or were wounded. Three different times they gave us replacement drafts to take the place of so many casualties. Many of them suffered the same fate.

While recovering from his wounds, in the hope of clearing his guilt, Glenn attended therapy sessions. He still considered himself a sinner and a murderer when recalling that Chinese officer and the photos of his family. No matter that it was war, no matter he was fighting for survival, the remorse was too much for him. Admitting he wasn't a praying man or someone who had ever shown interest in the ministry, the first time he did pray was at the Chosin Reservoir when he was asking any God who would listen to keep him alive so he could see the sun rise one more time.

> I saw several chaplains while in the hospital, trying to deal with what I now know were flashbacks. The last chaplain I saw helped me identify what was happening and facilitated me to put a label on myself on how I was seeing myself as a murderer. I didn't have a clue as to the dynamic that was happening. In retrospect, it was a time of confessing the guilt, the pain, the remorse. It was a time of agony, but there was a beginning of relief in all that was jammed up inside. I began to move what was inside to the outside. It took more than a few years for that process. Then the chaplain challenged me with the gospel and asked me the question, "Is what Christ did on the cross sufficient for the forgiveness of your sins?" Then, after a long pause, he asked, "But the important question is, can you accept His forgiveness?" I heard the Lenten message of mercy in my head.

This was the beginning of Glenn's spiritual journey, on his way to becoming a minister and traveling the world doing missionary work. Glenn said he wishes he could say there were ringing bells and significant moments of spiritual enlightenment, but there weren't. His head believed, or wanted to believe, but faith in God was miles from his heart. His struggle persisted for years while he worked odd jobs—washing dishes at diners, delivering milk and newspapers. Armed only with skills he learned in the Corps, Glenn told future employers he had learned to shoot and kill people, and he was very effective at it. Of course, that wasn't the answer business owners were seeking. Glenn went on to express that he'd always had an interest in flying but was never able to become a Marine Corps flying cadet because he had zero experience. So he took flying lessons, earned his pilot's license, and joined Magnolia Aviation in Laurel, Mississippi. He spent the next five years crop-dusting mostly cotton fields in Mississippi and Alabama, and during winter months dusting giant anthills that were taking over the fields.

> *I kept feeling a call to ministry, I recall; I know (with) the things I've done I could never be a minister, having killed people in Korea and breaking all the Ten Commandments at least three times. But a minister took me under his wing and gave me the spiritual education I never got. And one time, when sitting in on a meeting, he told a fellow minister, "Is this argument over, or do we need to go outside?" And right then and there I said, that's my kinda guy. Maybe I can even be a minister.*

Glenn even had run-ins with members of the Ku Klux Klan (KKK), whom he described as "big, strong, Alabama farm boys."

> *A few clan members cornered me in the local drug store and told me, "We're coming for you, preacher." And I told them, I hope you're a good shot because I am. All I had at home was a BB gun, but they never did come to lynch me. They did burn a cross in my front yard and I was relocated to Atlanta through the church. But not every Southerner is like that. Folks from Alabama are wonderful people. Many grew up as poor dirt farmers like me and get along with anyone of color. There's a rather negative picture of the poor Southerner and it's not true.*

As a missionary, Glenn traveled for over ten years to Africa, Ecuador, Honduras, and many Caribbean islands. When he turned seventy, the church wanted him to retire. Laughing, Glenn said that he told the bishop, "Get your toughest youngest man and we'll see who can do more pushups." The church let him serve several more years, assigned to hospice and working with combat veterans in their last moments. Glenn then talked about one of his hospice patients.

> *I noticed a Marine Corps flag outside the veteran's door, and his wife told me that he had served in Korea. I told her so did I. I went in, and although we never knew each other in Korea, we shared our experiences with each other, and I truly believe it helped ease his conscience. Ultimately, he passed away. After the first meeting with him, his wife was listening at the door and when I came out told me that she had never heard any of those stories. She went on to tell me that she thought he didn't love her anymore after he got back from Korea because he was quiet and distant. I told her, no, that's not what was going on. He was dealing with demons and what happened to him in Korea.*

3. Glenn Galtere, USMC: Thou Shall Not Kill

(From left) Collin Wilson, Glenn Galtere, and Ryan Walkowski pose for a picture after Glenn's second interview.

It took two visits with Glenn in Florida to complete this chapter, and was well worth the time. At the second meeting I was accompanied by Collin, my travel partner and documenter, and Glenn and his lovely wife showed us a scrapbook of newspaper articles his mother had kept while he served in Korea, which gave us a huge amount of Korean War details that have been invaluable in the development of this book. Thanks Glenn, for sharing so much.

> *I'm grateful to this day, I must of went through combat training three or four times before I saw combat. One time, by the Reservoir, there was a constant stream of tracers coming from both sides. It was so thick, if you stood up you were dead. It sounds stupid, but I'm grateful to the Corps that they gave me that kind of training before they put me in a place where people would shoot at me. If I met a Chinese soldier today that was there when I was, I'd thank him for his bravery. Sounds stupid, but I sort of admired them. They were fighters.*

Chapter 4

Bob O'Keefe, USMC
Battling Bob O'Keefe

Corporal, U.S. Marine Corps—Dog Company, 2nd Battalion, 1st Marine Regiment, 1st Marine Division. Interviewed July 29, 2022, Toms River, New Jersey. Born 1930.

Every night they prepared themselves for battle. They prepared by blowing bugles, loudspeakers, and whistles. The loudspeaker would go BOOM, BOOM, BOOM. Then they come down the hill towards us. Looked like Custer's Last Stand the way we were dug in at Koto-ri. O.P. Smith said to Chesty Puller, "You gotta hold this road open or we don't get outta here!" So that was our job, to hold that goddamn main road open.

It was Michael Lombardi, a family friend, who suggested that Bob O'Keefe was a must interview, and that Michael would facilitate a meeting that would include a ceremony at their city's Town Hall. He even suggested I speak about my project. After about a week of my corresponding with Michael, he arranged a phone call with Bob's family so I could explain my mission and the basics of the interview procedure. I think it's safe to say they were impressed with my dedication to remembering Korea, the Forgotten War, especially after learning I was only twenty-nine years old.

Arriving at Toms River, a charming 225-year-old town on the New Jersey shore, Collin and I were greeted by Michael, himself a veteran and decked out in military dungarees, who took us to the Town Hall to meet Bob's son Mike and daughter Beth and the other family members who were preparing the rec hall for the event. The stage had been set for the interview—the Town Hall, the local motorcycle club honor guard, and even a bagpiper who'd play the Marine Corps hymn. Collin and I went to work setting up our small display of war photos and the Korean War flag featuring the signatures of each veteran we'd interviewed—soon to include Bob O'Keefe's. We had about two hours before the ceremony, so Mike took us to meet Bob, who was outside, enjoying the balmy weather. Mike asked to be notified when we were done and left. No time was wasted. Bob went right into it.

I forget when they attacked South Korea, but I was on leave up at the lake with my sister and her husband and a girlfriend I knew at the time. And uh, we were lying on the beach at the time, and my brother-in-law went to get hot dogs, and he comes back and tells us there's a war broke out in Korea. I said to him, well that's over by Japan and the Army is over there, so they probably won't need the Marines.

And my brother-in-law said, "No. All military personnel are supposed to report back immediately."

With only six months left on his enlistment, this was not the news Bob wanted to hear. (Note: Because of the Korean War, President Truman added another year to all enlistees' hitches.) Soon Bob was in Kobe, Japan, where the Marines were organizing and making ready to invade Incheon, South Korea. When that day came, the mighty U.S. military machine went to work. What seemed like the entire 1st Marine Division were loaded onto LSTs (the transport labeled "landing ship, tank") and left Japan to meet up with the rest of the fleet heading to Inchon. On September 15, the landing craft, with the 1st Marine Division, the Army's 7th Division, and various supporting units, cruised toward Inchon Harbor's formidable seawall.

Bob O'Keefe in his U.S. Marine Corps portrait.

Some forty thousand men surprised the six-thousand-man North Korean Army and turned the tide of the war by taking the stress off the embattled Pusan Perimeter. Among the many warships blasting the shoreline was a historic battleship.

I saw the Missouri *and all the other ships as we loaded in the landing crafts, and I told myself, well, this is real! Then we hit the beach at Inchon, and the first thing I saw was a kid named Miller get killed. Another one who got hit was Dombrowski. He was a Master Sergeant and got hit in the arm. The blood was squirting out like a geyser. The corpsman was right there and bandaged him up and put him right back on the landing craft to a hospital ship.*

The Inchon landing is regarded by many scholars and military historians as one of the most flawlessly executed and decisive military operations in modern warfare. The resistance was tough, but the Marines and Army units, after taking Inchon in 72 hours, started the march and advanced to Seoul. Bob dug in with Oberg, a Navajo Native American, who Bob said "wasn't a nice guy." Oberg would send Bob and the only Black Marine in the platoon to set up a listening post with com wire and a field radio. There was a lot of scuttlebutt about a North Korean counterattack with tanks on the prowl, but no one knew where or when they would hit the line.

We went out about a hundred and fifty yards; we called back every fifteen minutes and I said to this colored boy to make sure you call back every fifteen minutes. I asked him if he wanted the first watch or to sleep. He said, "No, I can't sleep, so go ahead." He and I were talking, and he came from Montclair, New Jersey. I can't remember his name but you're going to hear some terrible things here. We were laying in the hole we dug, and he said to me, "I hear a clicking sound, and I smell fish." I said to him, "I don't think so. We're like fifteen miles inland now, how could he smell fish?" But he said to me again, "Well I smell fish, and I hear a clicking sound." As we were talking, he said to me, "I have two enemies here. The North Koreans and the Clan." I'm Irish, so when he said "Clan," I thought the Irish Clan. And he said, "No, there's a lot of Southerners here on this line." He said to me he worries about it, so I told him to keep his nose clean and everything will be okay.

While Bob dozed, his foxhole buddy was still hearing the clicking that was getting louder, with the fish smell getting stronger. At about four in the morning, Bob woke up to find his foxhole buddy wide awake. Bob described his feelings as always being on edge, even with nothing happening; there was always an eerie feeling.

I told him, "Why didn't you wake me up?" He told me he couldn't sleep. I asked him if he called back, and he said, "Yeah, I called back." He told me to sit and listen, so I did. I didn't smell the fish, but I heard the click. Now I could hear it, so I said I'm going to call back to the lieutenant. First his assistant wanted to know what I wanted, but I told him, "Never mind, put the lieutenant on." I told him we hear a clicking out here and my buddy smells fish. He said "fish." And I said, "I'm telling you what's going on." So, I asked him, "Can you get us a flare to see what's out there?" Well, he calls back to the Missouri, *'cause we are still within range—fifteen miles, and they had a twenty-five-mile range with the battleship. When I heard that battleship go, I said to the colored boy, "We gotta get outta here! He just called back to the* Missouri *and this is gonna look like Times Square here in a minute!"*

Bang! The star shell exploded, and Bob and his foxhole buddy were running for their lives toward their line. Bob was yelling and screaming, "O'Keefe, O'Keefe, don't shoot, don't shoot!"

We went through trip flares, landmines. I don't know how the hell we made it through there. God almighty was with us at that moment.

Reaching the safety of their line, the two Marines hopped in the reserve hole they'd dug earlier. The clicking they'd heard came from five enemy T34 tanks slowly, stealthily, inch by inch, advancing for a counterattack. Luck would have it that when the star shell went off, the North Koreans froze, but only momentarily. The tanks then broke through the lines, wounding and killing a lot of men in Bob's company. All hell had broken loose, and the entire line opened fire on the tanks and North Korean troops.

Bob O'Keefe during his interview with Collin Wilson and Ryan Walkowski.

> The colored boy, my buddy, was starting to panic, because a tank came right up on the hill by us. He said to me, "We gotta get outta here, we gotta get outta here!" I told him, "We can't. We gotta stay where we are because the whole line is firing all over this hill. North Koreans are in front of us, and our weapons are back there, we can't do a goddamn thing." I told him, "Let's stay here, because Easy Company is just starting to come over the road."

Bob saw a red-headed Marine armed with a bazooka, zigzagging and dodging around the tanks. Bob didn't know his name but said the Marine must have known that a T34 fuel tank was exposed at the vehicle's rear. Knocking out three of the enemy tanks with precision shots to those vulnerable targets, the bazooka man moved to fire on a fourth vehicle but was killed as Bob watched. While the tank crews were escaping from their burning vehicles, they were picked off by Marine sharpshooters. The battle continued, with the North Korean counterattack stopped in its tracks by textbook Marine Corps tactics. Next stop was Seoul.

> The next day we were heading towards Seoul, and a man named Joe Ervin came to me and said, "Hey Bobby, that colored boy you were with..." and I said, "Yeah." He said, "He got it." I asked him, "What do you mean?" And he told me, "He's dead." I said, "You gotta be kidding me. He's dead?" As we're moving, he's telling me this, and said what happened. I asked, "Did a sniper get him?" He told me he got shot in the back. I don't wanna say anything but what he was telling me, the Clan was out

to get him. You had to watch yourself over there, you know what I mean? I felt bad when it happened, but then you gotta move on.

Bob explained that the primary mission for the 5th Marines was to take Kimpo Airfield, with the 1st Marines ordered to the main route into Seoul and the 7th Marines to head further north around Seoul to catch any fleeing North Koreans. This was when Bob said that the officer leading the 1st Marine Regiment was Lewis "Chesty" Puller, the most decorated Marine in the history of the Corps, and a veteran of campaigns fought before and during World War II. I asked, "So, you knew Chesty?" Bob replied, "Yes, personally." Reaching the outskirts of Seoul, Bob and the 1st Marines were positioned on a hill overlooking the capitol, while Puller was planning the next day's attack.

You're not gonna believe this, but I'll tell it anyways. There was a female reporter by the name of Marguerite Higgins, and she took photos for Life Magazine. Chesty Puller was on top of this hill with us, looking down at Seoul, and MacArthur comes down below the hill with his crew. He wanted to talk to Chesty Puller, you know. His aides come out and Puller turned around and said if the General wants to talk to me, he'll have to come up here, because he's trying to set up an attack to take the capitol. And he did, he stayed there and I'm on the side of the hill in my foxhole and MacArthur passes us with his entourage. Whatever went on with Chesty up there, I don't know, but the next day we went into Seoul.

Bob described Seoul as "totally demolished, nothing like the beautiful, flourishing city it is today." Patrolling the right side of the boulevard entering the city, he noticed that the Marines advancing on the left were being targeted—getting hit and falling to the ground. Bob found an alleyway, and with a few Marines, crept around the corner to find the sniper. (Author's note: This dramatic scene was captured on film, saved in many Korean War photo document files, and in it, you can see Bob to the right, clutching his M1 Garand.) While checking things out, the Marines spotted a muzzle flash in a nearby church steeple.

I said they're in that goddamn church there, you could see the flashes. So, I said I'm gonna go out and get a tank. And here's another thing ... they had barriers along the road, and we couldn't bring the tanks in, because we didn't know if there were explosives under them. But I went and told them everyone is getting slaughtered because there is a church up here with two snipers, I think. So, this Captain Crock said, "To hell with that barrier," and ordered the tank to go through and nothing happened. The tank pulled up, and I got behind it and get on the phone and tell them up a little further, up a little further. Here the driver hops out and runs into the alleyway and starts firing with a carbine. I told him, "What the hell are you going to do with that pea shooter? Get in that tank and blow that goddamn church up! Everyone is getting slaughtered here!"

During the sniper fire, two Marine chaplains approached: Father Keeney, who was Catholic, and a Protestant padre whose name Bob didn't know. Keeney suffered a near-fatal chest wound but survived. The Protestant chaplain suggested they cross the street, but Bob snapped, "You can't, they have us zeroed in." Despite Bob's warning, the chaplain started across but made it only halfway. He was hit.

He got halfway across, and he got it. He made it to the other side and was leaning against a wall and I hollered, "Are you okay?" And he waved back. I went back to Worfield, that was the Marine's name. Anyways, I told Worfield, "I'm getting the tank." The tank moved up and he told me over the phone that he sees it and then he blasted it. Warfield and I went to the church to check it out and there were two snipers.

The battle turned into urban warfare—building to building, door to door, against an understrength North Korean force of around seven thousand men, facing roughly forty thousand American warriors (7th Army Infantry Division and the 1st Marine Division). Although outnumbered, the North Koreans had the advantage of a heavily fortified city, with machine-gun emplacements and snipers in strategic positions everywhere. The barricades that Bob mentioned earlier had to be cleared, taking the Marines about an hour at each position, as they advanced and swarmed over the city. Bob made it clear MacArthur wanted the capitol taken and handed over to the South Koreans as promised. Although Marines carried on with house-to-house engagements, artillery barrages could be heard in the northern outskirts, Seoul was declared secure on September 25, 1950, on the three-month anniversary of the war.

When we got to the capitol building, what happened was one of the Marines went up on top and raised the American flag over the capitol building. That didn't go over too good, know what I mean? So, they had to go back up and take it down and put up the South Korean flag. But it was funny at the time.

The next stop for Bob and the 1st Marine Division would be Wonsan Harbor in North Korea. The leaders in Washington were cautious on whether the enemy should be pursued over the border that separated North and South Korea. Threats from China were not taken seriously. General MacArthur was seeing a glimpse of total victory with South Korea free of the North Korean Army. The People's Republic of China, in late October and early November, attacked the entire advancing UN front but pulled back in what seemed like a full retreat, as mentioned in other chapters of this book.

We boarded the ships and went around Korea to Wonsan. What happened was it was mined. We had to stay on the ships until they cleared the mines out of the harbor. We were there like four or five days on the ship. Anyways, Bob Hope was on shore with the Army doing a show and told them the Marines are out on the ships doing "Operation Yoyo." He apologized later. When I came home, I ran into him and told him, "That wasn't nice, you called us Operation Yoyo. We secured that whole goddamn area." But he apologized. I was only making a joke to him though.

The next stop for Bob O'Keefe would be one he'd never forget.

There was one main road leading from Wonsan to the Yalu River. It forked past a reservoir called Chosin. Only small skirmishes were taking place during November, with the 1st Marine Division strung out along an eighty-mile road. Bob even remembered playing football in North Korea at Koto-ri, where the 1st Marine Regiment was stationed with Chesty Puller. The talk was buzzing that everyone would be home by Christmas. On November 27, 1950, the U.S. Air Force and 1st Marine Air Wing boasted control of the entire peninsula and celebrated by distributing Thanksgiving dinners to all the troops across South Korea. Among the 1st Marine garrison at Koto-ri were the 41st Commando or Royal Marines—nine hundred Brits led by Colonel Drysdale. The 7th Marines were located the furthest, at Yudam-ni, while the 1st Marine Regiment was in reserve at Koto-ri. On November 28, reports began trickling down that Marine and Army units further north were being hit by an overwhelming force, not yet known to be Chinese. Each night, enemy troops poured around the loosely consolidated Marine and soldiers, outnumbering them ten to one. Soon the Chinese surrounded the 1st Marine garrison at Koto-ri. That's when Chesty Puller gave his famous quote to rally his Marines: "We've been looking for the enemy for several days, now we've finally found them. We're surrounded. That simplifies our problem of getting to these people and killing them."

Every night they prepared themselves for battle. They prepared by blowing bugles, loudspeakers, and whistles. The loudspeaker would go Boom, Boom, Boom, then they came down the hill towards us. Looked like Custer's Last Stand the way we were dug in at Koto-ri. O.P. Smith said to Chesty Puller, "You gotta hold this road open or we don't get outta here!" So that was our job, was to hold that goddamn main road open. They were hitting us every night. Daytime they didn't hit us because of our air support.

I asked Bob about the use of napalm.

The prop jobs, what ya call 'em, the F4U Corsairs? They could fly low and the jets at the time just couldn't do the job. And they were dropping a lot of napalm. And they were from the carriers. And you could hear them flying around waiting for daybreak so they could see the Chinese going back to wherever the hell it is they went to hide. Anyways, we secured the area and waiting for the 7th Marines to link up with the Army and 5th Marines, and they come down and we formed a full division of mixed units. Then we went down to Hungnam, and that's when I went into the hospital from severe frostbite. I'm disabled from Korea, but that's okay, I'm here.

Bob witnessed the same human waves of fanatical enemy forces mentioned over and over throughout this book. He also experienced gruesome hand-to-hand combat, which he was reluctant to discuss.

While advancing out of Koto-ri, they'd come across multiple road obstructions. When the column would stop, the Chinese swarmed all over the stalled Marines. During the long journey to the evacuation on the coast, the "Mickey Mouse" winter boots issued to our forces created as many casualties as did the Chinese. "Mickey Mouse" boots are cold-weather foot attire supposed to keep feet warm, but with one flaw: While constantly on the move and fighting in the hills against the Chinese to protect the column, the ground troop's feet would sweat, and would freeze at the moment they stopped marching or fighting.

> *The Indian I told you about, Odberg, told me, "I wouldn't wear those." And I said "Why?" We had these combat boots on, and they look comfortable, and guys were putting them on, right? He looked at me and said, "Yeah, they'll be cutting their goddamn legs off, just watch." And that's exactly what he said. I said, "You gotta be kidding me." But I listened to him. I kept them though, just in case, and it got to be thirty below zero and I was about to put them on and Odberg told me not to. He was right. When I got to the hospital, they were cutting the legs off guys with those boots on.*

There were huge sighs of relief when, ten miles from the coast, Bob and his buddies saw the evacuation ships lying offshore. Upon reaching the coast, the U.S. Army 3rd Infantry Division took over the perimeter to allow the battle-weary Marines and GIs to board the ships. Seventeen Congressional Medals of Honor would later be awarded to those heroes who fought during the harrowing two weeks at the Chosin Reservoir. I could tell from the look in Bob's eyes that he was reliving those horrific moments, so I eased up the questioning.

It was almost time to move to the community center, when Bob shared one more story of an R&R (rest and recreation) in Japan, with Odberg and a few other Marines—all recovering from frostbite. They decided it was a good idea to catch a Japanese boat and hit a local bar. Turns out, the place was filled with World War II Japanese veterans, so the moment a few Marines walked in, the tensions rose.

> *We're in the back room and we can hear the band playing and everything. Well, this Japanese guy goes up to get some drinks, and everybody is having a good time. He said, you guys stay here, and he went up and got Sake. I couldn't drink it if I tried, I said, "That's horrible, I can't drink that." But we were sitting in there and we said to each other, "Where the hell is Odberg?" So, I went down the hallway and opened a door and saw him at the bar. And here he's talking with his Japanese bullshit, you know. So, I said to the other guys come on let's go in and I ordered beers for everyone. So, Joe see's this big piece of asparagus and asked if I wanted to try it and I told him, "No, don't you see what they use for fertilizer around here?" Anyways he gets sick, and that's when I looked around and noticed all these Japanese veterans of the war. There was one bathroom, and this Japanese broad went in there. Well, Joe gets sick and runs in there and this broad comes out screaming because he's puking. I turn around and the place is collapsing and I'm going, "HOLY CHRIST!" During all this, some candles got knocked over and the place is on fire now. We get outside and I look at Odberg and tell him, "The boat isn't there, what do we do now?" Odberg said, "Let's go out the front." Well, all the Japs out front were pissed. Well, here comes the Army MPs and they got off those trucks and they beat those Japs like hell and scattered them. So, they grab us and take us back and they wake up Chesty Puller. Odberg was the first to talk to him, then us, and we told him that Odberg ordered us to go with him. Chesty looked at us and said, "If I didn't need you guys, you'd all be in jail for six months!"*

Just then, Bob's son came to tell us everyone's starting to pile into the community center, so we packed up and headed down. There must have been about a hundred guests who came to pay tribute to Bob for his military service, including other Korean War veterans. Michael Lombardi opened the ceremony, recounting Bob's history in the Corps. When it was my turn, I proudly talked about my mission, adding in the details which brought Collin and me to interview Bob, who was presented by the mayor of Toms River with a flag that had flown over our nation's capitol building. A fifty–fifty drawing was held, and half the money raised was given to us to continue our travels. What a wonderful and helpful gesture! After the ceremony, before returning to the O'Keefes' for a farewell party, I had the opportunity to chat with Howard Openshaw. who had served with the 11th Marines during the outpost phase of the Korean War. Much of what I learned from Howard would wind up in some of these chapters.

Even though Collin doesn't drink, we weren't going to pass up the opportunity to cut loose with a surviving member of the Chosin Few. A half hour or so went by, and that's when Battling Bob O'Keefe left us with words you might hear only from an old Marine:

"Well, I'm going home, I'm loaded!"

CHAPTER 5

Jim Hostetler, USMC
Marines Don't Cry

Private First Class, U.S. Marine Corps, Fox Company, 2nd Battalion, 7th Marine Regiment, 1st Marine Division. Interviewed January 29, 2023. Lewisburg, Pennsylvania. Born 1928.

Do you believe in God? Because I can tell you, He exists. Before I shipped out, my mother-in-law gave me a small Bible with a dollar stuck in the page of Psalm 91:7–12. What happened to us on Fox Hill is exactly as that Bible verse is written.

As my Veterans Page on Facebook grew, so did the outreach from other documenters. Zack Wolf, who was interviewing World War II, Korea, and Vietnam veterans, reached out, offering to connect me with a surviving Korea veteran he'd recently met. When he told me there was a Marine who was at the Last Stand of Fox Company during the Chosin Reservoir campaign, I knew I had to meet Jim Hostetler, who'd suffered two battle wounds.

The story is that Fox Company did everything possible to hold a crucial pass high in the mountains of North Korea just west of the Chosin Reservoir, through which harassed Marine units could safely withdraw to fight another day. While the exploits of Fox Company are well documented in the book *The Last Stand of Fox Company*, and in the previous chapters, my goal was to have someone who was there tell the story from the viewpoint of a man who'd fought and lived through that hell.

Zack helped get me in touch with Gene, a friend who looks after Jim Hostetler, and he was most receptive to Collin and me meeting this veteran, suggesting I give Hostetler a call. I punched in the numbers and waited patiently as the phone rang. When I heard "Hello, this is Jim," I introduced myself, explained my mission, and said, "I understand you were with Fox Company at the Toktong Pass."

You just gave me goosebumps son; how did you know I was with Fox Company at the Reservoir?

I told him about Zack Wolf, and about Gene filling me in, and said I'd be honored to come and speak with him. Jim listened quietly as I explained my dedication to our Korean War veterans. He seemed impressed, and mentioned how gratified he was to learn I've gone nationwide documenting his brothers in arms. We agreed to

January 28, 2023. This worked perfectly, since I'd already lined up three other East Coast sessions. Jim and I continued to talk on the phone when he painted a picture I could never have imagined of the infamous Last Stand:

> *Do you believe in God? Because I can tell you He exists. Before I shipped out my mother-in-law gave me a small Bible with a dollar stuck in the page of Psalm 91:7–12. What happened to us on Fox Hill is exactly as that Bible verse is written. It says, "A thousand will fall at your side." After the six-night battle, we counted exactly one thousand dead Chinese. "Ten thousand will fall at your right hand." After we fought our way out, an estimate of over ten thousand Chinese were said to have been killed in the surrounding area. It also says you will be gifted a long life; I'm going to be ninety-six next year!*

The next step for Collin and me was to arrange time off with our bosses, who were most cooperative. We scheduled two stops in Pennsylvania, one in New Jersey, and another on New York's Long Island, all of which we completed in three days, also adding in two new interviews and two follow-ups. All of those were with Marines. On the drive, Collin and I listened to the audiobook version of *The Last Stand of Fox Company* and could hardly believe the savagery of this battle.

This historic engagement, where Fox Company faced substantial factions of two Chinese regiments determined to throw them off the hill, has been documented many times, with different perspectives. Because Jim was there on the ground, smack dab in the middle of all this insanity, you know his story has to be the true gospel. And it all began with his enlistment in the Corps in 1945, and just missing World War II.

> *Being that I graduated later, I was only in the last three months of the Second World War, and never shipped out. In those days everyone was patriotic, so my whole class, except the guys who were 4-F, joined up. There were three of us going into the Marines.*

Jim was trained to be an aircraft technician and was working on newly developed Marine jet fighters when World War II ended. Most enlistees were released from their service contracts early, but believing he'd be recalled, he reenlisted because, as he put it:

> *The Soviets were acting up and there was no point in being a drafted Marine. So, a buddy of mine who had been a sniper Marine on Peleliu, and another buddy who was a machine gunner with the 1st Marines, figured we might as well get into the Reserves. So, we joined a line company infantry Reserve outfit, and this is the only time the Marine Corps lied to me. Before I signed the papers I asked, if something happens will I go back into the Marine Air Wing. They told me, "Oh yes, you'll go and be trained for jets." Well, that was a lie! I joined the Reserves in January of 1950 and on June 25, 1950, the war broke out.*

Before being shipped to Korea, he took leave, went home, and put his personal affairs in order. He missed the September 15, 1950, landing at Inchon, but in late

October he took part in the landing at Wonsan, North Korea, where UN forces would begin their push north. Part of the first round of replacements, he was assigned to Fox Company, 2nd Battalion, 7th Marines. At this phase of the war, because Allied forces had thoroughly beaten the North Korean Army, it was believed that it was all in the bag.

I went in with the first replacement draft as a rifleman at Wonsan, North Korea. At the time, Wonsan harbor was the most mined harbor in the history of warfare. Anyway, we had to wait a couple days as they swept the harbor for mines so we could land. I went in there and that's when I was placed with Fox Company. We went through Koto-ri, Hungnam, a few others, and all the way to Hagaru-ri where we got a new captain for Fox Company, and we thought he was insane. We had been there for weeks. We all had beards, and our hair was a mess, and he made us shave and get cleaned up. Then he would start giving us rifle inspections; we thought he was nuts. But he had been on Iwo Jima and was awarded the Silver Star for bravery. His name was Barber.

Jim Hostetler in his Marine Corps portrait.

Captain William E. Barber commanded Fox Company, 2nd Battalion throughout the Last Stand battle against a numerically superior Chinese force that attacked the Americans for six straight nights; the campaign is regarded as a monumental feat in Marine Corps history. For his leadership and actions on Fox Hill, he would later be awarded the Congressional Medal of Honor.

The story of this historic fight, as told by Jim, is that Barber received orders from O.P. Smith, Commanding General of the 1st Marine Division, to take Fox Company to a crucial pass just seven miles west of Hagaru-ri … and hold. With only minor skirmishes confronting advancing Marines and UN Forces pushing north, the war was thought by most to be about over. What no one knew was that small Chinese units were sent to lure them in with the intent to spread out the 1st Marine Division and other UN forces and allow the Chinese to infiltrate the gaps and annihilate the unwitting allies.

> *The Fifth and Seventh Marines went up to the Reservoir, with Chesty Puller and the First Marines staying in Koto-ri. My company, they dropped us off at the Toktong Pass to guard the pass. I don't know if I told you, but we found out later that it was forty-two below zero, seventy-five below wind-chill factor on that hill. On November the 27th, I was in a bunker with a fella by the name of "C." The Chinese hit us two o'clock in the morning, killed a lot of people and bayoneted a lot of people.*

As the Chinese intervention unfolded, the next six nights were more than just a battle of survival for Fox Company: The entire UN front was in jeopardy. Captain Barber knew if Fox Hill and the Toktong pass fell into enemy hands it could very well mean the destruction of the entire Division. Jim and Fox Company—228 Marines—soon found themselves surrounded and encountering vicious nightly attacks by never-ending masses of Chinese. Flares lit up the battleground, while sounds of bugles and horns rang without end as the enemy poured in from all sides. This was the first time most of these young Marines experienced this frightening tactic: shadows and rocks suddenly turning into rows upon rows of men in quilted uniforms, charging forward and screaming, "Marine you die, Marine you die." Over the next hours, the fighting seemed as if it would never end. Throughout the night tracers filled the air, and deafening hand-grenade and mortar-shell explosions turned men deaf. It was a long, long night. Then, just as the sun rose, the Chinese vanished, disappearing into their daytime hiding places.

> *I don't know what time, but it got daylight and "C" had the fire port, and I had the entrance to the bunker so they couldn't get in. My fire team leader Smith was over to the right, and there were two guys out to my left in a slit trench. I called over to Smith to tell him we're moving over by the two guys in the slit trench to form a better field of fire. So, "C" and I moved over to the right front of the slit trench and there was four of us in there, two fellas by name of Gonzales who were Hispanic, and they were cousins. Once nighttime came, it got so bad, they ran right through us.*

The Chinese implemented grenadiers—soldiers inserted in the waves of attackers who carried sacks and baskets full of hand grenades, hurling them as they ran toward the Marines. The hail of hand grenades almost seemed like they rained from the sky, with Marines using their entrenching tools and rifles as baseball bats to knock them away. From what Jim told me, and what I've been able to research, the Chinese who hit Fox Company and the surrounding Marines and UN forces were a well-trained and well-equipped army, not the typical human waves later experienced where some would not even carry a weapon. Another detail is that many in the Red Army were equipped with captured American weapons from the Chinese Revolution of 1949, when the United States backed Mao Zedong's enemy.

It got so bad with those Chinese carrying sacks of hand grenades, that we fell back to where the other Marines were forming another line. So, the first guy out was Roger Gonzales, and they shot him through the back and shoulder. He got back to the line and crawled in the hole with a guy from Pittsburgh by the name of Bob Kersner, a friend of mine. He died in Bob's arms. Bob and the other Marines were taking and stacking frozen Chinese and using them as sandbags. Bob took Roger and piled him up on the top of the pile to protect himself. Bob survived the war and went to the family of Roger and explained to them what had happened, and what he had done, and that even though Roger was dead, he may have saved his life.

We'd been hearing many gruesome stories on our journey interviewing Korean War survivors, but we were shocked as Jim relayed this account: so difficult to imagine stacking the dead body of a friend on a pile of other corpses to use as a shield.

The next guy out of the hole was "C." I was facing one way, and he was facing another. They threw a grenade in, and he took ninety percent of the blast. It hit me in the back, but it was minor. He crawled out after getting hit and made it to the Third Platoon command post and died there. I was the third one out, and I don't know how far I got from the hole when they threw a hand grenade. I never heard it land, and it went off near my head. I got seven scars on my face; pieces went through my cheeks, and I still have a piece of shrapnel behind my left eye yet. Luckily, I never lost my eyesight, but anyways I came to. I must have been knocked out and I thought I was blind. I put my hand up and could see blood and everything, so I knew I could see.

This was only the first night on Fox Hill.

The Chinese were successful, breaking through on all flanks, but the gallant Marines would shrink their perimeter to consolidate their fire power and regain the ground lost during the day. When the fighting died down, Jim was sent to the aid station to have his wounds checked.

There was snow all over the ground and we had fixed bayonets, so I stuck my rifle in the snow outside the aid tent. A Marine walked in front of me, and he had a bullet hole in his forehead from a small caliber. He walked in. I couldn't believe it. The corpsman there took out a swab and swabbed the inside of the wound and sent him back on the line.

After his wounds were dressed, Jim was told there wasn't much else that could be done. He was ordered to help deliver much-needed ammo to the frontline. His body was full of grenade fragments, two bullets torn through in his shoulders ... and he was sent back to the battle.

When I came out of the aid tent, somebody had taken my rifle, so I saw another one in the snow, and I picked it up. So, I had all these hand grenades, so I started up towards the line. The Chinese had the higher ground above the road. A sniper fired at me, and I went to the ground. I got up to start climbing again and he fired again. And I go to the ground again. Some Marines up above told me, "Come on now, he can't hit ya." I get up a third time and he fired again. So I turned over and I could see his position in the rocks. I had that strange weapon, so I fired Kentucky windage at him and I don't think I hit him 'cause I could see him skipping across.

With each nightly attack the Chinese slowly whittled away at the shrinking Fox Company. But not without coming up against all the firepower the Marines could give them. Hanging on by a thread, in their fearless attempt to survive, the Americans slashed and stabbed with their bayonets, swung rifles as clubs, beat the attackers to death with their bare hands and helmets.

Unfortunately, there were snafus: Wrong supplies were airdropped, and water canisters froze before they hit the ground. Even with the odds stacked against them, Fox Company never gave way—determined to fight to the last man and hold the pass at all costs. It appeared it was going to come to just that. The second night, every wounded Marine who could still fire a rifle joined the defensive line, braced to repel the next Chinese onslaught. And sure enough, it came. The blaring bugles, clanging pots and pans, the flares, and once again, the Chinese were right on top of the defenders.

The second night, all wounded had to get in a line—a perimeter, it was so bad. So, they put me in a hole, my hands and feet were frozen. I was wounded twice, and they put me in a hole with a lieutenant named Brady. He was shot through the shoulder and in the hole we were butt to butt. Anybody coming his way he was going to take care of, and anybody coming my way I was going to take care of. The back of my head was facing the outside of the perimeter and that was the only time I swore at an officer in the Marine Corps. That night when it opened up, you couldn't even stick your finger out of the hole without getting it shot off. I don't know where I was gonna go. There was no place to go, but I was gonna get outta there. He said something to me, and I told him, "You son of a bitch, your head is lower than mine!" He told me to squat down some more, and I did. So he probably actually saved my life. On the fourth night I was in a slit trench with a bunker on the end of it. Platoon Sergeant Otis was in the bunker, I was in the middle of the trench, and the forward observer, Campbell, he was at the end of the trench. Campbell was calling artillery fire in on the hills around us, so he would tell me the coordinates and I would tell Otis, and he was on a radio back to Hagaru.

At daylight, once again, the Chinese withdrew. The sights that sent shivers up and down Jim's spine started with a five-inch sapling tree just a few feet outside his foxhole—cut in half by machine-gun fire that could have cut him in half. Then there was the frozen godforsaken hill before him, painted red with blood and covered with dead bodies. The surviving Marines were practically walking corpses, suffering from debilitating frostbite, fatigue, and thirst, with a casualty rate of over eighty percent. Against the odds and the overwhelming number of Chinese attacking each night, they still held the pass.

Before Fox Company moved to the Toktong Pass, the 11th Marines set up field batteries on the perimeter of Hagaru-ri to provide support, if needed. Although they were outnumbered, in some cases almost ten to one, and cut off, the fire support provided by the 105 howitzers proved to be their saving grace. The Americans and other UN forces were still surrounded, facing complete obliteration. But the UN forces owned the air, which along with the howitzers delivered accurate and devastating support. Hagaru-ri was just seven miles east of the Toktong Pass. Five miles north, the rest of the 7th Marines at Yudam-ni began their march to the Toktong Pass. General O.P. Smith, stationed at Hagru-ri, knew Toktong was crucial to the 7th Marines making it back and was scrambling to devise a plan to consolidate all Marine and Army units at his site, from where they could fight their way out.

> *They took a battery of 105s, and instead of keeping it and putting it, you know, in the center, they moved the artillery out to the perimeter. They did this so they could reach us at Toktong Pass. There was other artillery at Yudamn-ni, which I think was five miles. The mountains—I get confused, I don't remember if they were eight thousand feet or five thousand feet. Lieutenant Colonel Davis tried twice to get down and help us. I think they also tried from Hagaru, but they couldn't get through to help my company. Now I didn't see this, I heard this, but Davis stood on a six-by truck with the headlights shined on him and he told his people we're going to help Fox Company, and nothing is going to stop us. So, they did. They fought their way down through the mountains to relieve us. The guy I told you who was a machine gunner in the Second World War, he was in Baker Company. In fact, we were in a circle, and the guy I grew up with was there fighting with us. I didn't know which company had fought their way to us. Getting off track here, but Davis became a Marine Corps general. When they opened Quantico for us, not for what I did but for what the company did, we were heroes. Davis was there and the Commandant of the Marine Corps was there, and Davis spoke. When he got up there and was speaking, he said every time they got screwed up and didn't know where they were going or whatever, he focused on that bright star, so they knew where they were going to get to us. When he was telling us that he started crying, that's how moving it was—that star hanging over us.*

Referring to one of his earlier comments, I asked, "Did you know it was the Chinese when you were first hit?"

> *No, when they first hit us, I didn't know what was going on. Because we had everybody whipped. During the Second World War, we supplied China (with) Thompson submachine guns and all kinds of weapons. Here they had Thompson submachine guns and all the weapons we used during the Second World War. They were using a lot of the same stuff we used, and they used Russian burp guns and stuff. But I didn't know they were Chinese. We had plenty of small skirmishes before we knew they were Chinese and we radioed to MacArthur to tell him we were running into Chinese. General Almond, who was in charge of the 10th Corps, which the Marines were under, his statement was, "You're not scared of a few Chinese laundrymen, are ya?"*

The nightmare finally ended when the rest of the 7th Marines punched their way to the Toktong Pass, gathered the remaining Marines, and fought their way to Hagaru-ri. As Jim was finishing his story, I couldn't help but marvel at the fighting spirit of this man. Wounded multiple times, battling subzero temperatures and an enemy that seemed to never stop ... this Marine is a survivor.

I was told later that eighty-seven Marines of Fox Company come off that hill and I hear only eleven of that eighty-seven were not screwed up from frostbite or being wounded or something. We fought our way down to Hagaru and they had a perimeter and air strip. The Greeks were flying in also, and I was flown to Japan on the same plane as Captain Barber. From Japan I went to Midway on the way to Hawaii. I told them in Hawaii, while getting my back rubbed by nurses, that if you're not going to send me home, let me lay here. Going from forty-two below zero to getting your back rubbed by pretty girls was nice.

Jim's next stop was the Philadelphia Naval Hospital but he doesn't remember how long he was there. After recovering from his injuries, he was placed in a National Guard Company in Philadelphia, then transferred to the Virginia National Guard in Norfolk, and finally shipped to Camp Lejeune, where he served the remainder of his enlistment with the 8th Marines, 2nd Marine Division.

Jim Hostetler holding a Bible open to Psalm 91, verse 8, with a dollar bill marking the verse; next to him stands Ryan Walkowski

It was during the battle for Toktong Pass that Jim made a vow that if the good Lord would spare him, there would be no more sinning on his end. During the heat of battle, Jim had seen the verse from Psalm 91 unfold before his eyes, and promised he would change his ways should he survive this horror.

He did not change.

Jim admitted that he went right back to his old sinful habits, which he continued until he attended a reunion where he met an old friend, Captain Walter Hiskett, who had become the Chaplain of the Marine Corps and was a key speaker at the event. Saying that he always believed in God and faith, Jim added … "I never walked the talk."

> *I have severe post-traumatic stress disorder, I come home from the reunion, we stayed down there for five days and got drunk and cried. We fought the battle. I come home from there, fourteen nights I couldn't sleep. You're not gonna believe it, but it's true, I slept by myself away from my wife. I got on my knees and started praying, that's it. That's it! That's it! I'm not gonna say one thing and do the other. Marines don't cry, their eyeballs leak, and my eyeballs leak. I stood up. I stood up and boy, I felt all these bad memories hit me at once and I thought what the heck. I just devoted myself to God. We went to visit my wife's mother who lived to be ninety-six and she gave me the Bible with the dollar in it when I went to Korea. While my wife visited her, I was visiting with a retired ninety-one-year-old minister and I told her my story and she told me, "Jimmy, Satan was losing you and he was throwing everything in the book at you." I lived it and some people don't believe. But they can believe whatever they want. But I lived it. You can call me a religious fanatic or cuckoo. Well, all Marines are cuckoo. But it makes sense to me.*

Jim's story of both survival and faith was over. He graciously invited Collin and me to stay for a while. We took photos. He asked, "Who is driving?" Collin replied, "I am." Jim went to the fridge and brought me an ice-cold sixteen-ounce Miller Lite. There wasn't any way I was going to pass up an opportunity of having a beer with this gallant Marine. Before we left, Jim signed a dollar bill that I would place on Psalm 91 in my grandparents' Bible. I expressed once again to Jim and his friend how grateful we were for the meeting, and for him telling us his Korean War story, adding that I was glad he allowed strangers into his home so willingly. Jim's friend responded by pulling up his shirt, revealing a concealed-carry pistol, and commenting, "We took proper precaution." We all shared a good laugh.

Saying my goodbye, I told Jim that "we're off to interview other Marines, the furthest being in Long Island." His reply humbled both Collin and me:

> *Amazing, simply amazing what you two are doing.*

Chapter 6

Elroy "Sonny" Roeder, U.S. Army
My Pal Sonny

Corporal, U.S. Army, E Company, 23rd Infantry, 2nd Infantry Division. Interviewed January 24th, 2023, Rothschild, Wisconsin. Born 1929.

The moment I got off the ship in California I took my uniform off because people looked down on us. It was almost just like during Vietnam. No one cared at all what we did or where we were.

Elroy Roeder was my first interview, at a time when I wasn't thinking about a book. My primary goal was only to learn about my grandfather's wartime experiences—he never spoke of his involvement in the Korean War. Elroy Roeder's neighbor, after seeing my Facebook posting, contacted me, stating that living next-door to him was a ninety-two-year-old Korean War veteran whom she'd be happy to ask about being interviewed. After a few days, she got back to me, saying that she'd reached his daughter, who'd be expecting my call. Elroy's daughter Lisa was thrilled that someone was interested in speaking with her father, telling me that he'd fought there in three of the bloodiest battles—the Punchbowl, the infamous Heartbreak Ridge, and Bloody Ridge. I was beyond excited and expressed that he only had to talk about what felt comfortable. The last thing I wanted was these old warriors bringing back unwanted memories. Lisa also said that he'd been interviewed by the local school, as well as by someone writing a book about Korea. Since this was the first veteran I'd ever talked to about his combat experiences, I didn't quite know what to expect, or even how to go about it.

Elroy answered my call, and in a friendly manner asked what I wanted to get out of this. After I told him about my grandfather, he said to call him Sonny, and to bring some beer over during the next Green Bay Packers game.

I'll tell you whatever you wanna know if you can believe it. Most people think it's a bunch of bullshit, so I never really tell anyone 'cause they think I'm lying.

My first question for Sonny would certainly be why people would think he was lying. I showed up with the requisite six-pack and was warmly greeted. Sonny had everything laid out—photos from Korea, his medals in a shadow box, maps, and his 2nd Division Company yearbook. I was as green at interviewing as I was when I first became an apprentice electrician; I didn't know a damn thing. Setting up my camera, I explained that I had no idea what I was doing and that we were going to figure this out together. Sonny laughed, and that was a good thing.

My first question was indeed, "Why do people think your combat stories are bullshit?"

Everyone would always look at me and laugh and say, "Oh bullshit, that never happened, that's not what combat is like." When the school interviewed me, those kids' eyes got so damn big when I told them my combat stories, it's like they didn't believe me. I don't blame them. Some of the things I've seen I couldn't even believe myself.

Elroy "Sonny" Roeder in his military portrait.

Because Sonny was born and raised in the Wausau, Wisconsin, area not far from my hometown of Birnamwood, I felt an immediate connection that relaxed us both. Sonny started with being drafted into the Army at the beginning of 1951, not too long after marrying in October 1950. Even with the threat of conscription, he and his fiancée opted to marry anyway. A few months later, Sonny was on his way to basic training at Fort Leonard Wood, Missouri, where he was also trained as an engineer.

We practiced laying mines, demolitions, stuff like that. Building bridges. But soon as I got to Korea and entered at Pusan, I was thrown a rifle and told I was reassigned to a heavy mortar platoon and headed towards the front line. Talk about feeling like a rookie again.

Sonny arrived in Korea in August 1951 and was immediately shipped to the front line. He had no idea where it was. (Ground troops often didn't know their locations, or even which day it was, which is why many of my veterans' recollections are random and not in the order of when they occurred.) Loaded on trucks that drove all night, the transients arrived at their destination, where Sonny was assigned to Easy Company, 23rd Infantry, 2nd Division. His first engagement was the Punchbowl, a battle already raging on his arrival. A new member of a sixty-millimeter mortar platoon, even though he knew nothing about mortars, Sonny quickly became acquainted with his new team: an ammo-bearer, a gunner, and a forward observer. Mentioning that it was hard to remember exact details about the Punchbowl that happened seventy-two years ago—a lifetime for most people—he solemnly admitted that he can never forget the dead bodies.

> *I saw a lot of bodies lying around and rotting, that's the first time I'd ever seen a dead person just lying there. Chinese, North Koreans, innocent people, children. But I was surprised it didn't bother me, as bad as that sounds.*

Sonny remembered that his company suffered the most at Heartbreak Ridge, a battle that raged for a month and two days, with both sides suffering staggering casualties. One estimate is that UN forces lost 3,700 men, with the Chinese and North Koreans suffering over twenty-five thousand.

I knew a little about Heartbreak Ridge from the Internet and documentaries, but to be sitting across the table from a veteran who served at one of the bloodiest battles of the war was surreal. Sonny said they'd fight their way up the hill, charging into a storm of small arms and automatic rifle fire, and for every hand grenade GIs would toss, the Communists would throw three.

> *The worst part of the whole experience is you're going uphill while they're shooting down at you. A lot of the way up they had ropes to guide us because almost every GI carried a heavy load, rifle, ammunition, grenades.*

He described Heartbreak Ridge as a wasteland, nothing left of the hill but a bombed-out, desolate piece of ground. There were mounds of dirt with shattered stumps everywhere, from the heavy bombardments that splintered every tree from direct hits and air bursts. With all the vegetation blown away, it was a soupy mix of mud from the constant rain. Sonny explained further about Heartbreak.

> *A game of who could throw who off the hill, fight up the hill just to be thrown off, then back up in the slopes to take the ridge. There were people running up on top of the hill, and who the hell knows who they are, but you just know you're walking into a trap. But our squad leader said, "Keep walking, keep walking." And then all hell broke loose.*

The waiting Chinese and North Koreans poured into the approaching platoon a devastating rain of firepower. Sonny jumped behind what was left of a giant tree, somehow dropping his entrenching tool. When he'd reach out to retrieve it, a burst of machine gun fire sprayed the area, riddling it full of holes and pushing the shovel further away. The Communist forces had waited until the approaching GIs were zeroed in, then dropped a murderous shower of heavy mortars. Quickly withdrawing while grabbing the wounded, Sonny and the platoon made their way down the hill. Sonny said this fierce firefight was only a prelude to what they would later face.

I never got a scratch; they really laid those mortars and grenades into us too. They killed a lot of guys and wounded even more. I never got a scratch though, and I couldn't figure out why not me, because one way or another they all got hit and that was the worst part.

It was maybe on the third time, Sonny recalled, that they finally broke through and eliminated the Reds from Heartbreak Ridge. Over the next few weeks, he remained on the front line, defending the hill from further onslaughts of superior forces trying to throw off the outnumbered UN troops. Shelling continued throughout the day—until nightfall, when the enemy would attack in waves of screaming warriors. During one of the bombardments, Sonny was frantically digging his hole deeper when he saw two of his buddies taking shelter in their hole, laughing as their way to cope with the intensity and madness of the barrage. Sonny said he could see the rounds flying through the air. One round landed between his two pals, killing both soldiers—just a few feet away, as Sonny helplessly and forlornly looked on. The constant barrage never seemed to lift, in what seemed like a lifetime. Sadly, another friend, dug in and hiding in his hole, took a direct hit.

Elroy "Sonny" Roeder standing below Heartbreak Ridge; original inscription said, "Yours truly, back from the frontline."

He starts yelling, "I'M WOUNDED, I'M WOUNDED!" And I hollered back at him to stay where he is and don't move, nobody can help you right now. After the bombing stopped, the medics came out and grabbed him along with every other wounded man. We got organized and here came round two and it started all over again.

Before the next bombardment, Sonny was debating whether to dig a new hole or jump into a foxhole occupied by two other GIs. He opted to stay. The barrage started again. The GIs took a direct hit.

(There) were two other guys in a foxhole that I knew that I was going to jump in. It's a good thing I stayed where I was. Otherwise, I'd be dead. Just luck that's all it is, just plain luck. I did a lot of praying while I was on Heartbreak.

Sonny also recalled hearing the downed GIs screaming in pain and crying for help, but nothing could be done. The Chinese were boobytrapping the wounded and the dead. For Sonny, this was one of the worst parts of the war into which he was drafted. I can't describe my feelings listening to him tell these gruesome stories, to which I could only reply with "Wow" or "Jeez." Sonny went on to say that the Chinese were incredibly sneaky night-fighters: Mornings would find GIs still in their foxholes, sometimes close friends of his, with their throats slit. To adapt to these kinds of in-the-dark tactics, the Americans strung empty C-ration cans at the front of the line to alert them if anyone was approaching. They also learned that when there were two in a foxhole, one soldier remains awake while the other sleeps When they were finally relieved and sent down for a few days' rest, only about twelve GIs walked off the hill of the platoon he was with.

Elroy "Sonny" Roeder posing with his Bible that he carried while fighting on the frontlines of Korea, most notably at Bloody Ridge and Heartbreak Ridge. This photograph was taken during one of Ryan Walkowski's many visits.

I used to carry a dozen or so hand grenades with me, and whenever I heard movement or those tin cans rattle, I'd roll one down the hill. Sometimes it was the rats feeding on the dead bodies and other times it wasn't. One thing is for sure, Heartbreak taught me a lesson and I wasn't going to take any chances.

Later in the battle, there was little daytime activity, except for sporadic artillery from both sides—reminding each other they were still there. That was the only time Sonny got some sleep. Besides the random shelling, Sonny described it all as "Like a picnic, just lay on your side in the sun and do what you can to rest." If the GIs weren't moving along the frontline, they'd hunker down in their foxholes waiting for the night, waiting for the dreadful sounds of bugles, waiting for another frantic enemy assault.

One afternoon, Sonny volunteered to join a squad of French soldiers heading out on patrol, accompanied by a forward observer who was to spot enemy positions for artillery and heavy mortar crews. He described it as just walking along with nothing going on and it being a rather nice day, when a foul stench stopped them in their tracks. It was the strong smell of garlic—part of every Chinese soldier's diet, along with rotten fish heads. The wind was right, and they knew they were approaching a Chinese squad. Next thing, all hell broke loose, one of the deadliest crossfires he'd ever witnessed.

> *I called out to my French partner and asked if he could smell something. Yeah, he told me. Here was a goddamn Chinese patrol and we came up almost on top of them. Here this commander gets on top of a rise and yells down to us that we're on our own. Jesus Christ, I didn't know what to think, but that Frenchman I was with was thinking the same, so we jumped and made our way back.*

Not speaking the language, Sonny motioned to his French partner to jump off the side of the ridge where it was sandy. Without hesitation, the Frenchman followed, and they dropped about fifteen feet to a soft and safe landing. The next few hours were spent finding their way back in the dark of the night to friendly lines, following a marked path through a posted minefield. Sonny again mentioned his luck, considering that many men on that patrol were captured.

Sonny recalled another night seeing the remnants of a French listening post staggering in, one soldier with a missing leg and another who'd been slashed by a bayonet. Sonny offered to help the second man, who refused, indicating he was okay as he stumbled down the hill to an aid station, stuffing his guts back into his stomach with every painful step.

> *I couldn't believe what I was seeing, walking with one leg, and using a rifle as a crutch, and that poor guy holding his guts in. I couldn't believe he was even still alive, let alone walking. They were tough fighters, them French.*

Sonny had been right, another Korean War tale hard to believe … but true. He went on to talk about a fresh replacement who'd become his foxhole buddy on Heartbreak Ridge, with battle-experienced Sonny doing his best to explain how things are, how they go, and what the rules are for each hole being fifty percent alert. New guys were always placed with a veteran. His name was Libby, related to the Hawaiian family that owned Libby Fruit, a well-known fruit canner. Sonny tried explaining that one man sleeps while the other stays awake, and hand grenades are kept out and ready, and don't even think of putting your rifle on safety.

> *I told this kid, all right now, I'm going to take first shift, and you sleep. So I did that and after a few hours I woke him up because I started getting tired. I closed my eyes wondering if I could trust this guy. Well, I woke up to him snoring. Boy, was I pissed off, and I really laid into him too!*

Sonny chewed Libby out, warning the rookie he'd shoot him if he ever fell asleep on his shift again. After a repeat incident, Sonny didn't shoot him, but kicked him out of his hole and never saw him again or heard about it from his officers.

Are you trying to get our throats cut? Cause that's how you do it, you dumb bastard. I'm not going to die on account of you, I told him.

Sonny later befriended a Frenchman named Luke who spoke fluent English, and I'm hoping if this book finds its way overseas. If Luke is still alive and sees this story, maybe he'll reach out.

One morning after being relieved, he ran into Luke, who invited him and his buddies to join their squad for dinner of freshly baked bread, homemade soup, and a promise of French wine.

Christ, them Frenchmen were something else, I absolutely loved them guys, and Christ, the food they had ... best meal I had in almost a year. Drinking with them, I got half a jag on just hanging around them. They were fun guys though, definitely the kind of guys you want on your side when it hits the fan. Wish I had exchanged addresses with Luke. He was a good buddy.

Sonny asked Luke how he ended up in Korea—whether he'd been drafted, or however it works in France. Luke related that after killing a *gendarme* (policeman), he was imprisoned on notorious Devil's Island. Turns out, Sonny was a buddy to a guy who was technically a murderer. The story, as Luke told Sonny, is that a *gendarme* came to an *auberge* (French tavern), looking for Luke, who landed a punch right between the officer's eyes—a blow that instantly killed the cop. At Devil's Island, Luke was given the opportunity to join the French Foreign Legion. He did, and was sent to Indochina (Vietnam), where the French were fighting a furious but fruitless battle. When the Korean War broke out, he was told that if he volunteered to go to Korea and survived, he'd be a free man and able to return to Paris, something he was anxious to do. Luke agreed and was shipped over as part of a French Battalion assigned to the U.S. 23rd infantry. The 23rd was finally sent down from Heartbreak Ridge, leaving the hill to the French, who later took a severe whipping but held the front line and the hill. Sonny has always hoped Luke got out alive and returned to his home in Paris.

We were good buddies and always chummed when we were down below the hill. I wish to this day we had stayed in contact 'cause I never knew if he made it or not. Those guys were fearless, especially Luke, always shaved and wearing perfume aftershave. I always told Luke that they're gonna smell you. But he smiled and said, "Then I die looking and smelling good."

After Heartbreak Ridge, Sonny was involved in more skirmishes, hill after hill, outpost after outpost, never actually knowing where he was, except that the enemy was a hundred yards or so right in front of him. Often taking over the Communist's trenches and foxholes, he and his buddies would, more times than not, dig them bigger and deeper.

Sonny and his company were being trucked to the frontline in one-ton trucks when a tire on his vehicle went flat, causing it to stay behind while the rest of the convoy drove on. Truck after truck passed while they waited for a wrecker to come along and repair the flat. Just before dark, with the tire finally fixed, they were back on the road headed north.

It was getting late already, and getting dark fast, and I don't think the driver really knew where he was taking us. He was going north all the time, and we finally came to an encampment of an entirely different unit who let us post up for a few hours before they headed out.

With little faith in the driver, they got back on the road. Just before daybreak the truck began bouncing and weaving as it drove over abandoned foxholes, meaning they were mistakenly and dangerously back on the front line. Before long, the vehicle and its passengers were totally exposed, which is when the driver realized his error and turned south toward a safer position. In the morning light, the GIs could see the bad guys dug in on their side of the line, and to this day Sonny can't figure out why the enemy never took a shot. The driver managed to find the road and finally headed in the right direction, but still almost managed to get the truck stuck in a rice paddy.

He must have driven a couple miles on that road along the front line and we never got shot. When we finally linked back up with our outfit, they sure had a laugh about us. Yeah, it sure was funny. I thought, damn driver near got us killed.

As winter approached, so did the reality of having to post up in a foxhole or trench and freeze your ass off in the bitter North Korean cold. Sonny recalled not much going on, except for small skirmishes he described as "Just a way to keep each side busy." He admitted that even after seventy-two years, he still hasn't shaken the shivers of that North Korean winter. He also talked about the Mickey Mouse boots issued to the troops as actually being warm, but if your feet sweated too much, you'd be prone to frostbite. Sonny countered this by wearing regular GI socks and constantly changing them to keep his feet dry. Recalling that changing into new clothes only happened once every month or so, he added that he was lucky to be wearing long underwear.

On Christmas Eve, the Chinese played holiday carols over loudspeakers along the entire line and tried to convince the GIs to surrender and be home with their loved ones by the new year. Braced for an attack that never came, instead they were attacked by propaganda, but enjoyed the Christmas music.

All night long they played them carols over them damned old loudspeakers. Between each song they would tell us to surrender and go home. Then they would tell us between songs our girlfriends and wives were cheating on us.

Sonny then related being rotated to a different company on Christmas Day, and being given a hot turkey meal with all the trimmings. The Chinese started shelling the front line, but it was indirect fire with no damage, and the Americans, while savoring a traditional Christmas meal, enjoyed watching a free fireworks show.

> *Christ, they had everything mom would put out at home, and even gave us ice cream. Boy! Was that a treat from living off C-rations for so long. Then all of a sudden VROOM, here comes their shells, but they weren't hitting a damned thing. We just sat there and watched them land while we ate.*

In the spring and summer of 1952, the war became the Outpost War, with scheduled patrols sent out to capture prisoners or set up ambushes. Sonny recalled that any fighting was primarily against the Chinese, since UN forces had practically annihilated the North Korean Army. It was mostly taking hills and outposts, locating stashes of left-behind supplies, clothing, and weapons, as if the enemy knew the GIs were coming.

> *We had them whipped and beat and they knew it. Any we came across, they ran before we got there.*

The time came for the war to be over for Sonny, for him to be rotated home. He boarded a troopship that sailed to Oakland, California, from where he flew to Fort McCoy, Wisconsin, for his discharge and was told to find his own way. While hitchhiking, he was offered a ride back to Wausau for twenty dollars. It was a lot of money those days, but Sonny wasn't going to turn it down. He just wanted to get home anyway and damn the expense. Because there was no fanfare, no warm or special welcome, the only good thing about returning to the states, he regretfully said, was seeing the Golden Gate Bridge; other than that, he couldn't wait to get back home.

> *The moment I got off the ship in California, I took my uniform off because people looked down on us. It was almost just like during Vietnam. No one cared at all what we did or where we were.*

Even Sonny's barber didn't show appreciation for his time in Korea.

> *Gosh damn barber goes, "Well, where the hell have you been? I figured you started going somewhere else." And I told him no, I was in Korea fighting, and he just shrugged it off and said, "Oh, I didn't know that." No one gave a damn, so that's why I never really talked about my military career.*

Back home, there were disappointments. Not only didn't his neighbors care about what he'd done in Korea, neither did his former employer at the Coca-Cola bottling plant, who'd given away his job. After talking with his Veterans Service Officer, who informed the employer that Sonny's job was legally protected, Sonny took on his old position with his old foreman, but, he said,

> *I just had a feeling he was going to try anything he could to get me fired. I got a few paychecks, and I left and went to the papermill, and I haven't drank a single bottle of Coke since then either.*

6. Elroy "Sonny" Roeder, U.S. Army: My Pal Sonny

Elroy "Sonny" Roeder with Ryan Walkowski after he signed Ryan's Korean War veterans flag. Elroy was the first veteran Ryan ever documented. Ryan started having Korean War veterans sign a flag a year after he started interviewing, and he made sure to get Elroy's signature on it.

His new employer was Weyerhaeuser Paper Company, from which he retired after thirty-six years. Residing now in Rothschild, Sonny was one of the Wisconsin veterans I introduced to South Korean photographer Rami Hyun, who was also interviewing Korean War veterans for a South Korean blog. Sonny seemed to appreciate that I was there to help him get through Rami's accent, especially since at age ninety-three he was also hard of hearing. I tried my best not to laugh when Sonny looked at me, asking for help to better understand Rami.

What the hell is he saying? I can't understand a damned thing. He's got too thick of an accent and my hearing is shot.

I reassured Sonny that if there's one thing he could take away from our meeting, it's that I give a damn, or I wouldn't be here. As a result, we developed a solid friendship. I often stop in to see how he's doing, bringing him fish fillets after he told me that all his friends are dead, so he doesn't go fishing unless someone in his family takes him. That really tugged at my heart, so I told him that I'd get him out on the lake as soon as possible. It's impressive to me that at ninety-three, he still hunts turkey and whitetail deer, and is interested in getting back out on the water. I always enjoy my visits with Sonny, which are not always about Korea. We crack a few cold beers and chat about anything and everything, as we plan that promised fishing trip. Seems I have a soft spot for these old-timers—these Korean War combat veterans, especially my pal Sonny.

CHAPTER 7

George Sousa, U.S. Army
The Survivor

Corporal, U.S. Army, F company, 23rd Infantry Regiment, 2nd Infantry Division. Interviewed October 11, 2023, San Diego, California. Born 1930.

I watched my two good friends get killed right before my eyes—from you to me away. An enemy tank round took my entire squad out, and I was the only one who wasn't killed.

My associate Collin and I had planned a trip to Washington, D.C., to attend ceremonies honoring the seventieth anniversary of the Korean War armistice. We'd be privileged to see the unveiling of the addition to the Korean War Memorial, featuring the names of every fallen American combatant, as well as KATSUA (Korean Augmentation to the United States Army, who'd been directly attached to U.S. forces). The South Korean government had donated millions of dollars to complete the monument, so among the day's highlights were Korean diplomats addressing the impressive crowd that included a large contingent of American veterans. After the ceremonies, Collin and I waited at separate exits, handing out flyers promoting our documentation of Korean War veterans. We were then invited to a downtown hotel to meet Lou Ann Shrink, niece of a Medal of Honor recipient, who was more than willing to share her uncle's story.

On November 6, 1950, Ann's uncle—2nd Lt. Robert Dale Reem—and his Marine platoon were on their way to Chosin Reservoir, where they engaged in a fierce firefight with Chinese forces. (This encounter proves that the Chinese did not wait until the end of the month for their surprise entry into the war, as many believe.) While rallying his men to defend against another attack, a hand grenade landed in the middle of the group. Reem, without hesitation, threw himself on the explosive, shielding his men from the blast. This selfish and courageous act cost the lieutenant his life but saved his men. For this selfless action, Reem was posthumously awarded the Congressional Medal of Honor.

After our fascinating chat, Ann introduced us to other veterans with whom Collin and I sneaked in some short last-minute interviews.

Then we headed to the bar off the lobby, where I noticed an old-timer sitting with someone I assumed was his son. I introduced myself and explained my mission.

He asked us to join them and have a beer. How could we say no? George Sousa was his name, and his companion was indeed his son. Sousa told us that he was with the 23rd Infantry Regiment and was wounded on Heartbreak Ridge. He added that if we ever made it to San Diego, we'd be welcome to stop by for an interview, even though there were "some things I don't want to remember." We exchanged numbers.

A few months later I called George. We agreed to meet on October 11, 2022, at his home in the hills outside San Diego. It fit my schedule perfectly, since I was also able to line up two other California interviews.

I was rather impressed with George's neighborhood—not that I thought he'd be living in squalor, but I didn't expect a gated, affluent community. George met me at the end of his driveway, along with his friendly golden retriever, who in dog years was probably the same age as George, who was ninety-three. He invited me to join him out back where he said he likes to smoke his daily cigar. There, George asked,

So, what do you want to know about Korea?

I told him I prefer that veterans tell me their stories, starting from the beginning, in their own words, and to feel comfortable with what they relate. Still recovering from the loss of his wife of sixty-plus years, George Sousa began his Korean War battle history with his arrival just as the 23rd Infantry Regiment was about to attack and take Bloody Ridge, which he described as

utterly bombed out to the point that when the winds came up there'd be dust storms.

This battle site had seen the U.S. 23rd Infantry and attached ROK 36th regiments facing numerically superior North Korean forces. Each night, bugles would blare, and the enemy would advance, screaming bloody murder, resulting in bitter close-in fighting (a recurring theme with every Korean War veteran I've met). Saying that Korea was a long time ago and there are things he doesn't want to revisit, George did talk of Bloody Ridge being so fierce he suffered severe combat fatigue and was ordered to check in at the nearest aid station. It was a battle site that unquestionably lived up to its name: 2,700 casualties for UN forces, and over fifteen thousand for the KPA (Korean People's Army). The KPA would finally withdraw and move to a ridge a few miles away, later known as Heartbreak Ridge.

All the killing, all the shooting, all the bombing, took its toll on me, and I just couldn't go on. So, they sent me down below to recoup for a few days before we made the next advance push. The next push was for Heartbreak Ridge. That's where I almost died.

George talked of numerous reports of enemy T-34 tanks roaming the area, but no engagements ensued. The first day on Heartbreak Ridge, his squad, along with a complement of South Korean civilians hauling supplies, made their way up the ridge, which was not yet fully taken. Orders were given to send up a few squads to probe for any enemy positions.

I had an uneasy feeling going up, knowing there were enemy tanks on the prowl. But orders are orders, and you gotta follow them.

His suspicions proved correct. As they inched up Heartbreak Ridge, a hidden enemy tank was waiting for any advancing UN forces. North Korean heavy armor consisted mostly of Soviet T-34s, provided by the Russians after World War II and which spearheaded the invasion of South Korea in June 1950, with overwhelming early successes against South Korean infantry and U.S. M-24 Chaffee light tanks. The South Koreans had few weapons to defend against armored vehicles, mostly American M9A1 bazookas. More tank engagements occurred with larger forces of T-34s when China entered the conflict later, but because they were dispersed with the infantry, tank-to-tank battles with UN forces were uncommon. This well-concealed T-34 got the jump on the patrol, firing a round in their direction, followed by a second. George, describing this scene with a weary and wide-eyed look, said he was scared "shitless," but thankful those first two rounds missed. Before the Americans could react—everything happened so fast—a third round landed in the middle of the group. For George, everything went black.

How I wasn't killed, I will never know. When that third round went off, I thought it was all she wrote for me. There is a level of survivor's guilt because why me and not them? I watched my two good friends get killed right before my eyes, from you to me away. An enemy tank round took my entire squad out, and I was the only one who wasn't killed. To this day, I still think about that—seventy-two years later.

George recalled not being able to move until he regained his breath and awareness. It seemed like an eternity. As he described this, all I could picture was the scene from *Saving Private Ryan* where Tom Hanks is on the Normandy Beach in dazed confusion, before fully returning to reality. How quickly it all happened ... that's how fast it was over. The enemy tank was

George Sousa, seen here in a photo that captures the moment he was awarded the Purple Heart while below the MLR in Korea, 1951.

gone, and George started to crawl, dragging his M1. He was picked up by some South Koreans. As they started back toward friendly lines they came under small-arms fire.

> *They dropped me to run, and I hollered, I'm going to shoot you dead if you leave me here. They must have understood me, because they came running back and grabbed me.*

Reaching an aid station and getting treated, George was then sent to Japan to recuperate. He figured this was his ticket home, but he was wrong. His medical leave did not count as time toward his tour in-country, so when his wound healed, he was sent back to the front lines, where he found that the war was vastly different. It had become mostly an Outpost War—military troop detachments stationed away from

George Sousa and Ryan Walkowski after George's interview.

the main force standing guard against unauthorized intrusions and surprise attacks, and where patrols into enemy territory would initiate.

George made it clear he didn't remember much from that phase of the war, as his unit was always on the move from hill to hill, trench to trench, constantly engaging Chinese. One event he did share was that on one outpost there was a damaged tank sitting in front of the line and his team was ordered to recover it with a tank retriever. They suddenly encountered inaccurate small-arms fire from the Chinese. While keeping his head down and eyes peeled for enemy tanks—a tactic he learned on Heartbreak Ridge—George spotted a bunker and went to investigate. Inside was a beautiful Asian tea set that a fellow GI started to "acquire," when George abruptly interfered.

I noticed a string attached to the handle, so I immediately stopped him. I told him, Don't! It's booby trapped! They got the tank ready to be hauled away, so we started to move out, and when I was far enough away, I took one shot at that tea set with my M1 and BOOM, the bunker exploded.

In 1952, George was finally able to rotate home in time for Thanksgiving, where he met his firstborn son. Celebrated as a war hero, he made it into the local newspaper, and he showed me the clipping, along with photos of his time in Korea. George finished the interview, explaining that before he went into the service his family ran a commercial tuna fishing company. When he came back, he turned it into a highly successful business with a fleet of boats, some with helicopter landing pads. His goal was to set his family up so no one would ever have financial worries.

I turned a business that went from using poles to being a multi-boat company. My family and I have been blessed to live a comfortable life.

I asked if he had anything else he wanted to touch base on, or talk about in more detail. He politely told me, "No, that's it."

It was a short but powerful interview—well worth the time. But something was nagging at me. Recalling that there were things he said he didn't want to remember, I was curious as to why he would bring up that one highly emotional and traumatic experience, which most try to forget. So I asked, "Why tell me you almost died and saw your friends killed?" His unforgettable answer before I shut off the camera was simple, yet significant:

That's a part of war worth mentioning. I survived, but they didn't, and I hope they're never forgotten with the work you're doing.

Chapter 8

Ed Gruber, U.S. Navy
The Navy Combat Correspondent

Journalist 3rd Class Petty Officer, U.S. Navy, Pacific Fleet Public Information Office, Pearl Harbor, Hawaii. Interviewed June 2023, Woodstock, Georgia. Born 1928.

As a kid during World War II, I questioned how, on D-Day and at those perilous Pacific island invasions, our young men—mere boys, could take their first steps out of those landing craft, how they could go into battle knowing the horrors that awaited them. Years later, taking my first steps on my first nighttime combat patrol with a Marine squad was the beginning to finding the answer.

Early in my search for interviewees willing to participate in my venture, Ed Gruber, then ninety-four years old, reached out from Woodstock, Georgia. A Korean War veteran, former advertising writer, and a published author, now retired, Ed said he had some interesting experiences but made it clear—no combat stories.

There are things I don't want to remember.

I told Ed, as I did every interviewee, that I didn't expect anyone to talk about or share unpleasant experiences which were better left unvisited. Via e-mail, Ed did share a few interesting parts of his Navy life that included working with John Wayne and Bob Hope. Also, as a Navy combat correspondent, he'd taken lots of black-and-white photos on his tour with the 7th Fleet on war patrol in the Sea of Japan, and during his time with the First Marine Division on the Korean Mainland.

My intended trip to Ed's neighborhood didn't line up with his golf schedule. I thought, how is golf more important than this project? Later, learning how critical playing golf was and is to Ed's longevity, I understood.

Golf is my medicine. As is my writing. They help keep my body and my mind young.

Soon, there was a quick weekend trip to Georgia, and a meeting with Ed that changed my life: not only starting a beautiful friendship, but instigating a partnership and mentorship where Ed would personally help shape me into some kind of writer. As you can imagine, writing this chapter on Ed left me quite nervous. But I'm learning, Ed. I'm learning.

8. Ed Gruber, U.S. Navy: The Navy Combat Correspondent

At our meeting, Ed said he'd be happy to check out my first efforts and do some editing. And he would help me find a co-author—since Ed, because of his advanced age, realistically felt he shouldn't commit to a long-term relationship. Turns out that resilient Ed stuck around long enough to get deeply involved in this book, so there was no need for a co-author. And I'm happy to say, at this writing he's ninety-six years young and still around. He also explained some of the machinations and complications of getting published. So there I was, being mentored by a professional writer with over seventy-five years of experience, helping to shape me as a writer and get this venture off on the right foot. What inspired me most, though, is that Ed believed in what I was doing to remember Korean War veterans. I think you'll agree, as you read on, that he was a pretty good teacher.

I don't want to write the book—the men you interview will be doing that. But I'll work it over as best I can, so it flows right and is readable.

Ed was born in 1928 in the Bronx, New York City, just before the Great Depression. His parents too, were New Yorkers, children of immigrants from Austria, Russia, Poland, and England. After Ed's birth, his parents moved to New Jersey, where his dad was a bus driver for the Interstate Line. But Ed's mother was unhappy away from her family back in the city, so they returned, and his dad took jobs at a leather belt factory in Manhattan, moonlighting nights as a taxi driver. When the Depression hit, the Gruber family survived with Ed's dad taking any job he could to pay the rent and keep food on the table. Ed remembered, at times, having nothing but beans served for dinner.

Growing up in New York in the thirties and forties, it was a safer, saner time then, but you still had to be tough. Because there were so many kids, when we played in the schoolyards or on the streets, if you didn't win a game of basketball, handball, or stickball, you had to wait another few games before you could play again. So winning was important. That's where I learned how to play smarter and to be ultra-competitive. The good thing was kids of all religions, races, and creeds, rich or poor, played together. It didn't matter. If you could play ball, you're on the team. And if you brought the ball, you were definitely on the team.

Ed's brother was born in 1943, which may have helped keep his father out of the draft, although he said his dad was eager to do his part. During World War II, the senior Gruber was a neighborhood air raid warden, with teenager Ed acting as a plane spotter.

Never saw an enemy plane flying over the Bronx. Wouldn't have known what to do if I saw one, anyway.

In 1946 Ed graduated high school without a clue as to his future. As a stop-gap, he attended the Fashion Institute of Technology, a Manhattan school devoted to turning out designers and production engineers for New York's famed garment industry. In his college classes were some World War II combat veterans who were the serious students Ed wasn't. He was only there for the ride—until he figured things out or got drafted. While he'd always liked writing poems and stories, since he was a kid, in his blue-collar family nobody ever said anything about writers making a good living. Besides, when he'd finish his two years at FIT in 1948, the government would still be drafting young men into the military. After graduation, remembering some horror stories his Army veteran schoolmates recounted, Ed joined the Navy.

> *I didn't want to end up in a muddy foxhole, so I enlisted in the Navy. The draft into the Army was for only two years, but the least you could enlist in the Navy was for three. I thought the extra year wouldn't be too bad, give me more time to figure out what I wanted to do with the rest of my life. If I played my cards right, I'd travel, meet interesting people, maybe learn a trade, and, because I was a street-smart wise-ass city kid, I'd beat the system. Believe it or not, I did it all—especially beat the system. When my Captain gave me my Good Conduct Medal, he said, "Gruber, this isn't for being good. It's for not getting caught."*

One of Ed's cousins was a World War II Navy vet, a submarine torpedoman, also a first-class hustler, conning his way through life. The cousin advised Ed to raise his hand when the company commander at Boot Camp in Great Lakes, Illinois, asked if anyone had ever worked in a post office. Ed told his cousin he'd never worked in a post office. "Don't be a jerk," his cousin said. "Do what I'm telling you. They'll make you the company postal clerk and you'll get time off from those boring classes and drills to go for the mail, bring it back to the barracks, sort it, get in some sack-time, and later at mail-call hand out envelopes and packages from their mothers and sweethearts. Being a Jew in the Navy won't be easy, but here you're a hero to a bunch of grateful guys."

And that's exactly what happened.

> *After boot camp, I was shipped to the Alameda Naval Air Station in California, across the bay from San Francisco. Because I had some college and could type, I was assigned to the Personnel Department of a Fleet Air Service Repair Squadron. First day, this lieutenant told me that he was giving me a very responsible job at which I could make a lot of money.*

The officer told Ed that underage sailors (you had to be twenty-one to drink in California) would be willing to pay well for ID cards with false birthdates, and even more for unauthorized Liberty Cards that allowed them to get off base. Plus, they would pay even more to expunge court martials and other misdemeanors from their service files. And Ed would be distributing and overseeing all these documents.

> *Immediately my city street-smarts antenna went up. Something wasn't kosher. I asked the lieutenant what happened to the guy who had the job before me. He smiled and said he was doing time at the Navy's Mare Island prison. I thanked him very much and told him that I thought I got the message.*

While Ed was enjoying his duty at the air station, and weekend liberties in San

Francisco, he came across an article in a Navy magazine that would change his life. It featured a school back at the Great Lakes Naval Training Station with courses that taught public affairs, photojournalism, writing, newspaper design and layout, operating and maintaining audiovisual and printing equipment, and coordinating with and escorting media—the whole gamut of public relations communications. It even included going on assignments for Chicago newspapers and radio news stations. Graduates upon completion of the extensive twelve-week course would become official U.S. Navy combat correspondents.

There is a God!

Ed applied, was accepted, and soon was on his way to refining his writing skills. He even covered a Chicago murder for one of the Windy City newspapers.

As he said, one of his goals was to travel. Travel he did, with his next assignment the Pacific Fleet Public Information Office (PIO) at Pearl Harbor, Hawaii. By the way, what I'm next about to relate, Ed may edit out. I hope not. Here goes anyway. His first time on a ship, the one he boarded in San Francisco to sail to Hawaii, the notorious cross-currents under the famous Golden Gate Bridge created some wild rocking motions that had Ed racing up ladders from below to the topside deck, only to barf over the railing—into the wind. He did tell me, though, that was the last time he ever got seasick.

> *At the Pearl Harbor PIO, at first, I was writing dull peacetime press releases about promotions, ship arrivals, and speeches for the Admiral. Also, babysitting VIPs and occasionally escorting them to the site of the USS* Arizona—*very emotional visits. But things reached a different level when my immediate superior Chief Petty Officer Bob Hampton got the go-ahead from our CO to design and build a radio recording studio. A twenty-plus years Sea Dog, Bob knew nothing about this modern technology, having been an engineman on combat destroyers prior to and during WWII—two of them torpedoed out from under him in the Pacific. This tour at the PIO was his first-ever shore duty. He overcame his lack of electronics technical knowledge with an uncanny ability to interpret instruction manuals, and with his brains and my brawn the two of us built a more than workable studio. In fact, with two monstrous Stancil–Hoffman tape recorders, the studio at the time was considered state of the art. Best part is, that Bob, his wife Vivian, and their two sons became my second family.*

Their first recordings were five-minute interviews conducted by Ed and a few of his PIO mates with young sailors and Marines stationed in Hawaii, recorded on small vinyl platters sent to the interviewees' hometown radio stations. Those were great for morale at the base and with the servicemen's families.

Soon, another PIO member came up with an idea for a Navy fifteen-minute radio show called *Across the Blue Pacific*. It featured a local Hawaiian musical group and either a dramatic story about Navy and Marine heroism or an interview with a celebrity who was visiting Pearl Harbor who had good things to say about the Navy.

Ed was the primary writer and director of the dramatic segments, as well as performing as an actor, engineer, and producer.

> *One of the dramas was about a heroic Navy deep-sea diver. We hit a snag when we couldn't get the sound effects right for the actor supposedly wearing a heavy diving helmet. We finally put a tin bucket over his head and inserted a microphone and it worked perfectly. Problem was getting him out of the bucket, but we finally got it done, leaving him with a pair of sore ears.*

Hollywood celebrities vacationing in Hawaii created many opportunities to have a real live star perform in the dramas. When John Wayne was in Honolulu producing and acting in a movie called *Big Jim McLain*, Ed's commanding officer contacted Wayne, who said he'd be happy to help. Overnight, Ed wrote a script and next morning—well, let's let Ed tell the story.

> *We were all ready for Duke. Trouble was he wasn't ready for us. Our mega-star showed up with a mega-hangover. He couldn't read the script. My CO found some bourbon in his desk drawer, which he kept for medicinal purposes only. We spiked Wayne's coffee and that got the job done. Wayne was more than complimentary when we were done, and even suggested I write a script for an up-and-coming young man working with him on the film. I did. That actor was James Arness, who later went on to become famous for* Gunsmoke.

Other Hollywood talents Ed wrote scripts for and directed included Walter Brennan, Ann Blythe, and Ruth Roman. Among those who gave interviews were the Andrews Sisters, Carmen Miranda, and Peter Lawford.

> *On liberty weekends in Honolulu, I was doing what most sailors did—hit the beach, the bars, and chase girls. But one Saturday, walking near Waikiki Beach, I was passing the Ft. DeRussy Service Club. Curious, I entered this huge theater to see at the piano a pretty lady—the director of the club, surrounded by some service guys, and they were all singing. So I joined in and the next thing you know, in my spare time I'm putting on shows at the theater, singing, emceeing, and dating the club director. Life was good.*

In June 1950, Ed was ordered to join BAREX50, an expedition sailing from San Diego, via Seattle, to Pt. Barrow, Alaska (northernmost point of the North American continent), where the Navy had oil exploration teams. Since huge cargo planes were still on the drawing boards, and there was no airstrip at Barrow anyway, the research teams had to be resupplied once a year—amphibiously. This could only happen when the winter's ice had drifted offshore, making the beaches accessible to LSTs (landing ships) loaded with cranes and large equipment, and smaller amphibious boats transferring food and gear from large transport ships lying offshore. Ed's job would be writing the fleet's newsletter and press releases and taking photos.

> *I'm on liberty—sitting in a San Diego bar on Sunday, June 25th with a bunch of other sailors and Marines—waiting for the ships to be loaded, and a couple Shore Patrol guys barge in, banging their nightsticks on the mahogany bar. And shouting that*

everybody should get back to their ships, bases, and stations on the double. And that we're in a fucking war! My first thought was gee, I just missed WWII, but they made one just for me. I hustled back to my ship, the USS Seminole, *and met with the fleet commander, who told me to forget about press releases. That we're now in a news blackout, so I should just focus on taking pictures and putting out the newsletter. He wanted the crews to get the straight news, not scuttlebutt.*

The expedition sailed north and returned without a flaw, with the only distractions coming from the Russians in Siberia trying to jam the fleet's radio waves—with little success.

Back at Pearl Harbor, Ed's next assignment was to interview another mega-star for a Navy radio newscast: Bob Hope, who was landing at Hawaii's Hickam Airforce Base, coming to Hawaii to tape his popular weekly *Chesterfield Cigarette Radio Show* before a military audience.

It was a mob scene at Hickam. I'm fighting my way through the crowd of reporters and photographers. As Hope's stepping out the door of the plane, I'm yelling, "Make way for the little guy. Let the little guy through." Hope leans down and says, "Hey sailor, you want a good interview. Meet me at the Royal Hawaiian Hotel later, and I'll give you private one." How lucky could I get?

The hotel room door was opened by Hy Averbach, Hope's producer and announcer. "So you're the little guy Bob says almost got trampled. He's in there. Don't knock. Just go on in." Ed did, finding Bob lounging on the bed in polka dot shorts and undershirt. "I see you survived. Thought for sure you'd get trampled. How do you want to do this?"

I told him any way that makes him comfortable. He graciously said that he wanted me to be comfortable. "Let's do it." The interview went well, with Bob complimenting me after, saying he thought I did a very professional job. Then he asked, "Hey, do you know any sailor with acting experience? We've got a skit in the radio show I do with a Navy guy." I quickly said, "Yeah. Me." He had Hy bring in the script and we ran through it. "You got the job." There was a rehearsal next day with actress/singer Gloria DeHaven and Les Brown—leader of the famous Band of Renown that accompanied Bob on almost all his USO tours. The show went well, but there was a technical glitch and we had to do a repeat performance a day later. On the way, I was sitting with Bob in the military limo, and we were talking baseball, since he was part owner of the Cleveland Indians, and I was an avid New York Yankee fan. Suddenly it got quiet, with Hope turning to me and asking, "Do you think they'll like me?" Of course I was stunned, but managed to tell him that he's Bob Hope, and he'll have them in the palms of hands the moment he steps on stage. He looked at me and said, "Thanks, Ed. I needed that."

A few months later, Hope called Ed and asked if he'd be Hope's emcee at a USO show in Pearl Harbor at Bloch Arena (where Ed played point guard on the Pacific Fleet basketball team). Before the show, Ed asked Bob for an opening line, which turned out to be, "I worked for Bob on his radio show a while back, and I'm still waiting for my check." Which Ed said went over like a lead balloon. After he introduced Bob, the comedian's opening line was, "Sorry about the no-pay joke. I gave it to Ed, but I keep the good stuff for myself." Leave it to the master!

Ed's time in Hawaii couldn't have been any better. There were tropical beaches, snorkeling, spear fishing, basketball, performing at the Service Club and dating the pretty Director, and writing for *Across the Blue Pacific*. Also, he was escorting VIPs and Hollywood celebrities such as the famous Andrews sisters to the site of the USS *Arizona*—not the impressive monument of today. Then, it had only a catwalk and flagpole, but was still the somber scene that brings tears to the eyes of its visitors.

> *For some recklessly macho reason, I was looking to validate the "combat" part of my Combat Correspondent classification. Otherwise, I felt like an imposter. I wrote dozens of requests for Korean War duty, but my reluctant CO declared me more valuable here (his words not mine). But a new CO agreed that the experience would be beneficial to my scripts and, because there was some kind of stalemate in the war zone, I wouldn't be in harm's way. He gave me the okay. I chose beer-buddy Dean Musgrove, from Iowa, to tag along, and soon our orders were cut and we were flying from safe, serene Hawaii to exotic Tokyo, where we would be planning our Korean itinerary. By this time, I should mention, because of the war, my three-year enlistment was turned into four.*

After a few days in Tokyo picking up fatigues, boots, lightweight sleeping bags, and .45-caliber Navy Colt pistols, they flew from Tokyo to Itasugi on the Japanese island of Fukuoka, where they climbed into the rear gun turret of a vintage Avenger Torpedo Bomber. These historic World War II aircraft were being used as shuttles between the fleet, Japan, and the Korean mainland—carrying mail and small cargo and, as Ed commented, "Two scared-like-shit sailors."

> *Our destination was the aircraft carrier USS Valley Forge, sailing with the 7th Fleet in the Sea of Japan off the east coast of Korea. Our pilot's objective? Find the carrier, land on it, with the hope that the tail-hook snags a steel cable stretched across the deck. This was not on my agenda when I enlisted. When we spotted the carrier looking like a pencil floating in the ocean, we were told that Navy and Marine warplanes returning from a strike had landing priority. Finally, through our headsets, we heard the carrier's landing officer's calm but commanding instructions, resulting in the cable being securely snared—the incontestable high point of my then young life.*

The journalists checked in with the ship's PIO officer, who informed them that reports of a stalemate were hogwash. A lot of serious stuff was happening. The Communists, entrenched up north, were steadily increasing troops and supplies. U.S. Air Force jets roamed the Yalu River daily. Fighter-bombers from aircraft carriers off both coasts flew hundreds of sorties. Minesweepers were working round the clock. UN warships and ground forces were on constant patrol. As in all wars, rumors raged wildly, from a possible kidnapping of the UN armistice delegation to a general assault against the islands in Wonsan Harbor—Ed and Dean's next destination. The upshot? Even with no large-scale combat operations, there were a hell of a lot of small ones, although—as Ed remarked—"You can't call people trying to blow your head off anything small."

Navy combat correspondent Dean Musgrove, in a photo taken by Ed Gruber while both he and Musgrove were embedded with elements of the 7th Marines near Munsan-ni, Korea, 1952.

Our next crazy thrill was transferring from the Valley Forge *to the USS* Mispillion, *a tanker running alongside, refueling the carrier with diesel and aviation fuels. This insane stunt was via a hi-line or breeches buoy, an open cage on a line between two ships moving at sea. Thankfully, both skippers and crews had this dangerously delicate operation down pat, with Dean and me planting dry feet on the tanker's rock-solid but rolling steel deck. Got me wondering what the hell I was thinking when I came up with the idea of going to Korea.*

Sailing north, day and night, the tanker pumped precious fuel, sometimes replenishing two warships simultaneously at port and starboard: British, South Korean, Thai, American, and others. The third day out, an emergency dispatch ordered the *Mispillion*'s captain to cease refueling operations and proceed full speed toward Wonsan Harbor. Chinese shore batteries had hit an American frigate, wounding a sailor who required ASAP transfer to the *Mispillion*'s medical facility. Upon arrival, a small craft was dispatched from the tanker to the frigate to transport the casualty. That same boat then conveyed Ed and Dean to the USS *Brinkley-Bass*, a destroyer entering Wonsan Harbor, whose mission was to protect a South Korean minesweeper, while blasting its lethal five-inch guns at mainland targets.

I watched fire missions conducted by the Brinkley-Bass. *Right on target, striking the mouths of caves concealing heavy-duty, track-mounted cannons wheeled deep inside after firing rounds at UN island-based forces and harbor vessels. Considering the dense Chinese population, this was a make-work exercise. Overnight, manpower-heavy enemy cleared the debris, rebuilt the tracks, and next morning their guns were back in action. We weren't talking chop suey here.*

Then the two correspondents disembarked for Modo Island, only a couple thousand yards from Communist ordnance.

The Marine commander gave us free rein to explore, with a heads-up that the Chinese on the mainland often took potshots at moving personnel. We immediately encountered bitter, battle-hardened South Korean Marines guarding a detail of trench-digging POWs. No love lost here. One unforgiving sentry swung his carbine at the back of a foot-dragging captive, snapping the rifle's wooden stock in two. No whimpers from the prisoner, he just dug a little faster. I suddenly realized that something beyond my comprehension was going on. What it was, was war. And I wondered, as I'd become more involved, how I would handle this destructive and dangerous business. My thoughts were suddenly interrupted by two close-by explosions—mortar shells. No injuries, no bowel or bladder accidents, only ear ringing, increased beating of my heart, and a new and frightening sense of reality.

During Ed and Dean's stint on Modo, a South Korean Marine on another island accidentally detonated a Willy Peter (white phosphorus grenade), severely burning his arm. A small boat was dispatched to get the casualty to the *Brinkley-Bass*'s medical facility. This would be tricky since the transfer had to occur with the destroyer at full stop—leaving the ship an easy target for Chinese gunners on the mainland. Ed went along for the ride and to take pictures.

Ed Gruber posing for a quick photograph while gearing up before a nighttime combat patrol with elements of the 7th Marines near Munsan-ni, Korea, 1952.

The handover was successful—and quick. Returning to Modo, in total darkness, the boatswain gave me a chilling order—station myself at the bow and warn of any concentrations of telltale phosphorescence, eerie glows from tiny sea animals agitated by floating objects. He told me our objects were deadly anti-ship mines hovering close to the surface. I did spot a glow—to my relief, just driftwood.

After a few days, the pair of correspondents boarded an LST positioned outside the harbor. Improved Communist anti-aircraft fire was causing more UN planes to be ditched at sea. The LST's helicopter would rescue these pilots, and others downed from fuel shortages or malfunctions. One pilot Ed re-met, just pulled out of the water, was an aviator Ed knew from his days at the Alameda Naval air station.

> *Was he pissed off. Lost an expensive pearl-handled revolver when he hit the water and said something about getting even on his next mission.*

Next was boarding the USS *Richard B. Anderson*, a destroyer serving as a carrier escort. The task force commander sent word he wanted a debriefing.

(From left) Ed Gruber, Sergeant "Mac," and fellow correspondent Dean Musgrove pose for a picture before a nightly combat patrol near Munsan-ni, Korea, 1952.

> *He asked us how it was on the beach. I think we went a little macho when we told him, "It was rough, very rough." Even though booze is illegal on-board U.S. Navy vessels, he offered us a drink. "Never got it from me," he said, "but under these circumstances some rules can be broken and never talked about. Right?" Of course we agreed and shared some brandy with the generous, rule-breaking officer. Little did he know that the resourceful Marines on Modo had a major stash of beer and booze. Also not talked about.*

That wasn't the end of Ed's and Dean's imbibing on the *Anderson*. Later, some of the crew, impressed with these two grungy journalists packing .45 automatics, shared mugs of their hidden stock of homemade raisin jack, an illegal fermented brew that Ed said would curl your bell-bottoms.

Next, there was another hi-line transfer, this time to the aircraft carrier USS *Boxer*. Ed said something about a nasty hangover and not feeling a thing going across the choppy sea.

> *On the* Boxer, *we took hot showers, typed up some stories, and then experienced our first carrier take-off in another Avenger aircraft. No catapults those days, so*

Top: A squad of Marines walking the Panmunjom Peace Trail (which was illegal for wartime activities) to reach their outpost faster (photograph by Ed Gruber). *Bottom:* A Marine bunker, a great representation of life on the front line of the Korean War, 1952 (photograph by Ed Gruber).

the chunky old torpedo plane took a slight dip after the wheels left the deck, leaving a piece of my stomach in the Sea of Japan. Our destination was the Korean mainland, where we'd join up with the First Marine Division on the MLR (main line of resistance). After landing at the Seoul Air Base, we were Jeeped through the city of Seoul, where most buildings were gutted and there wasn't a roof in sight. I couldn't help but feel sorry for the locals. We arrived at the Third Battalion, Seventh Regiment near Munsan-ni, where we received an ominous indoctrination from the Company Commander. It went something like this: "The Chinese are just over there. Between them and us are hills and rice paddies—heavily mined. Be careful where you step. Welcome to Korea."

The officer asked Ed about the team's mission. Ed said it was to do hometown stories on Marines and gather background material for *Across the Blue Pacific* scripts and a Navy newscast. When asked how he gets this stuff, Ed said, "We'll interview Marines returning from patrols." The last thing Ed expected was the Lieutenant's next statement. "Wouldn't firsthand stories be better?"

I asked, "What do you mean?" In retrospect, I should have kept my big mouth shut. His response was that there was a patrol going out that night to ambush gooks who surprised his boys the night before. I told him we were checked out on rifles but had no combat training experience. He said his Marines would teach us, and that fighting comes before writing. He added, "It might be fun."

So began the first of Ed's several nighttime combat patrols with U.S. Marines in enemy territory.

Introduced to a young sergeant named Mac, who turned out to be a brilliant leader at only twenty-three years of age and veteran of the Chosin Reservoir ordeal, where he was wounded by three burp-gun shells across his chest, Ed asked him, "Why the hell are you here? You could be serving anywhere else in the world." Mac simply said, "I needed to prove to myself I wasn't chicken." Only another Marine would understand.

"**Ready for action**": elements of the 7th Marines on the front lines near Munsan-ni, Korea, 1952 (photograph by Ed Gruber).

A great example of bunkers used by Marines on the frontline of Korea near Munsan-ni, 1952 (photograph by Ed Gruber).

A couple hours before sunset, we found ourselves saddling up with two squads, plus a machine gun unit. A sergeant named Moore was giving the briefing, starting with "We're taking the Panmunjom truce road to our breaking-off point." I asked him, "Isn't that off limits?" "For sure," he answered. "So, if we meet chinks—no gunplay. We do our business quiet-like." The ramifications of that statement brought up bitter bile that seared my throat. What the hell was I doing? I thought of pulling out, but to come off as a yellow, sniveling, chicken-shit coward was no option. He went on, "We'll string com-wire, check in every ten minutes till we get to White Hill. I want us at the base by dark. You knuckleheads keep the fucking chatter down. I don't want the chinks to know we're there."

The riflemen—Frankie, Woody, Morgan, Tony, Tom, Tex, Shelton, Burnett, and the others—checked weapons, ammo, and canteens, with a lot of kibitzing and little tension. These were combat veteran Marines. Wearing camouflaged helmets and flak jackets, and armed to the teeth with carbines, extra ammo clips, and plenty of grenades, Ed and Dean were ready for their first patrol. Or were they?

Along the truce road they met no enemy. But Ed said he'd swear he saw one behind every bush. When they reached White Hill, it was dark—as Ed described it, "Pitch fucking black." The sun had dropped behind the peaks like a bullet. They worked up a sweat scrambling to their positions. By now, though, it was damned chilly. Ed said he was glad he brought along a field jacket. After securing the area, Sergeant Moore picked up the phone. It was dead. He sent a fire-team to check the

8. Ed Gruber, U.S. Navy: The Navy Combat Correspondent

Marines cleaning up in the spring where they kept their beer cool; such valuable commodities were watched carefully by a machine gun crew armed with a .30 caliber machine gun (photograph by Ed Gruber).

line, and they were back in minutes. "The line's cut, Sarge. Looks like a fucking gook got in formation with us coming up the fucking hill in the fucking dark and cut the fucking line." Moore turned to Ed and whispered, "Pass the word. Fix bayonets."

I didn't know I had any bile left when another batch erupted. Somehow, I passed the word to the Marine next to me, thinking it's one thing to toss grenades and fire bullets, but bayonets? Hand-to-hand combat? I began shaking on top of my shaking. For hours we were hunkered down, observing gun tracers over hills not far from ours, where firefights were underway. Wondering who they were, if ours would start, and when. And how Dean and I would hack it.

It was a long, cold, and uneasy night, especially when Mac, sensing Ed's anxieties, whispered, "Just before dawn they'll drop mortar shells on us, then blow those goddamn bugles. Think it shakes us up. We'll pop some flares. You'll be okay. Just keep your head down. And fling your grenades where you see shadows."

Then, my mind started working. I wanted to fire my carbine, toss grenades, do anything but nothing. Thinking some kind of action would be less fearsome than the wild and crazy mind-pictures filling my head. I discovered that an idle mind is a warrior's worst enemy. Nothing happening was torture.

Ed Gruber and Ryan Walkowski sharing a beer after Ed's interview, the beginning of a friendship and partnership.

At dawn, four too-close mortar rounds abruptly disturbed the violent images running through Ed's head and started his ears ringing, with enough force to shake sand out of the sandbags and give everyone a serious bounce. Then … no bugles, no flares, no shadows, no bullets, no Chinese attack. As the sun rose, the patrol cautiously eased down White Hill, making their way back without incident. "How about that?" Sergeant Mac cheered over a beer. "Your first patrol, you didn't hurt yourselves or nobody else. I'll take you sailors out anytime." Which, later, he did.

There were more dusk-to-dawn patrols for Ed, with their own very real, not-imagined horrors. Yet even with the bugles, flares, shadows, bullets and explosions, the screaming, the torn bodies and tears, Ed said his first patrol was his most fearful. The others? He wouldn't talk about them, except to say that they were probably as scary, but he was too busy to notice. Things happened, he told me, that he didn't want to remember.

> *But I will talk about the Brotherhood. The amazing regard every Marine had for his brother Marine. These were the guys that, if you had to go to war, these were the guys you wanted by your side. They knew their jobs, protected each other, not only looked for self-survival, but survival of each other. No mom, apple pie, God, or the American flag here. It was the brotherhood, a bond that only forms between those who've been in combat together, and that's what I experienced.*

Back at Pearl Harbor in July 1952, things didn't go well for Ed. There were nightmares and binge drinking. His CO chewed him out… "I don't know whether to court martial you or give you a medal. I ordered you to stay out of harm's way; but landing and taking off carrier flight decks, hi-lining between ships at sea, getting into firefights, and now boozing it up like a stupid drunken sailor. You look awful. I want you to get your ass to the rest camp on the Big Island and sober up. You get back and start writing like I know you can. When's your enlistment up? September?

Can't send you home looking like this. Here, take this damned Korean Combat ribbon with three battle stars, and show me you're the man you were over there ... the man who earned these."

> *I did. Haven't had a gin martini since. Went back to the States, got into the advertising business with international ad agencies in New York, Detroit, Toronto, got married, had kids and grandkids, and now I'm a reasonably healthy widower living in Georgia with a couple of books published—still writing, golfing, fishing, cooking, eating, drinking—moderately. And still breathing. I guess I'm one lucky ninety-four-year-old guy.*

Brotherhood. It's the one recurring theme from every veteran I've met. Heck, there's even a brotherhood developed between Ed and me. He's pushed me on my way to becoming become a decent writer. I'll forever be grateful that he believed in a young kid on what's been called a noble journey. I made a point of twice a year getting to Georgia, visiting with Ed and planning our next moves on this book. As evidenced in this finished product, everything he's taught me helped move this project along with amazing speed. I didn't have time to wait. I wanted all the veterans featured to be able to read their amazing stories. It's Ed's mentoring that made this possible, helping me make my homage to Korean War veterans a reality, a dream come true. There's more to be written, but this chapter about Ed Gruber is as good as it gets.

CHAPTER 9

William "Willie" Cybula, U.S. Army
The Polish Kid

Corporal, U.S. Army, Item Company, 5th Cavalry Regiment, 1st Cavalry Division. Interviewed January 31, 2022, Ringle, Wisconsin. Born 1931.

I had many nightmares that always involved Sergeant Beale. There was never one that he wasn't involved one way or another. Even when I was at home, he was still trying to get me killed in my dreams.

My journey documenting Korean War veterans was gaining momentum, with friends, family, and even strangers constantly contacting me with names of those who'd served. After Kyle Wincensten, my best friend, told me about his great uncle, I spoke to Kyle's mom, who filled me in with more background and suggested I make the call. Some of my earlier approaches to veterans had been met with various measures of reluctance—sometimes hostility, for expecting them to recall repressed memories; even warning me to never contact them again. This was not the case with Willie Cybula, who welcomed the opportunity to share his experiences.

On the phone with Willie, I couldn't help but notice his thick Polish accent, which was typical for many northern Wisconsinites. It reminded me of my Grandpa Sonny and made me even more excited about a face-to-face interview. Collin Wilson, my colleague, came along to help document the meeting. Willie and his wife made us feel right at home.

Before I could pose my first question, Willie kicked off the interview by asking me about my grandpa. I told him that his name was Sonny Walkowski. Which was followed by this surprise:

I knew Sonny, Smokey, Ervin, and all of them. They lived right down the road.

Willie was born on September 22, 1931, in Reid, Wisconsin, a town known as Pike Lake. He was the seventh of ten children—six boys and four girls, who all grew up during the Great Depression in a dirt-floor home with an outhouse and no electricity. He often shared a bed with his siblings, with the newborns sleeping with their parents. Despite these harsh conditions, Willie said he'd had a great childhood that taught him how to make the best of things. For first and second grade, Willie attended a public school. After that he was enrolled at St. Ladislaus Catholic School in nearby Bevent until the eighth grade, before dropping out to help his family. Willie also said the country kids' attire those days consisted of typical bib overalls and flannel shirts.

My father didn't believe in education and didn't know how to write, so that's why some of my relatives have different spellings for our last name, because he spelled our name wrong.

Before his September 1950 enlistment in the Army, Willie was working on the family farm with his cousin Dan Gorski. They both thought about joining the Air Force, but Dan changed his mind. So Willie joined the Army, which offered a three-year commitment as opposed to the Air Force's four. Having never been more than twenty miles from home, traveling for Willie was a completely new adventure, which began with being shipped to Fort Riley, Kansas, for his six-week training course. Then he went to Fort Belvoir, Virginia, for an additional six weeks of engineering indoctrination. Upon completion, Willie was given seven days of leave before being posted to Lawton, Washington, with his next destination Korea.

William "Willie" Cybula in his military photograph before shipping to Korea.

We boarded a troopship with about thirty-two hundred men for a fifteen-day trip to Japan. On the fifth day we hit a storm that only allowed us to move ten miles a day. Everyone was sick and some even died from sea sickness.

After a few days in Japan, Willie sailed to Pusan, Korea, where he boarded a train headed north, traveling in a railway car that had about thirty-two bunk beds.

The men who were in the bottom bunks could not even get in. They had us really packed in there, so some people didn't even sleep at all.

Reaching the front lines, Willie was assigned to I Company, 3rd Battalion, 5th Cavalry Regiment of the 1st Cavalry Division. While taking in his new surroundings, he sorrowfully discovered that his squad leader—a Sergeant Beale from Washington, D.C.—had an intense dislike for anyone of Polish descent, insultingly referring to them as them Polacks. The bigoted NCO immediately demonstrated his prejudices by assigning Willie to be a BAR (Browning automatic rifle) assistant, which required him to carry extra ammunition for the BAR rifleman.

I'm only five-foot-seven and weighed 130 pounds. I was the smallest guy in the squad, but he made me carry the heaviest load. He was a first-class asshole.

Darrel Clipps, from Oshkosh, Wisconsin, was the BAR man, armed with a twenty-two-pound weapon and twelve magazines. As his assistant, Willie had to lug an additional twelve magazines, as well as his own rifle with a full load of ammo.

We got acquainted with the troops that had been there since July of 1950. Only the squad leader and assistant squad leader were what was left of the original group.

After a few days the new arrivals were taken up a hill and shown the trenches and bunkers. While walking around, Willie discovered two dead Chinese soldiers: quite a shock, considering he'd been raised in a small, peaceful Catholic community and had never seen a dead body. A few more days passed, and the 5th Regiment was called up to help relieve a British Brigade surrounded by Chinese forces. Two previous rescue attempts had failed to help the trapped Brits. Willie's regiment was immediately met by stiff resistance, especially from a rocky cliff up the steep hill from where the Chinese lobbed deadly hand grenades.

I spotted one of the Chinese soldiers and fired a few shots at him. I wasn't sure if I wounded or killed him.

As the battle carried on, Steve Prado from Milwaukee, a member of Willie's squad and a former softball pitcher, called for everyone to pass him their grenades. Steve put his athletic skills to use, tossing thirty grenades at the Chinese emplacements. Two didn't make it, ricocheting and exploding among the friendlies—fortunately, with no injuries. After knocking out the machine gun with a shower of more grenades, the Americans made their way to the cliff's edge to meet the trapped British Brigade, which could now pass safely through their lines. Willie and his squad followed.

One of our troops got out of a foxhole and stepped back where he fell about thirty feet from the edge of this cliff and landed on a rock. He didn't appear to be moving, and we had no way to retrieve him. The Chinese regrouped and closed in on us, so our squad leader made the decision to leave him.

I asked Willy if he remembered dates and names of the battles. He replied that the guys on the ground were given minimal information, so he was never sure.

The Chinese moved in rapidly, attempting to surround the fleeing UN forces. As darkness fell, Willie's squad marched thirteen hours through the night that was so dark that they'd talk with each other so as not to get separated and lost. Eventually, they met and mounted American tanks, riding for about half a mile until they encountered a Chinese roadblock. The troops dismounted, scrambling to higher ground from where they returned fire. Next, they headed south, only to run into stiff resistance from enemy forces that had advanced ahead of the fleeing UN soldiers. They immediately set up a defensive perimeter to take the Chinese head-on: hordes of fanatic warriors attacking in waves across an open field. It was the first time Willie witnessed this terrifying tactic. The Chinese, however, met superior firepower in a battle that continued for almost six hours. Wave after wave approached, only to be gunned down, leaving bodies strewn across the landscape. Despite the mounting casualties, the Chinese still tried to break the GI and British lines. When morning broke and the battle was over, Willie said there were dead Chinese lying everywhere. He recalled barely being able to walk due to the number of bloody corpses.

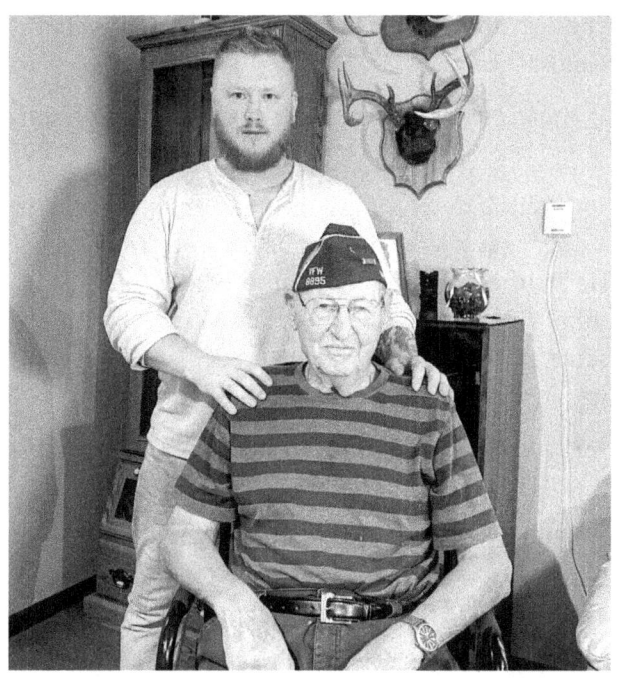

William "Willie" Cybula and Ryan Walkowski in Willie's home after his second interview for the book.

> *They were really coming at us, and we were firing like crazy. They couldn't match our firepower, so we just wiped them right out. The next morning all I saw were dead Chinese laying everywhere. and we collected weapons of all sorts, some even from the 1800s, and piled them into stacks ten feet high and burned them before we moved out.*

The next orders had the Americans heading west. Marching up and down hill after hill, the exhausted troops finally reached the frontlines. With trenches and foxholes already dug by South Koreans, all the GIs had to do was hop in. Willie did not remember which hill. At this point he'd only been in Korea a few days but had quickly become a combat veteran. As night came, a group of Chinese tried to throw the GIs out of the trenches, once again being met by superior firepower. Willie directed mortar fire that proved effective enough to force the Chinese to withdraw.

The next afternoon they were provided with relief and given food for the first time in almost three days.

> *Against what my Sergeant said, I ate a can of beef patties without warming them up and was sicker than a dog the whole next day. But I couldn't wait, I was so hungry.*

Willie described C-rations as not very tasty: in some cases, "not fit for even a dog." They were mostly beans and franks, beef patties, lima beans, and hash. He ate these for about a month before he could not stand a spoonful. I found this to be a recurring theme on my journey, with almost all the veterans saying the same about the rations, which were often leftovers from World War II: Throw in a water-purifying pill and pray they wouldn't get sick.

> *I survived most of the time on three soda crackers and jelly, or a chocolate, or jelly candy bar.*

It wasn't long before Willie was back on the frontlines performing daily patrols. On one mission, the squad came to a riverbank that had taken a direct napalm hit and they were horrified to discover eight barely recognizable charred bodies. Further down the river, they discovered more charred Chinese corpses that resembled stone statues. Considering his simple and innocent background, this proved to be traumatic for Willie—initially.

> *I had never seen a dead body before I got to Korea, and I hate to say, but you get used to it after a while. It doesn't bother you seeing so many laying around.*

On another patrol, Willie and his squad came across a wounded Chinese soldier with a broken leg, fighting off swarms of flies. The GIs loaded him on a jeep that took him to an aid station. Willie was later informed the Chinese soldier survived. That same day, while stopped for lunch, they were instructed to dig in. Sgt. Beale assigned Willie to a hole that had already been prepared. Willie thought this was great because it meant he didn't have to dig. As he retrieved his lunch—which he recalled was either beans and franks or lima beans—he was overcome by an obnoxious odor. He thought C-rations were bad, but never this bad. He tasted a spoonful and found it to be surprisingly tolerable. That's when he looked around the foxhole.

> *As I looked around the hole I was in, I noticed a decaying hand sticking out and quickly recognized that's where the stench was coming from. Now that I (could) see where it was coming (from) the stench became too much to handle, so I took my little shovel out and covered up the hand and continued to eat my lunch.*

Later, patrolling through a small village, one of Willie's squad members poked his head around the corner of a building. Suddenly, there was a loud BANG! The soldier's helmet flew into the air and his face was instantly covered with blood. A sniper had scored a direct hit. Shots kept coming, so the squad set out to locate the source and any other Chinese they could find. Once all the firing ceased, they examined the bleeding GI. Fortunately, he was only grazed. His helmet had saved the lucky GI's life.

During another patrol, just outside the town, the squad began taking small-arms and mortar fire. Digging frantically, Willie shoveled about two feet and hopped into his hole, praying he wouldn't take an incoming round. He looked up to see a soldier digging close to where the rounds were dropping. Willie tried to warn him, but he didn't listen—or maybe with all the noise, he couldn't hear. A mortar round blew him to pieces.

> *All I could see was his body go flying through the air, and land without his head and parts of his arm and shoulder on the right side. That was the most gruesome thing I'd seen while in Korea, and it really shocked me and left me stunned for a few minutes.*

After the firefight, the squad searched for the dead soldier's dog tags. The next day, the company commander instructed Willie and the squad to bring body bags and recover what pieces of the dead GI they could find. These daily patrols continued, always encountering Chinese forces, which kept Willie constantly on edge. He made it clear that more times than not, the Chinese would allow the Americans to pass through, then attack from behind in hopes of cutting them off. Once, someone yelled, "The Chinese are behind us, we're surrounded!" The entire squad hastily took up defensive positions and waited for movement. After a while, seven deer came out of some heavy brush, bringing sighs of relief, a lighthearted moment in a place and time where and when there were seldom lighthearted moments.

Hill 104, near Pork Chop Hill, was their next objective. One company was designated to capture the first hill. A second was assigned to the second hill. And a third ordered directly to Hill 104—the primary target. Sgt. Beale, Willie's bigoted nemesis, figured since Willie hadn't gotten killed carrying a heavy load, he'd make him point man on this assault. (The point man assumes the first and most exposed position in a patrol formation.) Against Willie in the lead, the Chinese began firing with small arms and automatic fire. Willie fired back, unsure whether he killed any Chinese, but he was accurate enough to cause the Chinese to flee. Company Commander Captain Longstraw didn't think they had met their objectives, so they moved on to the second hill, where they started digging foxholes. But they didn't have time to set up their identification panels. L Company on the next hill, believing Willie and his buddies were Chinese, inadvertently sent in a murderous mortar barrage. One soldier in Willie's unit, wounded earlier in the face by shrapnel and treated behind the lines, had been reassigned back to the unit for this assault. He was caught opening a C-ration can when the friendly fire came raining in. He immediately hit the ground, cutting himself on the can. He was later medically discharged and sent home. Once the mix-up was corrected and the mortar barrage discontinued, Hill 104 was secured, with Willie and his unit moving to a lower ridge. The following night, the Chinese launched a surprise attack, sneaking within yards of the American foxholes. In typical fashion, bugles blew, followed by flares lighting the night. The fighting was so fierce that the GIs practically aimed their weapons to the sky, killing

Chinese as they tried to hop in the holes. Willie recalled the fighting starting at 11 p.m. and lasting until morning, when the defeated Chinese withdrew.

> *I could hear a gurgling, but I didn't know what that was. As daylight broke, I noticed a Chinese soldier lying just outside my foxhole. He had the side of his face blown off and a hole in his throat. After seeing that, I just sunk back into my hole.*

Despite the severity of his injuries, the Chinese soldier was still alive. Willie had to listen to the gurgling caused by blood pooling in the soldier's throat before being blown out of the hole in his windpipe. The entire hillside was covered with Chinese bodies as far as L Company's forward positions. Willie also recalled a pile of ten dead Chinese soldiers next to a machine gun.

He explained that when a Chinese soldier was killed, his comrades would just toss his body to the side and keep on fighting. Following this battle, ten men, including Willie, were assigned to operate a listening post a half mile in front of the line.

> *That was one of the scariest nights I had in Korea. No one slept a wink all night, in fear if we did our throats would be cut. We were supposed to listen all night into the morning, and if we heard the Chinese coming, we were supposed to just run back to our line to warn the others. Luckily, they never came.*

Returning to friendly confines, Willie and his company were ordered to a river site where tents were set up for a few days of rest. The camp was alongside the Imjin River, so they had the luxury of hot showers with water pumped from the river and heated, providing the combat-weary GIs a rare treat. The troops often went weeks, sometimes months, without fresh clothes, often having only two pairs of socks. And one of the most important things in combat was keeping your feet dry. Whenever he could, Willie changed his socks and found a way to wash the dirty ones. After a few days, Willie and his company were sent back to the front.

> *I only had two hot showers from February 1951 until October 16, 1951, when I got wounded. Any other time we needed to clean up, we'd find a stream and do the best we could.*

About four months into Willie's tour, his BAR rifleman, Darrell Clipps, went home and was replaced by Clayton Arrowood from Los Angeles. Willie and Clayton got along great. Unfortunately, Sgt. Beale didn't have the same opinion, and often told Clayton that he was "good for nothin'," and one day he would take him over the hill to teach him a lesson. Not long after Clayton's arrival, Willie saw Sgt. Beale with two black eyes, a large scab on his nose, and two fat lips. Enjoying the sight, Willie also saw Clayton—wearing a big grin.

> *After our squad leader was out of hearing range, Clayton came over and told me, he did in fact take him over the hill to teach him a lesson, but Clayton said he beat the hell out of him instead.*

On the front line for a few weeks, the company was brought down for a week of R&R (rest and recuperation). They were assigned to an area, pitched tents, and were finally able to relax and get much-needed and welcomed sleep. Clayton asked Willie, "We aren't going to sleep on the ground again, are we?" Spotting a Korean house, Clayton went in, searching for something comfortable for them to sleep on. He returned with an armful of straw that, unknown to him, was saturated with lice. Clayton too became covered in lice from head to toe. Willie poured DDT powder all over him, and in a few moments the lice fell to the ground. Willie then poured the powder over the straw, killing the remaining pests in minutes.

Clayton looked at me with a big smile and told me, now we'll get a good soft sleep. He was the best partner I had while in Korea.

On October 2, 1951, Willie's company, along with the entire 5th Cavalry Regiment, began a push toward enemy lines in preparation for Operation Polecharge. The 5th Regiment got to about a hundred yards from the Chinese line. On October 3, the fighting kicked off. Willie recalled it lasting all day and all night, with artillery and mortars from both sides blasting each other continuously. A Chinese bunker had Willie's company pinned down with a murderous outpouring of heavy machine gun fire. Willie was chosen to blow up the bunker.

The lieutenant told me to drop my ammunition and rifle and take the ten-pound bag of TNT. I rejected that order, as I wasn't about to go up without my rifle and two bandoliers. Morning came and up we went.

At dawn, orders were given for a squad, reinforced with a tank, to head up the hill. As the squad pushed forward, Willie heard a loud swish, followed by an explosion. The swish was a bazooka round from a Chinese antitank team. The enemy raised up a second time, but the new recruits failed to return fire, allowing the Chinese to knock out the American tank. Without protection from the tank, the squad took off. Soon, another group of GIs came running past Willie, leaving him all alone. Then Willie also took off. The next day, when he was in his foxhole, the Chinese fired a single artillery round.

Suddenly, I heard a whoosh go right over my head, and I told myself, boy that was close. I stuck my head out of my foxhole and peeked around. The hill in front of me was higher, so I didn't think they would hit me. I relaxed down into the foxhole and heard the gun go off again and BOOM. The second round hit only ten feet or so away from me. Next thing I know, everything is dark, and I'm covered in dirt thinking I'm going to suffocate.

Shrapnel had struck Willie in his neck. He was taken to an aid station where he spent a few days before being sent back to the front. On the evening of October 15, he and the members of the 5th Regiment were sent back to take the hill, which they attacked the next day. While trying to knock out one enemy machine gun, a second one on their right flank opened fire. Willie took three slugs in his leg. Seven other squad members were also wounded.

> *I put a bandage on my wound and rolled over to a rock. There was a little hole underneath that someone else had dug, so I laid in there and I was safe. Neither the machine gun fire nor mortars coming in could hit me.*

Willie described being shot as feeling like "getting slammed with a sledgehammer." For about an hour and a half he stayed in that foxhole. Timing the mortar barrages, he noticed there was a short period when there were no nearby explosions. Debating whether he should make a run for it, Willie opted to go on the next three-minute break in the fighting. He got up, hobbled down the hill, and scrambled through a rice paddy with bullets flying past. Climbing a bank, he saw tree branches breaking in front of him as bullets were striking all around. After getting over the small bank and another hill, finally safe from direct fire, he still had a long way to go to reach friendly lines.

> *I got over the hill and walked for about a mile, but it wasn't easy as I was going downhill. I met up with South Koreans and they carried me down the hill to a M.A.S.H unit.*

The aid station medics determined that Willie should be transported by ambulance, which turned out to be a Jeep equipped with stretchers. While they were traveling down the road, Chinese artillery shells fell on both sides of the vehicle, but not near enough to do damage. Though out of harm's way, the Jeep driver got scared and started speeding. With the driver attempting to cross a river, the engine flooded. For a few fearful moments they were sitting ducks, until a GI in a three-quarter-ton truck came along and pushed the Jeep to dry land. At the aid station, it was determined his wounds were not that serious, so no morphine was prescribed.

> *They gave me a shot of penicillin on the inside of my leg and a canteen of water. I lay there all day and was not given anything to eat.*

That evening, Willie, and the other wounded were on a train to Pusan, from where they would board *The Constellation*—a Navy hospital ship. During the train trip, the wounded troops slept on wooden bunk beds. Willie described the bathroom as completely unsanitary and unsafe. If a GI or wounded soldier had to go to the bathroom, there was a two-by-four nailed across the corner of the rail car with a five-gallon pail under it, and a single roll of toilet paper. No medical personnel were on hand, so the soldiers attended to each other. They rode the train all night, finally reaching Pusan the next morning and being boated out to *The Constellation*. Starving, with many—including Willie—suffering excruciating pain, they missed breakfast, which forced them to wait on the ship until noon before finally being offered some food. After the welcome meal, while Willie was waiting for his wound to be cleansed, a medic gave Willie a shot of morphine—thirty-four hours after being shot. Eventually, a nurse arrived with a pan of water for Willie to clean up the best he could. He lay on his cot for two days before his wound was cleansed and treated.

9. William "Willie" Cybula, U.S. Army: The Polish Kid

I was awake but numb from the waist down. They started cleaning my wound out and I could see everything. The doctor had a round brush with no handles. He pushed it through the bullet hole and moved it back and forth while the nurse poured alcohol on it. I had a backache from lying there for three days, letting my wound drain, but they didn't want to give me another spinal. The doctor told me that I was a real tough guy, so he put nine stitches in my open wound without freezing it first.

Willie said that when the doctor inserted the needle and pulled the thread through to begin the suturing, it was one of the most painful things he'd ever felt besides getting shot. When the doctor finished, he poured alcohol on top of the fresh stitches, followed by another shot of morphine. After forty-five days in the hospital in recovery, Willie received the disturbing and disappointing news that he was being sent back to the frontlines.

That had a terrible effect on me, being put in harm's way over and over. But when I got back, the division was gearing up to move back to Japan, so I didn't have to see any more combat.

William "Willie" Cybula proudly displaying the Purple Heart he received from wounds sustained while fighting in Korea on "Old Baldy."

Snow covered the ground when Willie rejoined his outfit, and all he had were regulation combat boots, as opposed to the winter boots everyone else wore. He went to the supply sergeant to ask for a pair.

I told the sergeant I wear a size 9 and he told me they don't have that, so he gave me a size 11 for one foot and a size 13 for the other. I took them regardless, because I didn't want my feet to freeze.

Willie was soon shipped back to Japan, and in February 1952 boarded a Navy transport packed with five thousand other returnees that took eighteen days to reach the states. It was far from a holiday cruise ship voyage, with some passengers dying from seasickness, and the ship's galley running low on food. After reaching Fort Lawton, Washington, Willie was sent to Fort McCoy before being sent to Fort Ord, California, where his time was spent cleaning artillery weapons. He was then reassigned to an MP (Military Police) unit at Camp Stoneman, California, where his job was directing traffic.

I got into traffic control, and I loved directing traffic. After about a month, they put me on town patrol about forty miles from camp, two other men and myself. I stayed there until my discharge.

Separated from the Army in 1953, he returned to Wausau, Wisconsin, to work at Marment Corporation, until he retired in 1992. It was not a happy work climate. More times than not, at breaks and lunches, the employees would play cards where they had a table with cigarette ashtrays on each side. One day, unbeknownst to Willie, someone put a firecracker in one. When it went off, he jumped up and fell on top of the table. Willie said no one knew he was a Korean War veteran and that he suffered from shellshock—known today as PTSD (posttraumatic stress disorder).

Once they learned that I had shellshock, I was harassed quite a bit. When I would work the punch press, they would take a pipe and hit the big metal shroud behind it. If I was welding with my helmet down, they'd take a flat piece of aluminum and slap my worktable. They'd watch me jump and they would all laugh.

Another incident Willie related was about two final product inspectors—a foreman and co-worker who had okayed and shipped frames that were not up to quality. Willie caught the mistake and had to argue with them to correct it. Not long after this incident, Willie suffered a nervous breakdown and was hospitalized. When he asked the Veterans Administration doctor if there was anything they could do about it, the arrogant medic snapped, "NO!" Willy was told to stop complaining or risk being placed in an asylum for the rest of his life. This led to heavy drinking in his desperate search for relief, with massive hangovers, making the thoughts, memories, and nightmares even harder to bear.

I had many nightmares that always involved Sgt. Beale. There was never a nightmare that he wasn't involved in one way or another. Even when I was at home, he was still trying to get me killed in my dreams. To this day I have to sleep alone from my wife and with a nightlight on because of what I experienced in Korea.

In one dream, Willie said three Chinese were advancing toward him. As he fired at them, he realized Sgt. Beale had given him a rifle with a bent barrel. In another dream he recalled, Sgt. Beale had kidnapped Willie's family and was hollering at him like he always did in Korea. That, he confessed, was one of his worst dreams. Willie stated that all his dreams of Sgt. Beale characterized Beale's absolute hatred for anyone of Polish descent. Listening to this veteran during this part of the interview gave me greater insight into the struggles facing combat veterans every day of their civilian lives. Even worse is that Willie is from an era when they were told to just deal with it.

William "Willie" Cybula posing for a photograph while recovering in Japan from wounds received while fighting on "Old Baldy."

Fighting the Chinese was one thing, but having to deal with Sgt. Beale's constant discrimination was a war of its own. His hatred for Polacks was intolerable. I can remember when Private Wisnaski, from Pennsylvania, was killed, Sgt. Beale minimized it with "Oh, he was only a Polack." That was the attitude he had towards people of Polish nationality.

Willie acknowledged that when he arrived in Korea and was assigned to Sgt. Beale's squad, he was harassed and yelled at daily ... and that he was damned sure Beale was disappointed when Willie came out alive from the battle for Hill 104. Another incident that sticks out was Willie giving an old Korean he'd met some extra C-rations. When Beale found out, he raged at Willie and the squad for over fifteen minutes, insisting that if they didn't eat their food they should dispose of it. Another ordeal involved a twelve-year-old local boy who was hungry. Beale told the boy if he performed oral sex on him, he could have the can of C-rations. Regrettably, the boy gave in, Willie said with disgust and a very sad look on his wrinkled face.

> *That's the kind of person he was. He kept telling me he was going to make a man out of me, and I would tell myself, a person with that much prejudice wouldn't make a man out of nobody.*

Willie was one of my early interviews, providing an entirely different perspective. Being of Polish descent myself, I empathized, and I like to make sure he's doing well by continuing to stay in touch. I introduced Willie to Rami Hyun, a photographer who travels from his home in South Korea to the United States to document Korean War veterans. Willie was surprised and thrilled by Rami's appreciation of Korean War veterans. Rami photographed Willie in his VFW gear, providing him with an M1 Garand to hold as a prop. Rami then took pictures of both Willie and his wife. When Rami interviewed Willie, I set up my phone to record previously untold stories. After the photo shoot and interview, Willie sat in his driveway talking with us until nightfall. I was impressed to see this ninety-year-old veteran hop on his New Holland tractor and maneuver it into its storage spot. Willie said he asked his wife if he could get a toy, since he never had any growing up. "I'm not sure she expected a twenty-thousand-dollar tractor," he laughingly said. It was good to hear Willie laugh.

Willie is part of a dying breed, and I'm proud to say I've had the privilege of interviewing him, getting to know him, and enjoying every moment we get together.

Chapter 10

Vincent Salceto, U.S. Army
The "F" Word

Sergeant Major, U.S. Army, George Company, 7th Infantry Regiment, 3rd Infantry Division (Ret.). Interviewed July 28, 2022, Franklinville, New Jersey. Born 1932.

Once you hear shrapnel going past you, you never forget it. I told the squad we had to fall back and get out of this shit. So, I had a medic—Big John, he was a conscientious objector who did not want to carry a weapon. I tried giving him a weapon a couple times and he wouldn't take it. Anyway, he was our medic and was carrying the stretcher. Anyways, we get out of the shit and I'm counting the men, and we were missing four men, so I say what the fuck, man, and I head back out there.

I first heard about Vincent Salceto when a friend of his family noticed my Facebook page and reached out, saying I had to contact Vincent. In his words, "It'd be one helluva interview." I was told that Vincent, age ninety, was still very active on Facebook, so was encouraged to message him. In the meantime, his friend shared a news channel clip of Vincent's trip to San Francisco to visit the final resting place of his best friend David Ferrari, sixty-six years after they bonded in Korea. I was especially eager to hear from Vince, as the news footage I'd seen was extremely moving.

When Vince responded, he was agreeable to meeting, but added he didn't feel he'd still be around after dealing with the recent death of his son. We met the end of July 2022, and that's when I experienced an interview like never before.

Vince warmly welcomed Collin and me, introducing us to his wife, and taking us on a tour of his home, even sharing family pictures. We settled in the living room where he immediately began talking about his military career, starting off so fast and in such depth that I didn't have time to set up my camera, with the first part of the interview one I would never forget. Initially, Vince hesitated about being recorded, making it clear that he's not a politically correct advocate. I told him that nothing gets posted without consent.

You're going to have to do a lot of fucking editing in this interview. I guarantee you'll never have an interview like this again.

Born and raised in south Philadelphia, from the moment he was born Vince was a fighter. He said to me that his mother told him in later years the doctor told her moments after he was born, "this boy is going to be a fighter." The doctor wasn't far off. Italian and thus being in the minority in South Philly, Vince was in many fights.

> *I can remember fighting every day going to and from school. I know what being a minority is all about, and prejudice goes both ways. I remember one time a neighbor broke up a fight I was in and told me, if you wanna fight, join the Army. I never forgot those words, I never looked for a fight, but I never backed down.*

When Vince went to enlist in the Army and saw the number of inoculations recruits were receiving, he opted to join the Reserves, thinking he could avoid the shots. Of course, that didn't happen. His Reserve unit met in Philadelphia every Wednesday night for a two-hour training session. Before the drills he'd get into his uniform and hang out on a corner with his friends, describing them as kind of a gang. On his way to meet his buddies, almost every week Vince encountered a woman who'd ask, "Why is it that you're here and my son could be dead right now in Korea?"

> *So finally I got sick of this old woman asking me this, and told myself I don't need to listen to this kinda fucking shit. And I went in and asked to go on active duty.*

Transferred to the 79th Division, he was promoted to the rank of corporal. His first assignment was with a bomb squad and he was told, "In this outfit, you make one mistake, and that's it." While being shown a training film of a man disarming a bomb, the footage suddenly went white. It was then played in reverse, so the team could see the man disintegrating as the bomb exploded.

> *They cut the movie and the sarge told us this is why you only make one mistake on this job, and here I thought, what the fuck did I get myself into?*

After months of random assignments, he returned home, continuing to attend meetings, and still bumping into that same woman asking the same disturbing question. Vince recalled this making his blood boil. It's not that he didn't want to go to Korea, it was just not where he was assigned. Being in the Reserves, Vince didn't make enough money and bounced from job to job. His last job before going on active duty was working on the railroad laying spikes for new tracks. He laughed about it for a moment as he told us that he was the only white man on the entire crew, and that one older Black gentleman took him under his wing and treated him like one their own.

> *I was spiking and kept hitting the track and one of the Black fellas told me, laughing, "We can't have that shit going on." So they put me off to the side to practice, and I got pretty good at it. But those same encounters with that old woman finally drove me fucking nuts. I reported to the next meeting and told my superior I wanted to go on active duty, and he asked me, "Where?" And I told him Korea. He looked at me and asked, "ARE YOU FUCKING NUTS? You know there's a war going on right now, right?" And I said yes, and that was it, next stop was Korea.*

Transferred to the Regular Army, he was issued corporal stripes, with the sergeant's warning, "If you can't do your fucking job, we're going to take your stripes." Coming from the Reserves, Vince had one advantage compared to the draftees—he knew the drills. His mission was to help train the men.

Once I put my stripes on, they utilized me to move the privates around from place to place. I taught these guys how to make beds, how to march, manual arms. Everything I learned in the Reserves put me ahead of the curve.

After two weeks at Fort Lewis, he boarded a ship—along with 3,500 other GIs—and sailed to Korea. Assigned as head of the mess hall, he suffered from seasickness and went AWOL for three days, never leaving his bunk. He laughed as he recalled the incident.

I was sicker than a fucking dog, puking and getting it everywhere. I laid in the sack for like three days. This one day, an officer came through to check everything and looked up and seen me and said, "Hey soldier, what's your name?" I told him I'm sick and gave him my name. He told me I've been AWOL for three days. He asked if I had a job, and I said yeah, and he told me, "Get off your fucking ass and get to work."

Finally, shaking the malady, he was back running the chow line, which was an absolute mess from no one yet having their sea legs: puke and broken dishes all over the deck. After a few more days, people figuring out the ship's rolls began feeling better and were ready to put some food in their bellies. One night, a group of GIs asked Vince if he'd leave out a tray of sandwiches or pork chops for them to chow on. He told them he'd talk to the corporal running the kitchen. Looking at the corporal's name tag, he saw that it said Mize. (The next encounter Vince would have would be with Congressional Medal of Honor recipient Ola Mize, who earned that special honor later—in the summer of 1953, in combat in Korea.) Vince asked Mize if it was possible to leave some food out for snacks, and he would clean it up so it wouldn't be an issue. "I can't fucking do that, what the fuck do you think this is?" Mize snapped. "What the fuck is a matter with you? I got a fucking job to do, and so do you. We can't do that shit."

So, I looked at him and said, "Hey, what's your fucking problem?" He asked me, "Don't you know? I'm a super-duper paratrooper." The next thing I know we were throwing punches and beating the shit out of each other.

This altercation resulted in Vince and Ola facing the ship's captain, who ordered that this petty argument be put aside, making it clear that there are over three thousand troops on the ship who had to be fed, and it all had to be run like clockwork with no interruptions. The order was given to drop the bullshit, shake hands, and carry on with their jobs.

I shook his hand and told him "Ya know, I still think you're a fucking dickhead!" He got puffed up again and I told him, "Come on man, relax. I'm just busting your balls." But after that we got along great, but he was really on point. I mean that

Vincent Salceto (center) with two fellow GIs on a cold day in Korea.

guy was right on the money and never fucked around. I saw him a few times while in Korea below the MLR at the showers and I'd always bust his balls, and he'd get hot-headed but we both laughed it off.

In Korea, Ola Mize wound up with the 15th Regiment. Vince was assigned to the 7th Regiment of the 3rd Infantry Division. They'd meet a few times, with Vince describing the corporal as "cocky, but a good fucking guy."

When Vince joined his unit in Korea as a replacement, he discovered—to his surprise—that his squad leader was a seventeen-year-old kid.

I was talking to him about what's going on and I asked, "How old are you kid?" He said he was seventeen years old. I asked him, "What the fuck are you doing here, man?" And he said he volunteered, and I told him I did the same, but I couldn't believe the squad leader was a young kid.

The "kid" then told Vince, "It looks like you're going to take the squad over." Vince told him that he isn't taking over shit—that he's just a replacement, making it clear to the youthful squad leader he's going to pick his brain and learn every "fucking thing" he can about what's going on around here.

Vince was assigned a BAR (Browning automatic rifle) and soon befriended a Black soldier named Charlie White, also from Philly, who told him everything he knew, and what they'd been through as a unit, while also introducing him to all the veterans in the squad.

The first night online, I didn't know shit from Adam, you know. All I knew was the enemy was to the north, and we were to the south. Surrounded by mountains, I was assigned to a position in a gully. I noticed the barbed wire flattened and asked the reason for that. I was quickly told, that's where the Chinese came through the night before and that's why I'm posted up here with the BAR to stop them, because there isn't time to put new wire up.

As a replacement, Vince learned he wouldn't be meeting too many veterans, who had accrued the most points by being in combat and would soon be going home. As short-timers, they stayed behind the line. The startling revelation was that the FNGs (fucking new guys) did all the patrols and manned the outposts.

Vince was on his way up to the frontline where he would swap his BAR rifle for the M1. While on the way, a GI leaving to go home traded rifles with him.

Vincent Salceto having a smoke while wearing his parka on a cold day in Korea, below the MLR.

This fucking guy grabs my rifle and gives me his and keeps going. I shake the rifle and there's parts rattling in it, and I don't even know if this fucking thing is going to fire. I chase him down and tell him give me back my fucking rifle before I bust you over the head with it. He looked at me like I was nuts and said, "Are you crazy?" He wasn't gonna leave me with no piece of shit. Long story short, I had to give it up anyways because I end up getting the BAR again, which I later swapped out for an M1 that I carried for the rest of my time there.

The next surprise was that there was little to no ammunition to go around for the proper firepower needed to repel the enemy. Vince, asking for ammo, was given an eight-round clip designed for the rifle he'd just given up. He then asked, "What happens if they attack us?" He was told they had to hold the best they could. Vince told Charlie White "Fuck this," and that he would write a letter to the commanding general complaining that he's on the front lines in Korea and had to borrow eight rounds of ammunition.

A few days go by. I don't know if it's coincidence, but a few deuce-and-half trucks came up, loaded with ammo and hand grenades. Charlie looked at me and said, "What the fuck did you do, man, you're gonna get in trouble." I told him, fuck 'em ... take me off the hill then.

Another rather funny story was when Vince told us during the interview that his mother had mailed him regarding back taxes he owed and the seriousness of it. She explained to her son that not paying this will add up to even more that he owes once he gets home from Korea, even jail time. It was also during this part of his interview Vincent explained that all men serving in Korea did not have to pay postage: They would simply write "free" on it and their letters home would get mailed out on Uncle Sam's dime. With this knowledge, Vincent mailed the IRS a letter. "I thought what a fucking joke, you're going to lock me up over taxes? So, I mailed them and told them I am fighting in Korea and if they wanna do that then they can come and get me. Never did hear from them again."

Vince's area of operations was on the central eastern front near the Chorwon Valley and the Kumwha Valley, also known as the Iron Triangle. One day, with a tank assigned to the unit, they were hit by sniper fire. The tanker would sit below the hill during the day and fire when requested for night fire missions. During the day, the sniper was taking pot shots, so Vince told the tanker he spotted where the shots were coming from and gave him the coordinates, without realizing he was in the blast radius of the tank's cannon. When it went off, Vince hit the ground. The tanker jumped down to shake Vince to see if he was okay, but all Vince could see were lips moving and no sounds. The tanker told him he had to be checked out.

I said no, I'll be okay. Just let me rest. And I did and I was okay. My nose stopped bleeding, and I washed the burn marks off my face. The tanker told me if you go to the aid station, you'll get a Purple Heart. I told him I don't want no fucking Purple Heart, that's not why I'm here. I'm not here for medals, I'm here to do the right thing. I knew a lot of guys who got a scratch and got the Purple Heart, that just isn't me.

One tragic night, a forward outpost—receiving small-arms fire—lost communications. The outpost was about half mile forward of the troops and downhill, with a guide rope leading to it so no one would get lost. A few GIs were sent to reestablish communications and were never heard from again, so more men were sent, with the same disastrous result. Vince and the others were getting worried, but no one was willing to venture out, Vince, in his typical fashion, said, "Fuck it, I'm goin'." He hopped out of the trench and raced down the hill with his M1. Unfortunately, he discovered that the missing GIs had been hit by the Chinese, taken prisoner, and dragged off. Halfway down the hill, Vince almost suffered the same fate. Three Chinese jumped him.

We started tumbling down the hill and they're beating on me the entire time and one of them smashed me in my mouth and I knew my teeth were knocked loose and I was bleeding. I instantly grabbed my dagger (he'd picked up a dagger-like knife after a few days in Korea) and started sticking them, and I killed two of them with that knife. The third guy was trying to grab and take my rifle from me, but I held onto the sling and then I stuck him a few times. I sat there thinking, "Jesus fucking Christ, they knocked my teeth out," and then I started back up the hill.

This proved to Vince just how cunning the enemy was—luring GIs down and taking them by surprise. One of the Chinese he killed carried a pearl-handled German-style P-38 pistol that he appropriated and attached to his ammunition belt. One evening at the showers down below the MLR, Vince hung his up belt while using the facilities

Vincent Salceto geared up and ready for his patrol into no-man's-land. Vincent's area of operations was near what was known as "The Iron Triangle," Korea, 1953.

and out of the corner of his eye saw a hand reaching in and taking the pistol. Vince chased down the thief, who he discovered was also stealing military scrip currency from soldiers' wallets. Vince threw him against the wall of the shower house.

I told him, "Give me back my pistol and whatever else you took, or I'm going to beat the living fuck out of you." I then demanded he tell me what he's doing. He told me he's been stealing items to sell on the black market in the nearby village, while also taking all the military scrip to use in Japan when he would go on R&R. I told him from now on he's giving me 50 percent of his profits or I'm gonna beat the shit out of him and turn him in. And he did, and I ended up accumulating almost twenty thousand dollars in military scrip.

What Vince next shared was absolutely an incredible and laughable perspective of wartime con men getting rich. Vince said he never took part in anything other than getting his half for not turning in soldiers who were committing the crimes. When taking his squad to Japan for R&R, they lived it up in a whorehouse, spending the military scrip that was honored by the U.S. government. He'd tell the madam to put all the drinks—and other expenses—on his tab. It was here that Vince met a beautiful Japanese prostitute he'd see regularly on R&R and correspond with when he was back in Korea. Before he was rotated back to the states, he wrote her that there'd be no more R&R because he was going home and included in the envelope what was left of the stash, which amounted to almost twelve thousand dollars.

> *There was no fucking way you could ever take that much scrip in to exchange for real money because they would instantly know something was up and you'd get busted and locked up for theft. So, I mailed her the rest, and a few weeks later I got a letter from her saying she took the money and bought her own bar, and she wanted me to come live with her in Japan. I told her there's just no way I can do that, because I'm going home soon. Looking back, I wish I would have, and I often wonder if her bar is still there.*

Vince mentioned a friend, David Ferrari, who he said was like a brother, and that he trusted David with things he didn't tell others. Ferrari's name comes up again in this next harrowing story.

(From left) PFC Fetters, PFC Miller, Cpl. Redmond, and PFC Charlie White. These men were part of Vincent Salceto's "Misfit" platoon.

There was a greenhorn lieutenant assigned to lead a nighttime reconnaissance patrol. Vince stepped up and told him that rank doesn't matter when they're out there, and that he's strictly an observer and should do as he's told by the veterans who'd "been there, done that." The lieutenant was placed in the rear with the BAR man, whom everyone called Candy Bar because of the sweet treats he was forever eating. Reaching their first checkpoint, the squad took a ten-minute break. That's when Vince heard a disturbing sound. It was the lieutenant knocking his boots together and stomping on the ground, trying to warm his feet.

Vincent Salceto's "Misfit" platoon. Vince always made it clear he ended up with the GIs no one else wanted to deal with and bonded with them well (photograph by Vincent Salceto).

I told myself, what the fuck is that sound? So, I started checking the squad. Here is that lieutenant knocking his fucking feet together! And asked him, what the fuck are you doing?' And he told me it's cold and he's trying to warm his feet up. I told him, No shit it's cold, everyone is fucking cold. Now stop knocking your goddamn boots together, because that sound carries out here and they're gonna fucking hear us.

This was only the first disturbing incident in what would later become a living nightmare for the squad. At the second checkpoint, there was the same sound. Vince hustled back to the lieutenant.

I told him, look, you motherfucker, either you stop knocking your fucking feet together or we're gonna leave you out here. You understand me? You're going to get the whole fucking squad wiped out.

Continuing the march into the darkness, Candy Bar tripped and fell, striking the butt of his BAR on a rock, causing the bolt to slam shut and the firing pin to send off a shot.

I fucking cringed, I couldn't believe it, and all I could think was, you stupid mother fucker! And that's when all hell broke loose, and they hit us with a barrage of mortar fire.

Incoming was dropping and exploding everywhere, as Vince gathered his men, moving them out of the fire zone. Doing a head count, he was short of four soldiers.

With rounds still falling all around and shrapnel whizzing past his head, he saw his medic on the ground hugging the stretcher. Vince picked him up and rushed him back to where everyone else was huddled, and then went back to collect the other missing men. He found squad member Miller with his arms wrapped around a tree, grabbed him, and then saw Paul Tillis wandering aimlessly and looking scared.

> I don't know, and I still say today, I don't know if it was friendly fire or the enemy. 'Cause when it's coming in, you don't know where the shit is coming from, could be somebody fucked up, I don't know. If you could just visualize it. A full moon and calm night and rounds going off with shrapnel going everywhere. Once you hear shrapnel going past you, you never forget it. I told the squad we had to fall back and get out of this shit. So, I had a medic, Big John, he was a conscientious objector who did not want to carry a weapon. I tried giving him a weapon a couple times and he wouldn't take it. Anyway, he was our medic and was carrying the stretcher. Anyways, we get out of the shit, and I'm counting the men and we're missing a guy, so I say what the fuck man, and I head back out there. As I'm about to go back, Miller told me, "What are you nuts?" And I told him, look, either we all fucking go, or we all are fucking staying. I ain't leaving no one behind and that's fucking it!

Spotting a body on the ground, Vince rushed over and hollered, "Come on, man." Then a piece of shrapnel hit him in the leg and spun him around. Vince grabbed the man to pull him over, only to find his hand deep inside the soldier's open chest. A round that didn't go off had struck him, taking off his face, half his chest, and an arm. The man was David Ferrari. An instant of absolute horror engulfed Vince, with "a mixture of sadness, tears, and anger," is how Vince described it, saying he doesn't know how long he sat there holding his dead friend. Finally someone grabbed his shoulder. It was Miller.

Vince Salceto proudly displaying his dog tags during his interview with Collin Wilson and Ryan Walkowski.

> When I was sitting there holding Dave, I fucking lost it, man, I just fucking lost it.

I told myself I just can't fucking believe. I was so pissed off, and then I feel someone grab me and here it's Miller and he goes, "Vince, you gotta get us the fuck outta here, man!" I gathered myself and said, well grab him, because we ain't leaving him. I wasn't leaving shit there, man!

Vince reassembled what was left of his squad, put Dave on the stretcher, and headed to friendly lines, still dodging incoming artillery, mortar, and small-arms fire. As they reached a hill, a single shot rang out, and someone yelled, "What's the password?" Vince explained to me that passwords were usually short phrases or single words which included the letter "R," because Chinese had difficulty with its pronunciation, turning it into an "L." Vince didn't remember which password he hollered, not even knowing if it was correct, but it worked, and they were rushed up a path to a 2nd Infantry Division sector of the front line. A lieutenant snapped at them, explaining they were damn fools because they just walked through a minefield and they're lucky they weren't all killed.

Here this fucking guy is bitching and hollering that we walked through a minefield, and I told him, well, you guys didn't do too good of a fucking job, now, did ya? We got the whole Chinese army coming behind us, so let us through.

Safely below the MLR, Vince inspected everyone for wounds and performed a weapons check. That's when he discovered the greenhorn lieutenant had a crimped magazine for his M2 carbine, which basically rendered the weapon useless. Infuriated, Vince said he grabbed the carbine and, using it as a club, struck the lieutenant two or three times. Some of the squad wisely pulled Vince away ... and that was the last time Vince encountered that lieutenant. There was more Vince shared with us—but surprisingly, considering what he'd already admitted, he asked us not to put it on paper.

Sixty-six years later, Vince finally learned where his friend David

David Ferrari, in a photo taken by Vince sometime in the spring of 1953 before that fateful night when Dave would be killed.

Vince Salceto and Ryan Walkowski posing for a photo after Vince's interview with Collin and Ryan.

was buried. He and his family flew to San Francisco to make good on a promise he'd made in Korea. Passengers on the plane, learning of his mission, wrote commemorative notes and short messages on cocktail napkins for Vince. In San Francisco, at the Catholic cemetery where David is buried, there was a memorial service, with Vince placing his own Bronze Star for Valor on his friend's gravestone. Vince described it as a weight off his shoulders, and some closure to what happened on that distant battlefield so many years ago.

> *The nightmares never stop, but it did add a peace of mind to finally see my friend one last time and give him my medal. I didn't deserve that, he did. I'm no hero. The guys that never came back are.*

Vince's interview was everything he'd said it would be … an absolute roller coaster of a ride with Vince unapologetically himself, not self-censoring, and as you may have noticed, often saying fuck in what seemed like every other word. Unexpectedly, there were some stories told that he requested not being shared. But there is one more typically Vince-like story to be told.

Vince made the Army his career, retiring as a sergeant major. But in the 1960s, while he was teaching a class of recruits, a Jeep pulled up with a general and his staff who'd come to monitor the lectures being held in the field. The officer quietly watched Vince as he went through his lesson. When the class was over, the general complimented Vince, mentioning that not a single person was sleeping during his class (it was standard procedure during military lectures for people to fall asleep) because of his demeanor and the way he engaged with them. The general, about to move on with his aides, left Vince with only one piece of constructive criticism: "Don't use the word 'fuck' so much." Vince returned to his students.

They all wanted to know what was said and I told them. Fuck that guy, he doesn't know shit. They're just out here doing their job. And remember that each of you have a job to do and if you don't fucking do it right, it's going to get someone fucking killed, and I can attest to that.

Vince Salceto went on to say he had thought of canceling the interview, because seldom, if ever, did he speak about what happened to him in Korea, However, he added that he's glad he didn't, and that there's a guy like me capturing these stories.

After Korea, Vince had a long career as a Philadelphia police officer before retiring to a beautiful piece of property in Franklinville, New Jersey. Through all the great stories of Korea, the fistfights, and those crazy R&Rs, I can put it to print that Vince is without a doubt one of the kindest people I've ever met, with a huge and generous heart. There is more that can be said about my friend, but that would be a book unto itself.

Lastly, I would like to honor Vince's best friend:

In memory of David Ferrari
San Francisco, California
U.S. Army George Company, 7th Infantry Regiment, 3rd Infantry Division
KIA May 25, 1953

Chapter 11

Joseph Barna, USMC
Navy Corpsmen Are Angels

Corporal, U.S. Marine Corps, Weapons Platoon, Baker Co, 1st Battalion, 1st Marine Regiment, 1st Marine Division. Interviewed January 29, 2022, Freeland, Pennsylvania. Born 1931.

I can still see his face and smell the garlic on his breath. As he lunged at me, I was able to turn in time and his bayonet sliced my arm wide open.

Joseph Barna was the sixth veteran I documented on my amazing journey. His friend Frank Balon had messaged me, encouraging a meeting with "a proud Marine who'd served in Korea." This fit well with two other interviews I'd already scheduled in Ohio and Pennsylvania, not far from Barna.

Frank had described his pal as Marine with "a story that needs to be told," and he couldn't have been more right. Early on in my travels, I formatted a process that allowed the veterans not only to feel comfortable, considering the intensity and personal nature of the subject, but also to tell their stories at their own pace and their own words. This process worked especially well with Joseph ("Joe") Barna, who was as candid and forthright as any. When I met this ninety-two-year-old Marine veteran and his buddy Frank, they kindly offered coffee and snacks while I set up my recording equipment.

I owe seventy years of life to a Navy corpsmen—Jackie Kilmer. Was a friend of mine and he saved me at the battle for Bunker Hill. A few weeks later, he went to help How Company on another hill, and he jumped on top of two Marines to save them from shrapnel. He was killed. They gave him the Medal of Honor.

Joe asked me, "How many people know what the word hero means?" He went on to explain that it's a word not many people understand, and that he learned its truer and deeper meaning when he joined the military.

A boy never goes into the military wanting to die or to become a hero. Heroes are not born, they're made, sometimes within seconds of going into combat. I served alongside many heroes.

He was twenty-one when inducted into the Army.

But I ended up a Marine when a Marine sergeant selected me and five other volunteers to meet his monthly quota. There was a war going on in a far-off country called Korea.

Joe confessed that he didn't know if he could kill another human being, but after setting foot in Korea he soon got his answer. He added that he'd never met an American GI or Marine who said that he wanted to die, but if they did, they would die with pride. The unfortunate part is, as he said,

You don't get to choose between life and death in a war.

In only three words, Joe described life for a Marine in Korea: "Live or die." Every Memorial Day he's part of an honor guard, placing American flags on veterans' graves.

I have counted more than a hundred names followed by the words Korean War. Well, I guess I just beat the odds and I'm still able to remember what I maybe should forget. But I won't forget until that volley of rifles and taps are played over my grave, and that's why I'm here to tell you these stories.

Joe had recently released a book detailing his experiences in Korea, along with other life experiences through his ninety-two years. What he was going to tell me here on this day would be even more detailed, revealing memories he'd never put to paper.

Arriving in Korea in June 1952, he was immediately sent to the front and assigned to Company B, Weapons Platoon, 1st Battalion, 1st Regiment, 1st Marine Division. Joe described Korea as almost bare, with little vegetation or trees, as the result of relentless bombing and shelling from both sides. He vividly remembered getting off the truck and hiking for what seemed like forever, until finally arriving at a trench line filled with Marines. The truck driver stopped and told him, "Trucks don't climb mountains."

I thought I was climbing to heaven, but I would soon find out I was going to hell. I saw a lot of tired Marines all throughout the trenches. My first real battle came here a few weeks later. The mountain outpost I was on was called Bunker Hill.

At the top of the steep incline he reached his unit, where he was issued a devastating weapon—a flame thrower. Fueled with a mixture of gasoline and nitrogen, with a range of 100–125 feet, and a burn time less than a minute, it weighed a hefty sixty-eight pounds.

In Korea I stood five-foot-nine and weighed about 157 pounds. I was a small guy and here this lieutenant assigns the flamethrower to me. I asked, Why me? I'm just a little guy, and all the bigger guys carry rifles. But an order is an order.

Bunker Hill was a strategic piece of real estate. The Chinese knew if they took it, they'd control the gateway to retake Seoul. The Jamestown Line, as it became known, was the 1st Marine Division sector of the MLR (main line of resistance) that stretched across Korea in a jagged line. The Chinese had deep respect for the fighting will of the

Interviewee Joseph Barna posing for a picture with his M1 rifle, somewhere below the MLR near Bunker Hill, Korea, 1952.

U.S. Marine Corps, testing them day and night with constant shelling, and broadcasting demoralizing propaganda over huge loudspeakers.

Frightened by his first combat experience, Joe almost ran, but quickly realized that there was no place to go.

You're on a mountaintop ... and you're a Marine.

He hunkered down in his bunker, waiting out the Chinese barrage. Once the shelling stopped, he heard for the first time the bugles, bells, pot clanks, and yells of the approaching Chinese. Hundreds of flares lit up the night sky. His lieutenant turned to him and said, "You're on Joe. You're on!" Other Marines helped him into his flame-throwing gear. Leaving the bunker, Joe heard the Chinese screaming as they came up the hill, "Marine you die. Marine you die."

I looked over the trench line and thought to myself, oh my God. There must have been a thousand of them and they were all bunched up, you know. So, I lit the match and made one swipe to the right and one swipe to the left when they got within range. I must have killed a hundred of them, but they turned around, they retreated.

Joe befriended a Navy corpsman, John "Jackie" Kilmer, with the pair becoming foxhole buddies, a unique bonding and friendship formed only between men in combat. The respect Marines have for their Navy medics was evident; all that was needed in the heat of battle was for someone to frantically call out "Doc" or "Corpsman," and these "Angels"—their affectionate Marine nickname—were quickly at people's sides. Often armed with just a medical pack and a K-bar knife (Marine fighting weapon for hand-to-hand combat), these gallant medics would demonstrate extraordinary bravery and courage, tending to their fallen comrades. These are stories I've heard over and over from every Marine I interviewed, not just Joe, but this story is unique because Jackie, his best friend, was the man who would later save his life during a furious four-day battle on Bunker Hill.

> *I knew Jackie like I know Frankie here; I can still visualize him like I'm staring at you now. We bonded and talked about home to each other and shared stories about our families with each other. We would often buddy up in the bunkers too, and cook our C-rations over a candle flame, meals not even suitable for a dog, but we made do.*

In the summer of 1952, the Chinese hit Bunker Hill with a force that outnumbered the Marines eight to one. The battle was so fierce and devastating that Joe's company suffered eighty percent casualties. Frank, sitting in on the interview, said, "Joe, tell Ryan how they would attack again on Bunker Hill." Joe went on to describe it as being a quiet, dark night. Then all hell broke loose. It appeared every Chinese soldier carried a bugle, or was banging on a pot or pan, screaming and hollering their typical threats as they approached the entrenched Marines.

> *All around me I seen my buddies getting shot and killed. Some were crying out "DOC, DOC," and "CORPSMAN," or screaming for their mothers. I saw Jackie in the battle running all over and giving first aid to dying Marines and dragging others to safety. All we could do was continue to fight; this battle went on for four days. They even flew in two thousand replacements to reinforce us on Bunker Hill.*

On the fourth day, carrier-based Marine and Navy Corsairs flew in to provide much-needed support, dropping smoke bombs, creating screens which enabled the Marines to leave that "Hill from Hell," as it became known. Once below the MLR, the surviving Marines bivouacked in tents, getting the rest they'd rightfully earned.

Joe, showing me a photo taken by Jackie, somberly declared, "I had seen this sight almost daily. These are our boys covered up." It showed Marines on the ground, covered with camouflage ponchos. The caption read, "John Kilmer, Navy Corpsman Aug 52." Joe explained that it was a horrible sight because not even one of those dead Marines, he believed, was over eighteen years of age.

> *I will never forget the cemetery where they buried these poor Marines. It was the size of a football field and covered with white crosses. I saw ten coffins waiting to be buried and to this day don't know why they didn't send them home. Maybe they were too blown apart.*

Joe's next harrowing story was when wounded, bayoneted while carrying his flamethrower. The way he told it, the Chinese were shelling the Marines nonstop, in a deafening barrage that seemed to have no ending.

A photograph taken by Jackie Kilmer of dead Marines on Bunker Hill Korea, 1952. The inscription reads, "John Kilmer, Navy Corpsman, Aug 52. I had seen this sight almost daily. These are our boys covered up" (courtesy Joseph Barna).

Weapons fire was all over the place and all you could see were Marines and Chinese falling and hitting the ground, soaking the dirt red with blood. Once my flamethrower was empty, I became a sitting duck, except for the .45 pistol I had at my side, and the double-barrel shotgun taped to my flamethrower. I would always have a team of three or four Marines with me. They were my bubble, my protectors, my angels. Because the flamethrower is also a psychological weapon, the enemy would always try to target the operator and those around him. In my first days of battle, I saw another Marine flamethrower operator get hit and explode into a ball of fire.

One artillery round landed just behind Joe, knocking him down, with his flamethrower pinning him to the ground. Trying to regain consciousness and make sense of what had just happened, he saw an enemy soldier running at him with a bayonet on the end of his rifle. Joe turned and caught the bayonet on his upper left arm, suffering an eight-inch gash.

I can still see his face and smell the garlic on his breath. As he lunged at me, I was able to turn in time and his bayonet sliced my arm wide open. I quickly turned over with my sawed-off shotgun and gave him both barrels. I think I made twins of him. I cut him right in half, and that's when things started slowing down, and I was getting very sleepy. I could see my blood dripping off my arm onto the soil when someone said, "JOE, JOE." Here was Jackie, and he picked me up and carried me to a bunker where he stitched me up with a needle and thread and I rejoined the fight.

Jackie was the angel sent to save Joe that fateful night in Korea; angels do exist—ask any Marine who has seen combat. They come in the form of Navy corpsmen who go above and beyond. After Jackie cleaned and bandaged the cut, Joe returned to the firefight. Joe credits two people with giving him seventy years of life—Jackie Kilmer and another Marine whom we'll read about later.

During another massive attack on How Company, a call was put out for additional corpsmen to join the fight; Marines were going down like flies. In the middle of this battle, dauntless Jackie was in a bunker when another murderous artillery barrage hit the line. He packed his gear, ready to move out and help with the wounded, but was told by a sergeant, "Don't go out there or you'll die." Jackie told the NCO, "If I don't go out there, Marines will die." While he was administering first aid to two fallen Marines, shells were falling closer and closer. Jackie leaped on top of the two wounded Marines, shielding them from the blast. The heroic corpsman died with more than fifteen pieces of shrapnel in his body.

When the battle was over, Joe rushed to find Jackie below the MLR. That's when he heard the devastatingly sad news about his best friend, who died six days short of his twenty-second birthday. Joe, choked up, nevertheless bravely continued telling me the story about his foxhole buddy.

They gave Jackie the Congressional Medal of Honor for giving his life to save those Marines. After I arrived home in 1953, I was able to call Jackie's mother in Flint, Michigan. I told her he was the bravest man I ever met and my best friend. I carry a picture of my hero Jackie in my pocket every day, close to my heart.

Joe went on to mention the brutal tactics the Chinese used in their attempts to demoralize the Marines. One such act was to mutilate captured Marines, as examples of the grim fate that awaited anyone who might be next. Joe described it this way:

When you're fighting for your life, you do strange things. They were cruel people, those Chinese and North Koreans. They would capture somebody, and they would chop them up, and then they would announce on a loudspeaker and say, "Hey Marines, come get your buddy. He's resting right now." It's war and that's it, you're not going anywhere and the guys on the other side are still going to be here whether it's raining, snowing, hotter than hell, or negative degrees out. Nothing stops the fighting, and you can't go anywhere.

To top it all off, the Chinese would shell the Marines all day long … walking the shells from no-man's-land until zeroing in on Marine positions.

The second man he credited with giving him seventy years of life is a Black American named Bob Brown. When Joe became a short-timer—an enlisted man who was about to rotate home—he was assigned to support a patrol with his flamethrower. With only three weeks left in Korea, Bob Brown volunteered to take his place. Joe never questioned what color the Marine next to him was, because among Marines in combat, there was little or no prejudice.

> *That whole patrol was wiped out and I've never seen Bob again. He saved my life. I will never forget Corporal Bob Brown. He died for me and gave me seventy years of life. Death has no color preference, and neither do wars.*

Over the last few years, Joe's writings about his time in Korea have won multiple veterans' group awards. Plus, last year, Joe was the keynote speaker in San Antonio, Texas, at a graduating class of Navy corpsmen, which Joe described as surreal.

> *I was meant to be there, and finally after seventy years, I knelt and touched Jackie's grave and told him, "I'm here buddy and it's because of you." I gave a speech in front of the entire graduating class of corpsmen and shook all their hands.*

Joe went on to tell me about a few more heroes he knew in Korea, three Canadian boys who enlisted in the U.S. Marine Corps and were sworn in alongside Joe that fateful day he was inducted. Their names were Binkley, Breen, and Beauchamp. When in battle, one would be stationed in front of Joe and the other two would be on either side of him. A few weeks had passed when they were suddenly hit with a devastating Chinese artillery barrage. A shell came in sounding like a freight train, landing close to Joe and his men, and that's when everything went black.

Joseph Barna finally visiting his friend Jackie Kilmer's gravesite in Texas in 2024, seventy-two years after Jackie was killed in action in Korea.

> *I was thrown into the air, but somehow was not hit by any of the shrapnel. It was as though I was protected by a bubble. But the Canadian boys were all killed. These three boys died so I could live. They were truly heroes. I eventually stopped asking the question "Why not me?"*

Joe jumped twenty-five years ahead in his story to describe a time in the late

11. *Joseph Barna, USMC: Navy Corpsmen Are Angels*

Joseph Barna and good friend Frank Balon holding Ryan's Korean War veterans' flag after one of Ryan's many visits.

seventies when he was fishing with a friend in Canada. After a long day in the boat and catching fish, they decided to take in the sights and walk around the beautiful lake. While walking they passed a cottage with a small American flag featuring a gold star in the window. This is the kind of flag American families display when a loved one was killed in combat. Joe, without hesitation, knocked on the door. An elderly woman opened the door. He asked her about the flag, and she told Joe that her son was in the U.S. Marines and was killed in Korea.

I had already looked at her mailbox and I saw the name Beauchamp. Her son was one of the boys who died protecting me in Korea. I told the woman I served with her son, and I was there when he was killed. We both cried, unashamed.

Every veteran I've interviewed has become a friend, some closer than others. Joe and I have a special relationship; every trip East, I make sure to visit this gallant Marine, with every reunion being another special time in my life.

Finally, please join in a moment of reverence, in honor of one U.S. Navy and four U.S. Marine Corps heroes:

John "Jackie" Kilmer, Navy Corpsman—Congressional Medal of Honor

Bob Brown—Corporal, USMC
Binkley—USMC
Breen—USMC
Beauchamp—USMC

CHAPTER 12

Cecil Love, U.S. Army
The Old Bootlegger

Corporal, U.S. Army, 5th Regimental Combat Team. Interviewed July 2, 2023, Roanoke, Virginia. Born 1928.

My dad was caught once, my brother got caught twice, and my wife told me, "You know you're going to get caught one of these days making that damned old liquor." I told her, maybe so. The next damned day they did catch me. I had thirteen hundred gallons of apple brandy ready to be cooked off.

It was a new episode of *Moonshiners* on the Discovery Channel where I saw an interview with a ninety-five-year-old bootlegging legend from Franklin Country, Virginia. He was wearing a Korean War veteran's cap displaying a Purple Heart medal, and his name was Cecil Love.

This was too good to be true, and I knew Cecil had to be in this book. Searching for Cecil, I flooded the Franklin County Facebook pages with my posting, detailing my journey documenting Korean War veterans. Two days later, Cecil's daughter messaged me that her father would be happy to meet me.

Cecil had just moved to the Veterans Home in Roanoke, Virginia, and since this was post–COVID, I checked with the facility to see if there were any special visitor's requirements. I was given a go-ahead, and planned for July 1, which lined up perfectly with my day job schedule. I left for Virginia June 30, driving through the night, arriving in Roanoke early morning. I got some sleep at a rest stop before heading to the Veterans Home.

At the reception desk I was told Cecil's daughter had arrived a few minutes before. At this point, I'd honed my interviewing skills and was a lot less shy than during earlier interviews, but was still a bit nervous. Each time I'm on the threshold of a meeting, I'm asking, "Am I really doing this?" But I was quickly put at ease with a warm and friendly welcome from Wanda. Cecil, attended by a nurse finishing a routine checkup, opened the conversation with, "Sit down, son. My name is Cecil Love. How are you doing?" His old-fashioned good ol' boy how-do-you-do greeting set the stage for one of my most relaxed and colorful interviews.

At first we made some small talk, as I explained my missions as I do to every veteran and family member: how the session will proceed, and how their story will be represented. I mentioned that I needed just a few minutes to set up my equipment. He told me to set up wherever I'd like and to pull up a chair.

Cecil was born February 11, 1928, near Briar Mountain in Franklin County, Virginia, to Emmett and Ellen Love. Painting a vivid picture of what it was like growing during the Great Depression, he described how hard those times truly were. Cutting wood and spreading fertilizer for a mere fifty cents for a full day's work was one example.

> There was no work to be had unless you went to West Virginia to work in the coal mines. So, my Pa made moonshine liquor to provide for the family. With that, he even bought our family's home. It was a cabin on seventy acres of land, and he paid the bank note off in a week after getting it, after he bootlegged some moonshine and made a thousand dollars.

In terms of schooling, Cecil said times were so tough that all the students had to bring firewood to heat the one-room schoolhouse. The teacher rode a horse to school, and all the kids, including Cecil, walked to and from school with some traveling miles. Franklin County, like the rest of the country, was hit hard by the Depression; no one could afford a motor vehicle, so most transportation was done by horse and buggy or on foot.

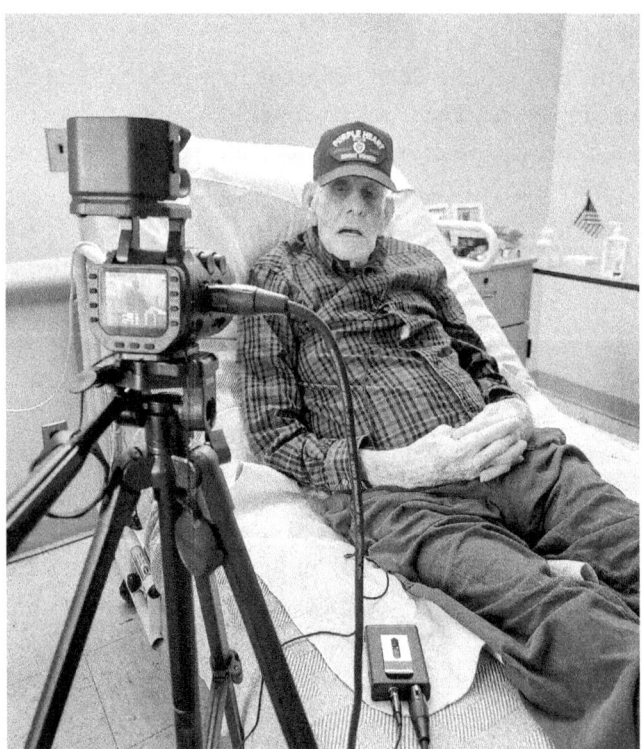

Famed moonshiner Cecil Love during his interview with co-author Ryan Walkowski at the veterans' home in Roanoke, Virginia.

> I quit going to school in 1936 when I was in sixth grade. The teacher taught us the basics—reading, math, trust in the Lord, and that if we used those things in everyday life, we'd be okay. We learned pretty good by her. But I stopped going and started doing odd jobs like hauling firewood and fertilizer, because there was money in it, and you could help provide for the family.

The illegal moonshine business? Not to get rich. Just a way of life and a way to survive those difficult times. The liquor his father and his brothers produced was out of pure necessity—if they didn't brew and sell moonshine, their families would have no food, not even the barest of necessities. Making the liquor was the easy part; the key challenge was being constantly on the alert for and eluding revenuers and ABC (Alcoholic Beverage Control) agents on the prowl to bust these illegal operations.

> *They would come up to the house and talk to my Pa, trying to convince him to sell them a jar, but we knew if he did that he'd go to jail, and they would raid the whole property until they found where we hid the liquor.*

The people for whom Cecil hauled firewood and fertilizer were running one of the biggest stills and whiskey operations in Franklin County, and that was thirteen-year-old Cecil's official introduction to the moonshine business. Sneaking over to watch the operation, he was spotted by one of the moonshiners, who asked, "Who toted all that wood up here for the still furnace?" Pointing to Cecil, one of the grateful bootleggers handed him some money.

> *He gave me a twenty-dollar bill. I thought I was the richest man in the country. My Pa said, "You better stay away from that racket." But I was hooked. You couldn't keep me away from making liquor if you tried.*

Over his lifetime, Cecil worked in sixty-two Franklin County distilleries—all illegal, of course. He graduated to earning almost fifty dollars an hour cooking and running moonshine, proud to be helping and providing for his family. Besides, he loved the action.

> *Sometimes "the man" would come up through the woods and you just run, jump over fences, and get away from them. I was never caught till that time in 2012 when I was eighty-three years old. I'll tell you about that in a little bit.*

Cecil described his mother as a strong and good Christian woman, who preached to him about not getting involved in that awful business, with it "being a first-class ticket to hell." Cecil however, had seen what it could provide, and nothing would change his mind. He told me, and I verified this later, that ninety-nine out of every hundred Franklin County citizens were in one way or another involved in the business of illegal moonshine liquor.

Laughing, Cecil said that more sugar, wheat, apples, rye, barley, corn, and cornmeal were sold in Franklin County than all of New York City. Cecil was an absolute wealth of knowledge, a dying breed of Depression survivors who did what they had to do. Each story he told was better than the last.

Cecil's oldest brother was killed in action in World War II and is buried in an American cemetery in Europe. When the Korean War started, Cecil put moonshining on hold for the first time when he was called up to serve.

> *I had a brother who had gone through school ahead of me by three years, and a first cousin and a neighbor. All of them got killed in World War II. Then I come along, and I'm going to Korea.*

Attributing some memory issues to his being ninety-five, Cecil couldn't recall anything worth remembering about basic training, except when his platoon was on a march and came to a hillside with high grass, where the recruits were ordered to cut the grass with their bayonets. Cecil told me, laughing, that they did just that—almost the entire hillside.

> *They would do whatever they could to break you down and aggravate you just to see what you could take. I never did understand why they made us do that, because it didn't teach us anything.*

Cecil entered Korea through the port of Incheon in 1952 and was assigned to the 5th Regimental Combat Team that was trucked up to the MLR northeast of Seoul. He described it as a status quo situation, where neither side did much to disrupt the other. Occasionally there'd be a mortar or artillery barrage from the Chinese, but it was mostly indirect and ineffective. From time to time there were pot shots from Chinese sharpshooters and snipers, but for the most part it was quiet on this section of the front line.

> *You never really know where exactly you are at, because they keep moving you. But often we were near Old Baldy and Pork Chop Hill, and even further west to Outpost Harry. I was in Korea for almost a year when I was wounded in action when the Chinese attacked the line.*

In January 1953, while fighting the bitter Korean winter, Cecil's unit also was in a faceoff against division-strength Chinese forces assaulting the surrounding hills in the hopes of retaking the city of Seoul. While wave after wave attacked their line, Cecil and his fellow GIs fought and gave the Chinese everything they had, even calling for self-endangering close-in artillery and mortar barrages. Typically in my interviews and travels meeting veterans, I heard that the Chinese had little to no regard for the lives of their own men. Often Cecil mentioned that the hills would be littered with enemy bodies left to rot, because the Communist forces seldom retrieved their dead. The U.S. Corps of Engineers members were often assigned to dig mass graves to bury the corpses, and this is where Cecil would see the one sight that disturbed him the most during his time in Korea. As the hillsides were checked for any wounded survivors, and for weapons, and with munitions to be collected to be burned, Cecil witnessed GIs smashing the faces of dead Chinese with their rifle butts to retrieve gold teeth.

> *It really did break my heart to see those mangled bodies get further mutilated. They didn't want to be there in the first place, and now they're having their teeth knocked out. I don't think a single one of those dead Chinese were over eighteen years of age, and here they are having their bodies smashed apart. It really broke my heart to see that.*

This cruel and grim scene occurred often—after each battle, with Cecil looking on with empathy for an enemy that just the night before was trying to kill him.

12. Cecil Love, U.S. Army: The Old Bootlegger   139

During one nighttime battle where the Chinese were successful in gaining ground on the Americans, Cecil was wounded—hit in the leg and stuck behind enemy lines. As the rest of his company pulled back to regroup, Cecil found concealment, hiding until the morning. Luckily, his buddies knew he was wounded and stranded, so next morning a company of U.S. Marines retook the lost ground and located Cecil. He was picked up by a few Marines and a Navy corpsman and hauled down to an aid station below the MLR (main line of resistance).

> *Next thing I know, I felt a pain in my leg, and here I was hit by a burst of machine gun fire and rolled down the hill where I hid myself until the next morning. I can't tell you how great it was to see those Marines when they picked me up the next day. To this day, at ninety-five years old, my leg still gives me trouble since that day in Korea.*

From a M.A.S.H. station he was transported to a hospital in Japan, where he remained for a few months. One surprise was hearing a familiar voice of a friend from Franklin County, Herbert Jones.

> *Once Herbert saw me all shot up, he started crying, but I told him I was all right, and there's no sense in crying. I would see him again when I was rotating home, and he started crying again, telling me he can't wait to get home. But I was back on the front line after I left Japan. We were fighting at Outpost Harry, Pork Chop Hill area, all over.*

Back in Korea, Cecil finished his tour of duty, accumulating those precious thirty-three points needed to qualify to be shipped back to the states. In almost all my interviews, the veterans said they volunteered for front-line action, which got them more points, more quickly. However, being wounded and hospitalized only meant that you'd be sent back out to earn the necessary points to go home.

Herbert and Cecil remained lifelong friends, with Herbert making regular visits to Cecil at the Veterans Home in Roanoke. On the first visit, Herbert again

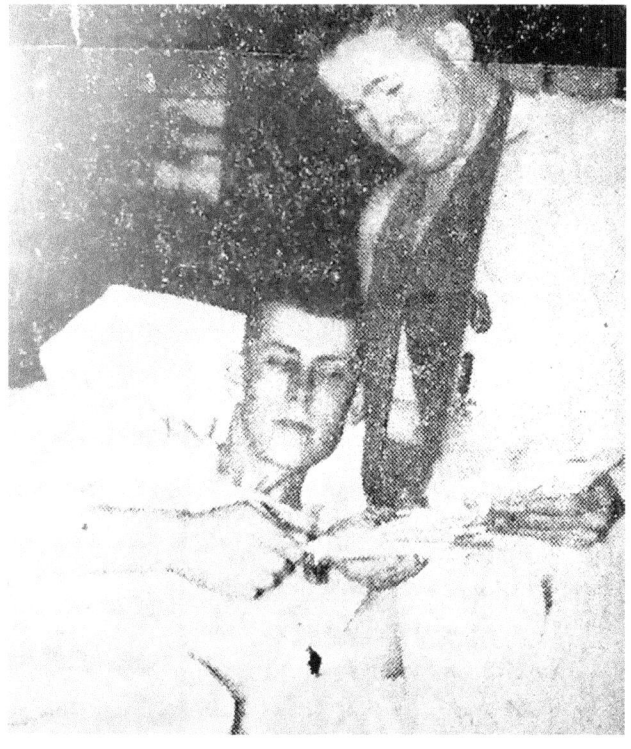

Newspaper clipping of Cecil Love receiving the Purple Heart while recovering from wounds in Japan.

started crying to Cecil about their ages, and how they were at the end of their lives, a recurring theme on my journey. The veterans I've interviewed know their days are numbered, and from their wartime lives and what they've been through, they generally accept that everyone has a checkout date. These heroes are not afraid of the truth.

While Cecil was totally open and honest about what happened to him in Korea seventy years earlier, there were certain experiences he didn't want to revisit. His combat wound still plagued him when he returned home, a definite handicap in his bootlegging business. One day, while he was visiting a still site, the location was busted by revenuers and ABC agents.

> *I ran like hell to get out of there. You can't get busted, or they'll throw the book at you, and you'll wind up in jail. It was tough to run on my bad leg from being wounded, but I got away and could hear the man chasing me yell, "Damn it, Cecil, you long-legged bastard, stop!"*

Back in civilian life, Cecil started a lumber company but continued dabbling in moonshine.

> *Once you get started, that's all you think about.*

Cecil mentioned that the ABC officers were not nice guys and would often physically abuse nabbed bootleggers and moonshiners. Many of the locals running stills were veterans, returning to what they'd always known, especially in the 1950s when jobs were scarce. As their relatives did during the Great Depression, they made and ran moonshine to survive.

> *A lot of the guys getting caught and beat up on were World War II veterans back from Japan and Europe. They got mistreated, and they'd come back and got to drinking and got to making liquor. Officers would raid 'em and beat them with blackjacks or whatever. You know, ole fellas already been punished enough, but they didn't care.*

Hearing these stories of bootlegging and making moonshine, I was surprised to learn that Cecil wasn't a big drinker, only sampling the product to make sure of its quality. "Never drinking to get drunk," he admitted. Yet Cecil would build what most would consider to be an "empire," which ran as far north as New York City, where he'd drop off a huge load and drive home with a paper bag sometimes crammed with up to $20,000. He also sold to famed NASCAR driver Junior Johnson, well known as a bootlegger, who'd sharpened his racing skills escaping authorities while hauling moonshine. Johnson would often take rides to Franklin County from North Carolina to buy brandy and corn liquor from Cecil.

> *Junior Johnson would often come up and I would sell him two hundred cases at a time. He would take those back to North Carolina and double his money. I knew every moonshiner and bootlegger this side of the Mississippi—Popcorn Sutton, Junior Johnson, even the Bondurants who got in a shoot-out during prohibition with the police. I've dealt with them all.*

Cecil Love many decades after the Korean War, running his moonshine still, tucked away in the woods. The barrels shown are full of peach mash, ready to make peach brandy.

Cecil quietly told me that he knows the day is coming when "It'll be time to check out." He said he has no regrets about anything, since he had a wonderful and exciting life and was able to "bless my family with a good upbringing." His daughter added that they were very fortunate for the money their father brought in making moonshine. Growing up, they didn't fully understand all the ramifications of that illegal business but came to the realization that it was just the way it was.

Is this chapter the most relevant or exciting, compared to the others in this book? I don't know, but I felt compelled to share Cecil's amazing saga because of it being pure Americana. I have no doubt in my mind that had I been around back then, I would have been making moonshine liquor with Cecil. Everything about it, from the mystique to the outlaw aspect to all the daring car chases, absolutely fascinated me. I couldn't help but be captivated by Cecil's tales of his bootlegging days and his time in Korea

Cecil said that lunch was ready. A good stopping point. But there was more.

My dad was caught once, my brother got caught twice, and my wife told me, "You know you're going to get caught one of these days making that damned old liquor." I told her, well maybe so. The next damned day they did catch me. I had thirteen hundred gallons of apple brandy ready to be cooked off. But they caught me before I had anything in the still and the judge ended up giving me a two-year suspended sentence, and that's the last time I fooled with it.

In 2011, eighty-three-year-old Cecil was finally caught. He'd been making moonshine for over sixty years. One of his rare and strange companions at the site was a black bear that would often come around to be fed by hand. Cecil said the beast waddled away up the hill and disappeared into the woods. A few minutes later, Cecil heard, "Put your hands up!"

I went to my still site and looked up and said, Lord if I'm doing anything against your will give me a sign. Fifteen minutes late, there was a gun in my back, and I was told to put my hands up. I didn't think He would answer that fast. I was thankful that the bear was gone because he was only used to me being out there and feeding him. I can only guess what would have happened had they been fifteen to twenty minutes earlier. That bear probably would have ripped them to shreds. But they caught me, and that's the last time I ever fooled with making liquor. I often think about it and wish I could run a still again, but I know my time is near the end at ninety-five.

After breaking down my recording gear and packing up, I said my goodbyes and was heading for the door when he called out my name. I turned, and that's when Cecil, a legend unto himself, left with me with a smile and a special sense of pride.

You know, son, you remind me of an old bootlegger.

CHAPTER 13

Bert Ruechel, USMC
The Widow Maker

Corporal, U.S. Marines Corps, Weapons Platoon, Baker Company, 1st Battalion, 1st Marine Regiment, 1st Marine Division. Interviewed October 30, 2023, Wausau, Wisconsin. Born 1930.

There were only two flame-throwers in our company, I heard someone yell, "Can I get in your hole?" So of course, I said yes. He sat there for a little bit then peeked up and shot that damn flame-thrower off. He took everything out that was in front of me. With that flame-thrower, nothing lives. It takes the oxygen out of the air.

The Marine with the flame-thrower who jumped into Bert Ruchel's foxhole was Joe Barna (Chapter 11), who was in the very same weapons platoon at the battle for Bunker Hill. A close high school buddy of mine, Cole Ruechel, had mentioned that his great uncle was a Korean War veteran and was willing to be interviewed. After my first contact, there was no further communication. I chalked it up as a loss, speculating he'd changed his mind, probably not wanting to talk about his wartime experiences. I didn't blame him. For many veterans, some of their wartime memories are pushed too far back to bring forward.

One day, however, I was surprised to receive a message from Dale Ruechel, Cole's dad, saying he'd shown Bert my Facebook page that included a video of Joe Barna talking about using the flamethrower on Bunker Hill, to which Bert immediately responded with, "Son of bitch, he hopped in my hole!"

As a valve technician, this was my busiest season with shutdown outages in full effect (when paper mills and power plants can have maintenance done), not to mention the coming deer hunting season that affected—and afflicted—most northern Wisconsinites, including me. Despite all that, Bert was a veteran I had to meet as soon as possible.

Dale gave me Bert's phone number, saying this Korean War veteran was expecting to hear from me. From my uncle's property, where I was prepping for the upcoming Wisconsin whitetail hunt, I called Bert. At first, we didn't talk much about Korea. Instead, our conversation was more about the Green Bay Packers, the NFL team we both love, which was disappointingly not playing to both our standards.

Well, come over in the afternoon after the game, I think it's a noon game today.

Hopefully they don't lose. We aren't doing too hot this year ... but any time after four is fine.

I finished sighting rifles with my buddies, gathered up my recording equipment, and headed toward Wausau. I'd been doing interviews across the nation, so it was a special treat finding a local veteran. I called Dale to tell him I was on my way. He said he'd try to join us but had just gone through knee surgery. Yet ... he did make it. Though it was a little tough for him to get around, he toughed it out and met me at his uncle's. My goal was not only to hear Bert's story, but to pitch to him the idea of a reunion with Joe Barna. A reunion after seventy-one years. How? I didn't know yet. First things first.

Bert welcomed me, escorting me into the kitchen where I waited while he washed and dried some dishes. When he finally sat at the table across from me, I explained that I hadn't prepared any questions, since this had all happened on such short notice, but I knew where he was deployed and in which unit, so I winged it with, "What was your first day in Korea like?"

You could tell, as he popped half a grin, this was a topic—a memory—he probably never talked about.

We were immediately taken to the front and there was I, another guy, and an officer who was leading us. I thought he knew what he was doing, but apparently, he didn't. They taught us in boot camp to never dive under a tank during incoming, because if it's hit, you're coming out of there in pieces. That lieutenant ran under the tank. It wasn't even two minutes and BANG! Me and that other guy stood there saying, "What do we do? What do we do?" And we heard someone yell, "Over here."

Bert Ruechel and Ryan Walkowski, Bert proudly displaying his Marine coat dungaree jacket with a painting of a Browning .30 caliber machine gun on it with the words "Widow Maker" and "Korea" on it.

Reaching the Marine who'd called, Bert and his

buddy dove for cover. Once in the hole, curious Bert popped his head up, only to hear the buzzing of bees swarming all around. When he asked, "What's with the bees?," the other Marine calmly said, "Keep your head down, those are bullets!" Welcome to your first day in Korea.

While this interview turned out to be a short one, what Bert shared that day was a machine gunner's personal perspective of the outpost war, which was as fearful and harrowing as any stories I'd heard to date. The battle of Bunker Hill, one of the bloodiest struggles involving the Marine Corps, was fought during this phase, and it was here that Bert soon met Joe Barna. Meanwhile, the Marine who'd warned Bert to lie low had more to say.

He told me to get down get down. And I said holy Christ, I ain't gonna live through the night. I asked him how long he'd been in country, and he told me six months. I told him, and you're still living? I can remember that and visualize that.

Bert didn't know the name of this hill along the MLR where he'd experience his first battle, a typical situation for Marines in Korea. The only time a grunt or GI might know his location was if he was manning a significant outpost whose name preceded itself. When I mentioned that Joe had told me he was all over Bunker Hill but spent most of his time on the northern point, Bert slapped the table.

That's him, then, I'm sure of it. There were only two flamethrowers on Bunker Hill.

Shifting conversation to the events of Bunker Hill, Bert went into detail on the fields of fire he and the other machine gunners would set up. Veterans and war buffs know about crossfire—interlocking machine gun fire with one weapon covering the left flank, a second straight ahead, and the third to the right. This tactic allows machine gun crews to cover and sweep the entire battlefield, or in this case the hill they're defending. It's a devastating and deadly strategy. Bert and other machine gunners with whom I spoke said the same thing: They would cut the Chinese down like grass with their .50-caliber Brownings. It's hard to imagine, but that's what happened, waves of humans being cut in half. The Browning model 1919 A4 fired over 500 rounds a minute, yet at times, even that torrent wasn't enough to slow the determined Chinese, who attacked more rapidly than they could be killed.

There would be a machine here firing to the right, a machine gun here maybe a hundred yards away firing straight, and then a machine gun here another hundred yards firing to the left. And whenever one machine gun nest gets pinned down, the others can fire toward them. I burnt barrels out and they get cherry red hot. All of a sudden, the barrel starts drooping down and you can see the tracers start falling. Then you put on asbestos gloves and swap the barrels out and just keep firing. And they would get damn close too, and it's scary.

I asked Bert, "What was your first experience like, seeing the waves of Chinese coming?" He balled his fist, grinned, and started pounding on his chest, going on to describing it like every other Korean War veteran: the flares, bugles, banging on pots

A field of dead Chinese after a nighttime battle against the 7th Marines. It's important for readers to understand what the wave-like tactics looked like and the aftermath of such suicide charges into machine gun fire (photograph provided by Robert Licker).

and pans, and screaming, "Marine you die, Marine you die!" "This," Bert declared, "was absolutely terrifying for a twenty-year-old kid ten thousand miles away from home." I then asked, "How much ammunition would you go through in a night?"

> *A couple crates I guess, a few thousand rounds. It doesn't take long when you hold that trigger down. Five hundred rounds a minute you're throwing out. I can't remember how many rounds are in a belt of ammo, but I do remember before one belt would be done, my assistant gunner would hook another one on and I'd keep firing. Like I said we burnt the barrels out and melted them.*

The next question was, "What was the life expectancy of a machine gunner?" Bert held up three fingers and gave this grim response:

> *Three minutes once the fighting starts. A machine gunner's life expectancy is about three minutes. You're the first thing they want to go after; they wanna take out the heavy weapons first.*

The Chinese swarmed Bunker Hill and surrounding outposts to gain ground to use as leverage during the peace talks going on just a few miles away. It's kind of ironic, but while these young men were fighting and dying, just a few miles away officers and emissaries were sitting across from each other trying to agree on terms to end the conflict. Most of my interviewees had identical comments about

The aftermath of the Chinese wave attacks (photograph provided by Robert Licker).

this stage of the war, that the killing was pointless. But the combat continued, ending the lives of many Marines and Chinese during these pushes on the 1st Marine Division-controlled outposts. The Chinese began their attacks on the Americans holding the hills with diversionary tactics in the hopes of catching them off guard, often sending shells into no-man's-land while methodically zeroing in on the Marines' positions. Then they'd begin their full onslaughts on Bunker Hill, sending in waves of fanatical Chinese.

> *There were no bunkers where I was, just trenches. There were a group of Marines just below me in a shell hole. I yelled, "Get outta there! Get outta there!" And they yelled that they couldn't. I hollered and told them to dig a hole there. And right as I did that an artillery shell hit them.*

Here was where Bert would meet Joe Barna. Amid all this chaos, Barna had hopped into Bert's machine gun hole to catch some cover and respite from the heavy fighting. Joe, using his flame-thrower, was shunting from one position on the trench line to another, unleashing his lethal weapon, when he stumbled across Bert's machine gun nest.

> *There were only two flame-throwers in our company. I heard someone yell, "Can I get in your hole?" Of course, I said, "Yes." He sat there for a little bit, then peeked up and shot that damn flame-thrower off. He took everything out that was in front of me. With that flame-thrower, nothing lives. It takes the oxygen out of the air. He sat*

Bert Ruechel's machine gun position along the front line of the Jamestown Line, specific location unknown, Korea, 1952.

there for a little while and got up and took off when there was break in the fighting. That was the last damn time anyone was going to jump in my hole.

What a coincidence: two Marines, not only from the same regiment but the same platoon, one here in Wisconsin only twenty minutes from me, and both sharing the same foxhole during the craziness of one of the most intense battles of the war. What could have been Bert's exact thoughts during the chaos of such an intense battle?

He took off, and I took the brunt of that. I said no more of that. They really started shelling and firing on my position, thinking that flame-thrower was still here. Could hear and see the mortars falling all around me. No more shooting flame-throwers out of my hole. They thought that flame-thrower was in my hole yet. And Christ, you want to talk about scary.

Now seemed a good time to pitch the idea of Bert and Joe reuniting after seventy years. Bert sat for a moment, popped a grin and said "Sure." The brainstorming began. Where, when, and how? The obvious place was my favorite local establishment, Kluck's Callon Saloon. Mark Kluck is big on anything that supports our veterans, even having military memorabilia in a display case in his establishment. I knew the family would be onboard, so I messaged Mark's daughter Amanda, who immediately responded with "Heck yes! I want to be there to see them." She approached her dad with the idea, and the next time I was there we settled on Monday November 13, a day the bar would be closed, so it would be a private event. The challenge was

Bert Ruechel with Ryan Walkowski after his interview and signing Ryan's Korean War veteran's flag.

getting Joe Barna to agree to make the trip from Pennsylvania. At first Joe wasn't sure and told me, "Well with Veterans Day coming up I'm very busy, Ryan, but after we will see. I'll put some serious thought into this." Sadly, his final answer was "No." But he'd be happy to do a Zoom call, adding,

> *It's a strange feeling, and almost unreal to speak to someone I was in combat with over seventy years ago. I'm not sure what I'm going to tell him.*

When I entered the bar, Mark and his wife Janel were doing a last-minute cleanup, I let them know the event would be covered by WAOW News Channel 9. It was a small gathering: Mark and Janel, their daughter Amanda Geurink, along with her toddler Grace, Bert's son and daughter-in-law, my friend Cole Ruechel who is Bert's great nephew, and my cousin Josh Cheyka, who was my tech support for the

Zoom call. I also invited Frank English, a veteran featured later in this book, since he too had fought on those same battlefields while serving with How Company.

The reporter from Channel 9 interviewed me about my "Remembering Korea, the Forgotten War" project. Then he chatted with Bert, asking questions about Korea and what he thought about the coming reunion. I'd never participated in a Zoom call, so I was out in left field, but luckily my cousin Josh helped get things going, and that's when the stories really began.

At first, Bert sat quietly, listening to the tales of battle Joe and Frank shared, occasionally chiming in. The rest of the group sat in total awe as these old Marines traded combat stories. When the Channel 9 crew went outside to get a n exterior shot of the bar, we all couldn't help but laugh when Mark told him, "Make sure you get my sign in the shot, so I get some advertising here."

The Zoom call then switched to Bert and Joe sharing stories of those terror-filled nights on Bunker Hill.

> *Joe, do you remember hopping in my hole and firing that flame-thrower off on me, and then you got up and ran. You shot that flame-thrower off, and the flames were just rolling down the hill all over. After you ran out of gas you got up and ran.*

Bert Ruechel and Ryan Walkowski during the reunion between Bert and Joseph Barna via zoom at Kluck's Callon Saloon in Ringle, Wisconsin.

Sharing a chuckle, Joe replied, "Yeah I guess I did, didn't I?" Joe also told the story of how Jackie Kilmer saved his life on Bunker Hill, giving him seventy more years of life, which allowed this historic and emotional reunion. During the call, I showed Bert the photo Joe gave me that Jackie took on Bunker Hill, of young dead Marines lying in the mud and dirt, covered by their ponchos, with the caption "John Kilmer, Navy Corpsman, Aug 52." Bert looked long and hard; you could see the emotion in his eyes.

Interviewee Bert Ruechel looking at combat photographs with "the thousand yard stare" after his Zoom-call reunion with Joseph Barna at Kluck's Callon Saloon in Ringle, Wisconsin.

I had seen this sight almost daily. These are our boys covered up. I saw it one day, there was three of us standing together. They had three of those big trucks, what did they call those—six-by trucks? Deuce and a half? They had Marines stacked seven high and three across with men on top of one another. I've seen three trucks like that with bodies. Anyway, we sat there, and we just stood there and looked, and I said to these guys, we could be on there. They were all dead.

It's moment like these that opened my eyes to what our veterans had gone through, making my mission that much more urgent and essential. Their efforts should never be forgotten.

When the Zoom call ended, we all sat around in somber silence. It couldn't have been more quiet. We'd been part of something very special. Then people began thanking me. But I told them, "It's not about me today. It's about these Marines. It's all about these Marines."

Chapter 14

Salvatore Scarlato, USMC
Now I Know Why I'm Here

Corporal, U.S. Marine Corp, B Company, 1st Shore Party Battalion, 7th Marine Regiment, 1st Marine Division. Interviewed August 10, 2022, and April 21, 2023. Born 1933.

I was told, "Why the hell do you want to join the Marine Corps? You'll end up face down in the mud somewhere, dying like a pig." My first combat experience found me face down in a rice paddy in human waste—that's what they used for fertilizer. And the whole time I'm thinking, that's what I was told.

A young Korean named Charles Kang reached out to me on my Facebook page. Commending my project, he said that his family owes everything to Korean War combatants, adding that if I ever came to Long Island, New York, he'd arrange meetings with at least seven veterans he's befriended over the years.

How could I say no? I started planning and was able to reach others who lived in nearby New Jersey. It couldn't have worked out better. I kept in touch with Charles, who graciously invited me to stay at his home with his family. I didn't want to intrude, but when I saw the rundown condition of my hotel, I gratefully accepted his offer.

Then came Salvatore Scarlato.

Charles Kang accompanied me to my first meeting with Sal, who was sitting at his kitchen counter playing solitaire and listening to music from the late 1940s and early 1950s. We got off to a slow start, with Sal somewhat reluctantly sharing his experiences with a stranger, but after some small talk, and my explaining the mission, he opened up with some short stories, going on to tell things I could never imagine.

So, what the hell is it? You just travel and interview old timers like me about what they went through in Korea?

That's it, I said. So what's your story?

Growing up in Brooklyn, and I'm sure it's the same now, we were just a bunch of wise-ass kids. Everyone was part of a gang of some sort, least that's what we called it back then.

14. Salvatore Scarlato, USMC: Now I Know Why I'm Here

(Note: This chapter bounces between two separate interviews with Sal. During the first meeting, there was no real timeline on his experiences in Korea, as he just rattled off stories.)

I always questioned anytime I could, as to why we were in Korea. Any chance I had, I asked that question to my superiors. I was always given the same answer, "Soon you'll see why." But until what I'm about to tell you happened, it never penetrated why. I'd seen what a bullet could do, what a bomb can do. I'd seen my buddies shot up so I was rather bitter about being there.

Shortly after arriving in Korea and sent to the front line, Sal and his platoon were on patrol when they came to a village where they found dead Koreans—men and women, with their hands tied behind their backs. While inspecting the village and offering aid to the few who'd survived, Sal came upon three orphans, one with a serious wound: two little girls and a boy. The girls were about eight years of age, The boy, maybe five, was crying and screaming. His hand had been blown off. Sal said he's never forgotten this horrible scene. Taking a bandage from his aid pouch and wrapping it around the wound, Sal called for a corpsman. A Navy medic raced over to tend the stump that was once the boy's hand.

This little boy was screaming, and I mean screaming. I thought I was going to go deaf, and he wouldn't let go of my neck after I picked him up. The corpsman came and dressed his wounds and flagged down a jeep and we took the little boy and his two sisters to an orphanage; it was a big orphanage and it's still there today.

Sal related that he picked up the boy's hand and put it in his pocket before getting into the jeep. Reaching the orphanage, they rushed the children inside where they were greeted by an Army chaplain and evaluated by the medical staff. The boy was rushed into the operating room, with the chaplain blessing him, and commending Sal for saving his life. Returning to the jeep, Sal waited for the corpsman, suddenly remembering something grim:

I was sitting in the jeep waiting for the corpsman to get back so we could get back to our unit and realized, holy shit, I've still got the little boy's hand in my pocket yet. I'd picked it up and put it in my front chest pocket when we took them to the orphanage. I rushed back inside and gave the hand to the surgeon, and he told me the little boy just died. I went berserk, I just went completely berserk.

The boy's death gave Sal the eye-opening and heartbreaking answer to why he was in Korea. He paused a few times while telling this story. I knew he was visualizing—reliving that horrifying scene. He went on to mention that he sobbed like a child and just couldn't seem to grasp the reality that the boy had died. Even back at his bunker on the front line, he couldn't stop crying. His fellow Marines offered what little comfort they could, encouraging him to drink some water and talk out the problem.

I believe in guardian angels, and you can believe this or not, it doesn't matter to me, because I know what I saw. When I got back to my bunker I was sobbing, and I mean sobbing. My friends and fellow Marines tried their best to calm me down. After a little bit I saw what I thought was a guardian angel. The figure looked at me and told me, "Now you know why you're here." And from that moment on, I was a different person. That's the day I became a United States Marine. I'm truly dedicated to the South Korean people. Anyone can tell you that, including Charlie here.

Charles and I sat quietly, finding it hard to absorb what Sal had seen and experienced. Sal went on to say that there isn't a day that goes by when he doesn't think about those children. He then touched base on his PTSD, making it clear that any struggling veteran needs to talk about it, get it off his chest. The meds they prescribe to so many veterans, in Sal's opinion,

> don't help anything, because you can't wipe memories away. It's just a bunch of bullshit taking medication for PTSD, I struggle with it every day of my life.

Charles asked Sal to take me to his basement. To this day, I've never seen a personal collection as impressive. Compared to any military and world history assemblage, Sal's basement was a virtual museum: mostly Korean War items, but also memorabilia from other wars that he'd collected over the years. Highlights from Korea included his poncho and a dagger-style fighting knife, along with just a few other relics, which were all he had left.

Sal Scarlato during his first interview with Ryan Walkowski.

> My father gave a lot of the things away I brought home from Korea, you know good old dads, they like to brag. But I got a story about this knife here I'm going to tell you.

Sal retrieved the all-black knife from a leather sheath hanging on a Korean War-era BAR ammunition belt. Holding the knife, Sal started

14. Salvatore Scarlato, USMC: Now I Know Why I'm Here

talking about what every veteran during my journey has mentioned, with only a few going into detail: about their war being fought with fierce hand-to-hand combat not seen since.

Sal Scarlato standing next to the poncho he wore in Korea.

One thing about Korea is, well, we fought Chinese, only Chinese. And one time we were hit pretty bad, and this Chinese fella, young guy, came running around the bend of this trench and I came around the opposite bend. He had this knife on him, this was his knife. We ran into each other; he swung at me and a big struggle happened. Maybe the lord is with me, maybe I'm fast. After the struggle I got the knife off him, and I killed him with it, there's still blood on it.

I didn't have words to react to his story. I was now holding that very knife. I returned it and dared to ask, "What's it like to kill a man with your bare hands?" He told me straight up:

One thing about doing something like this is, I felt like a murderer. When you fire a weapon at a distance, that's one thing. But when you kill a man with your bare hands, I felt terrible. I heaved like crazy. But after the first time it wasn't so bad.

At the second interview with Sal, a year later, I discovered that this bloody experience happened on Bunker Hill in 1952. Collin Wilson, my documenting partner, accompanied me on this trip, a quick and short turnaround—driving from Wisconsin to Long Island and back home in only three days.

I have these two young fellas here gonna do me an interview. Which I must thank them very much for continuing my legacy. Unfortunately, Korea was branded in 1988 as the Forgotten War when it's actually the Forgotten victory. People don't understand we won the war. We never went there to take over North Korea, we went there to push them out of South Korea.

This time, dressed in his blue sport jacket and wearing a VFW cap covered with military pins, there was no reluctance to share memories. Sal was ready to give one hell of an interview. (One medallion on his hat stood out—a Purple Heart pin. He'd never mentioned in the first interview that he'd been wounded.) He started with the news that he'd originally enlisted in the Navy, and when his hitch was coming to an end, he notified his recruiter he was going to join the Marine Corps. His recruiter made it clear that was the dumbest thing anyone could do.

> *I was told, why the hell do you want to join the Marine Corps? You'll end up face down in the mud somewhere, dying like a pig. My first combat experience found me face down in a rice paddy in human waste, that's what they used for fertilizer. They were opening up on us pretty good, and all that was running through my mind was that I was gonna die like a pig in mud.*

Sal mentioned that no one knew where the hell Korea was. They knew Japan, Indochina, and other countries, but had never heard of Korea. Sal went on to talk about his older brother, a World War II vet, conning him into joining the Naval Air Reserves, saying it was to save Sal's ass. In the Naval Air Reserve, you only fly when the weather is good, eat three square meals a day, sleep on clean, white sheets, and so on. The Marine Corps, which Sal preferred, was the complete opposite.

When Sal turned eighteen, because he was in the Reserves, he didn't have a draft number.

> *There was seventeen of us and we went down to the recruiter on J street in Brooklyn. Now you gotta picture this … my era was black pants, black pistol pockets—we were gangs. We went to the recruiter three at a time with big hair and cigarettes in our shirt sleeves. The recruiters looked at us and shook their heads and they gave us papers to test, and we all cheated. The Marine recruiter told us he wasn't gonna even grade us, he was gonna pass us because the Marines love wise guys!*

When he was ready for his discharge from the Navy, Sal's commanding officers tried to dissuade him from joining the Marines. "Are you out of your mind? Anyone who wants to join the Marines is out of his mind!" They did their best to convince Sal how good he had it with clean sheets, hot meals, and everything else that comes with the cozy gig.

> *I refused, and one of them asked me, "How would you like to die?" I didn't know how to answer, so I said—in bed. Then stay where you're at, he said, "because if you join the Marines, you're going to die face down in the mud or some rice paddy somewhere." But being thick-headed, I refused, and they gave me my discharge and letter of recommendation for joining the Corps.*

He made it clear that his twelve weeks at boot camp was quite the experience.

> *The DIs (drill instructors), all they did was yell at the recruits, but in a manner we learned. Their motto of "make you or break you," let me tell ya, they make or break you. If you're a wise guy, you're gonna change. If you're shy, they're gonna make you a wise guy, you follow what I'm saying? If you're fat they're gonna make you skinny,*

if you're skinny, you're gonna be fat. It's the way they train you. I don't regret it because they straightened me out. I came from a bad area where dope was becoming big, so that was the good thing going into the military. They gave me a break and that's the truth. Otherwise I would have been in jail. I was at attention one time and my feet were not pointed the proper way, so the DI kicked me. When someone kicks you, the natural response is to tense up and ball your fists. So, he says, "Oh, so we got a wise guy." He says, "Where you from?" I told him Brooklyn, and he asked "What is your nationality?" And I told him Italian, and he goes, "Hey, we got a gangster over here." So, he put me in this category with a few others.

When the recruits received their first haircuts, Sal, being a wise guy, told the barber to just give him a trim. Well, a DI heard him and didn't take kindly to that smart comment. He told Sal to pick up his clipped hair and go through the showers and not to dare drop a single strand. He threw his hair on the floor. Immediately, he was ordered to do twenty-five pushups—the beginning, he stated of "my pushup career."

To hell with that, I figured. How are you supposed to go through the shower with all that hair, so I threw it on the ground, and that was the start of my pushups. I had to do twenty-five, right there. They liked to pick a few guys who needed a little more attention than the others and use them as guinea pigs. I was one of them. I graduated on Christmas of 1951, and then went to Camp Pendleton for twelve weeks of infantry training.

This turned out to be the real thing. Sal and the other Marines had to crawl under live machine gun fire for the first time. Then they were told Korea is their next stop, that they're all going, and there are no two ways about it. So, the stage was set. Sal would be heading to Korea where his life would be changed forever.

They woke us up and said, "Saddle up!" You heard the old-timers talk about the Golden Gate Bridge and at two in the morning it's all lit up. It's gorgeous, a sight to be seen. It's even better when you're coming back, 'cause you're going home.

Twelve days later, the troopship docked at Kobi, Japan, where the Marines were given a few days to explore the city, only to be let down seeing so many beggars and young prostitutes—sixteen- and seventeen-year-old girls just trying to survive. Sal made it clear that this was a sad sight.

At nineteen years old you could care less, but as you learn things you realize what other people must go through. We made the second Incheon landing. Most of the troops used to come through Pusan and then you'd go to your unit.

Rumors had it that the peace talks were being moved to Panmunjom and the 1st Marine Division would be needed to protect the UN participants. It was about 8:15 a.m. when the rope ladders went over the sides of the ships and ammo boxes were dropped to the waiting boats, followed by the Marines.

In the back of my mind I didn't think it was reality yet, I didn't think this was a war yet, so they yell to go towards our station, and we get to the rope area and with certain calls you go down the ropes to the landing crafts where we would zigzag until we hit the seawall. We were forty-five hundred Marines and it still didn't penetrate, until the officer said, "Land of departure, Lock and load."

The Marines met little to no resistance, mostly scattered guerrilla fighters who didn't pose much threat to the more sophisticated U.S. military. Boarding trucks, they were driven north to ASCOM City, where they would receive their assignments. For Sal, it was Baker Company on the front line, desperately in need of replacements.

On the third day, I think it was, we went up to the MLR (main line of resistance), and you always traveled at between four and five because the Koreans and Chinese liked to fight at night. There were two trucks and two jeeps when we got hit by mortar and artillery fire, along with small arms. I jumped out and headed for a rice paddy and I went face down in the paddy. Koreans use human waste for fertilizer, and I thought I got hit 'cause I was all wet. I didn't fire my weapon right away; I was shaking and couldn't fire my weapon. and I got hit in the helmet by a round and it flew off. That was it, I threw up, had diarrhea, you name it. Someone came up to me and said, "You better start firing your weapon!"

This was the monsoon season, with rain like Sal had never seen, which put a pause to the firefight. The firing stopped as soon as the downpour began. A jeep was knocked out and a few Marines were hit. The troops were told to saddle up and move to what Sal remembered as Hill 234. At top of the hill, a sergeant told them to take posts in any bunker for now, and that they'd be placed in permanent quarters the next morning.

Me and two other Marines went into a bunker, and they kicked us out. We didn't know why at first, but we smelled. Smelled like you know what, and they told us to stand outside in the rain until we got clean, which we did, like dummies. It was pitch black. You couldn't see anything, and I mean pitch black. No moon, it was raining, and you don't know how scary it is when you can't see anything.

Sal and the other Marines were positioned on a reverse slope just behind the MLR, as a back door in case the Chinese tunneled below to attack from behind. The next morning, after a sleepless night out in the rain, the platoon leader introduced everyone and said he had some presents.

The platoon leader came to me and asked what's my name. So I told him Sal Scarlato blah, blah, blah, and he said they had a present for me. No one knew they were going to give us presents. We got something you're going to love, and he hands me a BAR. I asked if I could speak, and he said sure. I told him, "Sir, I don't know shit about a BAR. I can fire it, but don't ask me to take it apart!" So, I was scared. The death rate was three-quarters of an hour. A machine gunner was like fifteen minutes. Most the time the enemy goes after automatic weapons.

While he was told he looked the perfect size to carry the BAR, to Sal—who weighed 140 pounds—the math didn't add up. The BAR itself is a twenty-two-pound weapon, cartridge belts fully loaded are another fifteen pounds, plus everything else

Marines carry. The benefit was that he was never alone; he always had an assistant BAR man who'd be right there with an equal load of ammo. At first, Sal rejected the idea of carrying it, but after he got used to it, you wouldn't have been able to get it away from him unless, as he told me, "You couldn't pry it from my cold dead fingers."

I figured if I can't get you with one bullet, I'll get you with twenty. The next night I pulled guard duty on Outpost 2; we had three outposts. So, I went with a fire-team of four guys, and I didn't know them at all. They discussed who would sleep and watch, and they would fall asleep like nothing. And here I am shaking outta my wits. When it gets dark there, it gets black, you may be high up in the mountains, but it's black. If you light a match, they'll see you a mile away. Soon as the sun goes down, you start to shake. I know I did. The Chinese made sure to give us a welcome.

As soon as the sun went down, the Chinese attacked. First, they blew bugles. Next came whistles. And they always came at night. All defenders saw were shadows—all over the place, racing up the hill. During this battle, a Marine Sal didn't know was shot in the gut and fell on top of him. Sal turned to a corpsman, telling him to cover the wound. It didn't help.

You know what a short timer is? A short timer is someone going home in a week, or two weeks, and this poor guy gets shot in the gut, a belly wound. I put both hands on his stomach after a corpsman ran over and told me to do so. Here I am putting pressure on the wound and here his liver is, in my hand, I threw up on this. He is sitting here gasping for air and he passed away. I find out he's a short timer, and he's going home in a week. It was very horrifying when I first saw blood. The only thing prior to that was in the movie house, you know, or a butcher cutting a piece of meat, you know. It was very, very horrifying.

Sal compared the following months to being like a yo-yo: You go out, you come back, you go out and you come back, time and time again. There never seemed to be an end, just war, day after day, night after night. Rain, snow, sleet, cold, heat, didn't matter because there was always another battle to be fought. It was at this point in the interview Sal said that he's a firm believer in guardian angels and in his faith, and while he was in Korea, he would often think of his grandfather and his stories and see figures. A minister told him once that the figures are family members who'd passed on, looking over you and guiding you.

One major question Sal often asked was, "What are we doing here?" He would be answered with, "You'll find out." All the way up the chain of command, Sal received the same answer, "You'll find out."

I hated everybody; I hated the Koreans, I hated the Americans, I hated where I was. There was a lot of incidents and after I got hit on Hill 58, it made it worse. Hill 58 was known as "Siberia."

Located closest to L Company, the 7th Marine Regiment received orders to move to a new position—Siberia—only to find caved-in bunkers with bodies trapped inside. The call went out to bring in the engineers, but until they arrived, Sal and his fellow Marines became the laborers, spending hours digging out body parts of dead Marines. The smell and feeling have not left this old veteran to this day.

> *I was taking arms out, pieces of bodies out. You know how you get the dry heaves? I must have had it for about an hour. I just couldn't grasp any other smell. It was a nice, beautiful July day with a perfect breeze, but you could still smell death.*

It was supposed to be a secured area, but in the late afternoon the enemy attacked. The Marines took up their weapons. The Chinese moved in their usual wavelike tactics.

> *We heard the horns first, then the bugles and then the whistles as they came charging. I was firing this way and out of the corner the other way to my right, I saw someone throw something and it was a grenade. It went right for us and three of us got hit. He got the three of us and one was killed. I fell down the side of the hill and kept rolling until a mound stopped me. Otherwise, I would have gone all the way down the mountain. When I opened my eyes, I saw two gooks standing there and thought I just became a prisoner, but they were South Koreans.*

The two South Koreans were part of the Korean Service Group that hauled supplies and carried wounded off the line for UN forces. They called for a corpsman, who asked Sal if he needed a morphine shot to ease the pain, to which he replied "Yes." Shrapnel had struck Sal's right leg, causing the limb to swell to twice its normal size. Both hands and his neck had also taken fragments. While listening to Sal tell this story, I was amazed he made it out alive after that battle. He was put in a jeep and taken to an aid station which he remembered was part of Easy Company, and then by chopper to a Navy hospital ship sailing off the coast, where he recuperated.

> *A whirlybird flew me to the hospital ship and the pilot had a million-dollar smile, you know how some people smile, and it looks that way? Well, he was shaking my hand and saying something, but I didn't know what the hell he was saying. The whole way over he was looking at me and another wounded Marine on the side of this whirlybird, with a thumbs up with this big smile. So, when we landed on the hospital ship, he came over and grabbed my hand and said he's sorry he gave me a bumpy ride. I met him forty years later at a reunion of the 1st Marine Division, and we kept in contact until the Christmas cards stopped coming. A real nice guy. But now I was even more bitter and really hated Korea.*

Returning to Korea and the front lines, Sal became a scrounge for his colonel, often sent in search of whiskey. Since almost all GI gear and weapons were leftovers from World War II, and the Army often received the new stuff first, besides scrounging for whiskey, "which is worth its weight in gold practically in a war zone," Sal and other Marines would acquisition whatever food or equipment they needed. On the track to becoming the jeep driver for Colonel Funk, Sal was, unfortunately, caught in the act.

> *I used to go on a lot of whiskey patrols with a couple of guys for our colonel, Colonel Funk. He was like nine foot tall, this guy, real nice guy and down to earth, and*

he wanted to make me his Jeep driver until a few incidents got me in trouble. If we wanted food, we would steal it. If we wanted a Jeep, we would steal it. They caught me on the Jeep because it was a new one and the Army got those first while the Marines still had the junk. And that was a story of a different color.

It was during this time that the outpost phase of the wear had come to a standstill. There were still attacks, but as Sal mentioned, they were more to "keep the status quo." But his anger continued to grow, as did his hatred for being in Korea.

I was very, very bitter. I had to get outta here and I hated my officers. I had a chip on my shoulder, and always had an attitude. We had ROK Marines with us and one of the South Korean Marines became my good buddy. His name was Kim, and he would always tell me, "You watch your mouth. You watch your mouth. You're gonna get in trouble." But I didn't give a damn. I just wanted to go home because there was no end.

One evening, embittered Sal was saddling up with a Marine squad in preparation for another patrol. Kim gave him his prayer cloth to wear around his neck. (Most South Korean soldiers wore prayer cloths.) He didn't think anything of it, stowing it in his pocket. After the patrol, he tried to give it back to Kim but was told to keep it.

The incident with the assassinated villagers and the little boy he'd tried to save seventy-one years ago continues to plague Sal. Once again, he brought up the story.

I was crying, really crying, and so was the corpsman. When we got back, I told my squad leader, now I know what you mean when you told me I would find out why we are here in Korea. I just found out. To my knowledge we are fighting for these people, and these people are innocent and they're getting killed. That little boy had no life. That evening I was so sad, that entire day no one could come talk to me. My friends didn't wanna talk to me, nobody.

Sal went on to admit that this was the moment he became a Marine and a better fighting man. His hatred had him at a point where the enemy meant nothing; he didn't even want to take prisoners. But recalling the incident with the little Korean boy who never had a chance at life, and the caring shown by the South Korean Marine, helped bring empathy into his soul.

It was a horrifying experience, and thank God, because I went home in a few months after that. It was horrifying ... that's the only way I can explain it. You had no days or nights; half the time we didn't know what day it was or month until someone would say something.

Sal's last major battle was at Outpost Vegas along the Jamestown Line. By then he was a short timer assigned as "shotgun" on a truck. Outpost Vegas, along with Reno and Carson, were hit so hard by the Chinese that every able man was called to the fight. The 7th Marines, after furious battles, finally took back the hill complex. Sal believed the Chinese had no reason to take these outposts; they just wanted to see what the Americans would do to hold them. He also noted that this happened in 1953 when peace talks were well underway, which unfortunately didn't stop the fighting.

Our conversation took many twists and turns, and events were often not in sequence. At this point, Sal regressed, and again brought up Bunker Hill.

> *When Eisenhower got in, he came to Korea and said this is ridiculous—how this war is being fought. We can't beat these people because you need to cut their supply. Syngman Rhee wanted him to use the atomic bomb, so his hands were tied too. That would be the worst thing in the world ... you wouldn't be able to use that country for a hundred years.*

Between Bunker Hill and the Vegas Cities positions, an entire regiment was almost lost for what Sal said was "for nothing. The Chinese just wanted to test the Americans." Bunker Hill proved to be one of the most devastating battles involving over five thousand Marines. I could tell from Sal's demeanor that Bunker Hill was an experience he didn't want to remember or discuss.

When I asked him what winter was like, his answer was quick and short.

Sal Scarlato with friend Kim, a Korean Marine, below the MLR.

> *Cold, it was cold! They would give us new clothes and we would urinate in our trousers to keep warm because it was so cold you didn't want to whip it out to take a leak. And in our bunkers, we only had a little pot stove. It's like here, the further north you go the colder it gets.*

Surprisingly, the dreaded Korean winter offered a few advantages, if you could call them that. First, if a man was shot, he'd pack frozen snow on his wound to stop the blood flow. Second, to wash up, all it took were a few handfuls of snow. And last, when you needed to cool down your weapon, you threw it in the snow. It was after describing these conditions that Sal again touched on hand-to-hand combat.

> *The story I told you about on*

14. Salvatore Scarlato, USMC: Now I Know Why I'm Here

Sal Scarlato and Ryan Walkowski after their interview in Sal's basement full of military memorabilia.

> *how I got that knife? Yeah, well it's very hard when you're running in a trench while carrying a BAR to fight that hand-to-hand. You either want a knife, a .45, or a shovel. So, I used to carry a shovel, but one incident I had a knife, and I threw my helmet at a Chinese soldier, and I did what I had to do. And this time my buddy came running down the trench and he jumped over the body, and when he came down, he reached out to brace himself and grabbed the scolding hot barrel of my BAR. We had to kick his forearm to rip his hand off 'cause his skin melted to the barrel.*

Sal explained that the Marines' older BAR models didn't have carry handles; it was the Army that was provided with newer automatic weapons.

In the heat of the battle, Sal lost his helmet and was annoyed because inside were pictures of his wife—then his girlfriend—and other photos of his family. Inside it he'd written "Guinea,'" the slang name he allowed only his friends to call him. From others, it was an insult.

> *Only my friends called me that, nobody else because I'd hit ya. And this one time, a guy comes in our bunker and asks, "We got a guy in here named Guinea?" And he*

yelled, "Wait a minute. I got your helmet." He found out from someone else in our company what platoon I was in. We shared a good laugh over that.

We all had a good chuckle after I made the comment that I wouldn't know about all this since I was a dumb Polack. But, as Sal said, "It's all how you take it."

We shared an even bigger laugh when I told Sal I've even been called a "Mick a few times, but I take things with a grain of salt and never let it bother me."

Well, what the hell are you? Oh, you're Irish and Polish. Well, there's a combination.

We talked for a while about our respective heritages, with Sal telling me not to worry about it because even with his Italian heritage, he had a blonde beard and a red mustache. I responded with, "Well, I never met an Italian-Mick before," Again there were chuckles. Considering the tenor of the day, the laughter was a good way to finish, with Sal Scarlato ending our epic interview with one final statement:

I'm proud to have served, and even prouder that I'm a Marine who served in Korea.

Chapter 15

Paul Marsa, USMC
Box Me In

Sergeant, U.S. Marine Corps, George Company, 3rd Battalion, 5th Marine Regiment, 1st Marine Division. Interviewed April 17, 2022, Miami, Florida. Born 1934. Died 2022. Buried at Arlington National Cemetery.

Hey Ryan, I finally got to show Dad your page of what exactly you're doing and the pictures from your interviews, and his face really lit up better than I've seen in a while. Said he was so glad you're doing this and really seemed moved. He said he'd be glad to cooperate, I think it really gave him a little boost and made him feel useful again, so I really appreciate that.

That was the text message I received from Paul Marsa's son Alan, to which I immediately responded with the intent of arranging to meet ASAP. Since Paul was dealing with Parkinson's disease, I was in a race against time but managed to set up our interview on my next trip east, which would be starting in a few days. In previous correspondence, Alan had provided some background on Paul—that he was a Marine who served with George Company, 3rd Battalion, 5th Marines, mostly on outposts Dagmar and Esther. Alan had also mentioned that while Paul had told some stories about Korea, he never went into detail. Plus, Paul's memory most of the time was still very sharp but faltered at times. Obviously, any moments of confusion were due to his struggle with Parkinson's. This could be a challenging interview. Once again, I was greeted like family, with Alan serving snacks while I was setting up my recording gear. His father Paul, however, sat nearby—quietly. I was having doubts.

Surprisingly, Paul broke the ice.

First, I'd like to thank the cameraman and all his travels across the country. I'm in awe of you and your efforts, thank you. I don't know how you do it but I'm glad it's being done. Thank you.

And we were off to one fantastic interview.

Kind of a gung-ho teenager who'd just missed World War II action, Paul voluntarily enlisted in the Marine Corps in 1952. He was living in Newark, New Jersey, and working for a furniture delivery company. One day, while making a delivery across from the Marine Corps Recruiting Depot at Times Square in Manhattan with his friend Moe, they broke for lunch.

Moe and I were sitting across from the Depot, and they had a banner that said, "United States Marine Corps and Navy Recruiting," and Moe asked me, "Do you think you'd ever join the Marines?" I took one bite of my apple and said, "Sure why not?"

Paul described it being as simple as that. They went in, signed up for a three-year enlistment, and within two weeks he was in training at the Marine Corps Recruit Depot on Parris Island in South Carolina.

A DI (drill instructor) told Paul that he and three other Marines were selected to be replacements, and would absolutely be sent to Korea, a place Paul said he'd never heard of until 1950, when the war started. They were told to get used to their weapons: learn how to handle and fire them well, because "You're going to need them where you're going."

When I joined the Corps, that was the start of the best times and worst times. I had no idea what I was about to experience in Korea—horror, to say the least. But I am also grateful for what the Corps taught me.

Paul's advance combat training in the California mountains was cut short, and soon he was aboard a troopship sailing to Korea. The trip across the Pacific was exactly as every veteran has described—close quarters, bunks seven high, barely any room at all. Paul was the only veteran I'd interviewed who didn't suffer seasickness, but he was still anxious to get off the foul-smelling ship. The vessel stopped in Kyoto, Japan, for a short layover, a completely new experience for an eighteen-year-old kid from Newark who'd never left home.

The biggest place I'd ever seen was Manhattan. It was strange seeing the coast of a faraway place such as Japan. I have to say they were the good old days, the best of times, and the worst of times. I was anxious to get to the MLR to see what all the fuss was about. I wanted to see some action in the worst way. When I got there, I was in reserve, but I could hear the rumbling of artillery fire and machine gun fire every night.

Paul Marsa in his Marine Corps portrait.

Most of the time, the FNG (fucking new guys) were doing relay races while taking apart weapons: A Marine would run up and disassemble one part of a .30-caliber machine gun, and the next guy in line would do the same, with this sequence repeated until the weapon was fully apart and then reassembled. Paul felt that was extremely effective training, teaching the men to be quick and efficient under pressure, which they soon learned could save their lives in combat.

That day finally came. The reserves were called to the front of the MLR to relieve the battered and weary Marines who'd been fighting for weeks.

We went up by convoy in open-top troop trucks on dirt roads, with only a cow-light to point out the shoulder of the road. Once the trucks were close to the MLR, we began to receive mortar fire on our poor innocent convoy, which was very inaccurate. It was monsoon season, talk about miserable. Around-the-clock raining. It was miserable, a miserable time.

The weather on the way to the MLR proved just as hazardous to the Marines as the shelling from the Chinese. Along with the mortar and artillery barrages, trucks carrying the Marines were sliding off the muddy road, forcing them to stop short of their goal. There, the Marines were ordered to disembark, get organized, and begin marching up the hill in the pitch black dark and heavy rainfall. Their destination: Outpost Dagmar. With Paul having nothing but a poncho, backpack, and his M1, he and his slogging buddies arrived at their positions, only to feel the muddy sides of the dirt trench slowly engulf them while the battle-weary Marines they were relieving were familiarizing them to the situation. While scooping water out of the muck-and water-filled trenches, this is when Paul got his first experience with Chinese propaganda.

A female oriental voice came over a loudspeaker welcoming the 3rd Battalion, 5th Marines back online. Giving us due respect for our fighting ability, we were being complimented by the enemy for our past performance. It was kinda bizarre to me, and I didn't expect that at all.

To the best of his recollection, there was no exchange of fire that night, due to both sides being so miserable from the monsoon. Over the following days, periodically the storms would break, the sun would come out, and—as Paul described it— the Marines would take advantage of the sun beating down on the rocks to dry their socks and skivvies.

"Improvise in the field," my kids heard that their whole life, and my son Alan here, who is also a Marine, taught that to my grandkids. If you don't have something, you improvise in the field. The Corps taught me a lot and I'm grateful. The first time I had to improvise in the field, I was with a Marine named Everett Mason. I can't remember specifics anymore, but I know it was in the trenches with something that came about.

That "something" was a major battle when the Chinese mounted a heavy offensive across part of the MLR to test the Marine defenses on Outposts Hedy, Bunker

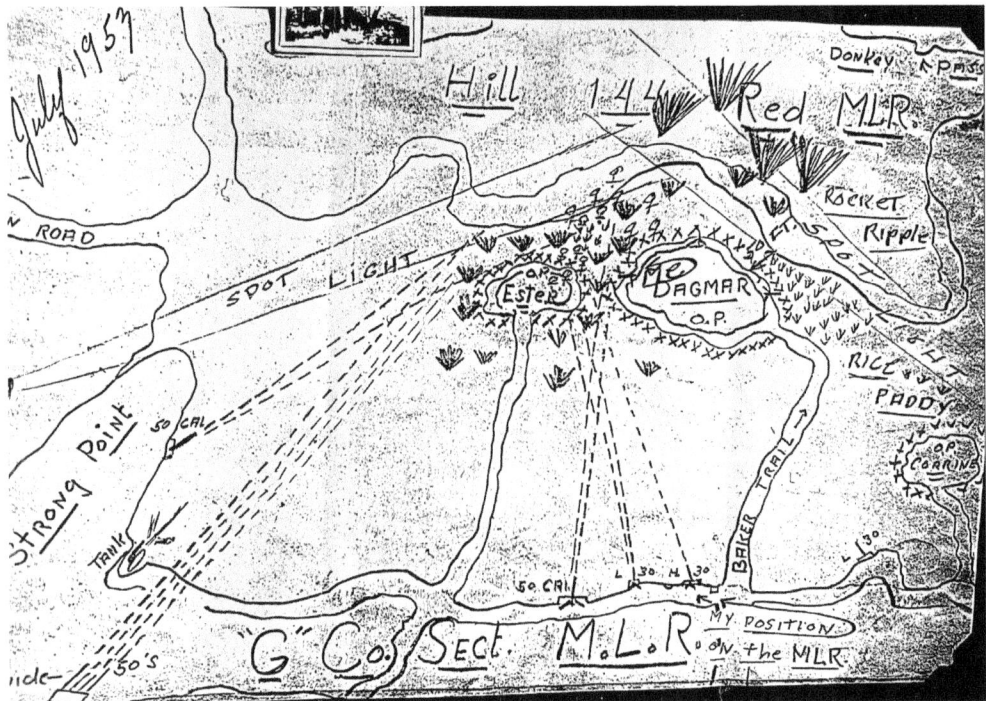

A map drawn by Paul Marsa, and provided by his son Paul, of his area of combat in Korea on outpost Dagmar, 1953.

Hill, Esther, and Dagmar. There are many online sources citing various figures of the number of Chinese infantries involved in that attack, but elements of two full divisions is what I'm confident putting to paper as the force which tried to break the back of the Marines. The fighting—some of the fiercest of the war—lasted four days, with the Reds unsuccessful at breaking through the lines, except for one outpost, Dagmar, where Paul took some shrapnel from an enemy hand grenade. At this point, Alan, Paul's son, asked his father to share how he got the medal. "Dad, were you on Dagmar when you got hit and received the Purple Heart?"

> *Being wounded, to me wasn't a big deal. It's not a big deal. But I got hit by shrapnel from an enemy hand grenade. After the fact, I was told I earned it (the Purple Heart), and we were all told to get into formation, and I was called out front. I thought right away, oh boy what did I do now. But they presented me the Purple Heart in the field, and I went right back to Dagmar.*

After receiving the Purple Heart, Paul had only a few days to relax and recuperate below the MLR, before being sent back to the line, to Dagmar. The next enemy attack, as Paul described, was "vicious" and "hard."

> *Esther was an outpost not far from us, and they were being overrun, and they were in deep peril. You know the fighting is close and hand-to-hand when you can hear .45 caliber pistols firing, and our commanding officer ordered a "Box Me In" (friendly artillery fired on your own position to help form a protective shield on*

and around the outpost), on Dagmar and Esther. I was manning a .30 caliber machine gun and had to fire across no-man's-land between UN and Chinese forces, towards the enemy that were overrunning Esther.

VT rounds (variable fused) were being fired by the 11th Marines, a heavy artillery outfit. These are timed to explode just above ground, thus inflicting wider ranges of damage. Paul and his fellow Marines dove into the trenches, foxholes, and bunkers, finding any cover they could. Paul described it as "Chinese being peppered and blown apart by the shrapnel raining down from above." But the Chinese kept coming. Once the artillery barrage lifted, Paul again fired his machine gun at the waves of Chinese, who now split their forces as they began attempted sieges on both Esther and Dagmar.

Paul Marsa geared up and ready for action with a Thompson submachine gun while on outpost Dagmar, Korea, 1953.

You had to be there to even comprehend it. We literally cut Chinese down and ripped them in half with our machine gun fire. Quad 50s were backed up on six-by trucks, and started opening up on the waves of Chinese, the number of tracers going through the air and zigzagging was absolutely surreal. They would open up with spotlights in five-second bursts of light to target the enemy.

Paul called this battle "Textbook Marine Corps": machine guns set up to catch the Chinese in a crossfire, backed by Quad-50s that fired 2,300 rounds a minute, creating a savage hail of bullets. His weapon overheated and the barrel had to be replaced more than once, quickly and efficiently. That earlier training had worked. The only illumination came from brief flashes of spotlights and flares, and thousands of tracers literally lighting up the night sky and the valley below the outposts. It was evident during this part of the interview, from the way Paul was relaying his experiences, that he was re-visualizing the horrors of that night on Dagmar.

There were moments in his telling of this battle when he would pause and close his eyes before talking again. I could easily see, by his demeanor and way he was speaking, that he needed a few moments to catch his breath before going on about this violent battle that only dedicated historians, and those who were there, know about. It was evident he held deep empathy for all involved, and that he only killed the enemy because it was war, and the truth was, if you don't kill them, they'll kill you.

I wondered if this old veteran could continue. But he did.

I don't know how long it took, but it seemed like forever. But I had to keep popping up out of my position and see over the embankment to make sure no Chinese were crawling up. Was very hard to see, very hard. The only light was the tracers and maybe a few flares, it almost seemed we were using everything we could out of our toolbox.

Paul related stories of other skirmishes, but due to his memory coming and going, he couldn't remember them all. One he did recall was while walking above the MLR hearing the whizzing of bullets, and suddenly a round striking right in front of him. He was targeted by an enemy sniper.

I was whistling along like an idiot, and I made the mistake very few Marines live to talk about. I think I was coming back from getting some chow when an enemy sniper started firing at me. I immediately dove down and found myself face first in the mud. Quite lucky during that experience, to say the least. Another time, I'm in a trench. I was nodding off and fell asleep. A Marine patrol was coming back in and when they hopped in the trench by me, a Marine landed on a dirt ledge and woke me up. I took my M1 with a bayonet and was inches away from cutting his throat. Just a few inches away from ending his life, and my life would have been ended too, for doing it. Not long after I grabbed either a Thompson or grease gun and I hopped out of the

Paul Marsa moments after receiving his Purple Heart for wounds received during combat on outpost Dagmar.

15. Paul Marsa, USMC: Box Me In

George Company, 3rd Battalion, 5th Marines, advancing under fire from Communist forces, 1953 (photograph by Paul Marsa).

trench and saw this Chinese soldier trying to get through the barbed wire. He paused and froze when he saw me, and I shot him. To this day I don't know why he was there by himself. He had a weapon, but I don't know what it was.

He described these experiences as "rather shaking," and wasn't certain if they occurred the same night. "With Parkinson's it's hard to remember, but I believed it to be."

Alan, trying to get a better picture of this encounter—as was I—asked, "Dad, why were you out of your trench?" Paul replied that he didn't know or remember, he just got out and that's when the encounter happened. As we rattled off questions to make sense and paint a better picture, Paul muttered, "I killed him."

I don't know why he was there or why I got up. Neither of us knew how to react at all. He must have been thirteen years old, and I was nineteen. We were both scared, but what am I supposed to do? So, I pulled the trigger on the machine gun.

I could tell that this wasn't easy for Paul; he sat there for a moment, rose, and then showed me photographs he'd taken in Korea. I'm sure it was to ease the mood, but these were never-before-seen pictures of G Company, 5th Marines in combat in Korea between late 1952 and 1953: pix of men advancing under fire on top of Outpost Dagmar, and even photos of bunkers being torn down, and trenches being filled when the cease fire went into effect. The photos sparked another story.

When the cease fire went into effect, what I think was 10 p.m. on July 27th, 1953, both sides shot off flares across the MLR, and it literally lit up all of Korea, at least as far as I could see. It was quite something, and you'd had to have been there to really picture it.

The interview concluded, and a week or so later I received a letter from Paul commending my work, along with a check for fifty dollars to help in my travels, which it did.

I regret to report that Paul passed away shortly after our June 11 meeting. Not long after, I was notified by Alan that his dad was on the waiting list to be interred at Arlington National Cemetery, which did occur on July 20, 2023. Alan later told me a story about telling his father that a nephew had taken his own life.

"Dad hardly ever talked about the bad stuff, only alluded to it occasionally. From the screaming nightmares, I knew it had to have been horrific. On the unfortunate occasion that I had to inform him of my cousin's suicide by handgun, he yelled at me to stop talking. They were very close, and he never raised his voice. He simply told me:

I've seen enough horrors in Korea, I don't want to hear anything else.

Paul's letter continued: "I realized my father was in some nasty stuff that he avoided talking about. He just couldn't go there, and only really touched on it when you interviewed him. That was the first time I heard him mention killing the Chinese regular at such close range. I could see his face clearly, that one obviously haunted him more than the hundreds he must have killed with the Browning machine gun."

When I began formalizing this chapter, I asked

Paul Marsa filling the trenches in after the ceasefire had been called, ending all hostilities in Korea.

Paul Marsa and Ryan Walkowski after their interview, posing with M1 Garand rifles.

Alan to help with any additional information, so what you just read is a collaborative effort to ensure that Paul's story is right. Alan and I have remained in contact via Facebook and social media and I'm glad, because he and his father showed this stranger the warmest hospitality and support.

Soon, I will visit Paul at the Arlington National Cemetery and pay my deepest respects to a good man, friend and Marine!

Chapter 16

Forrest Mullins, U.S. Army
Pork Chop Hill

Corporal, U.S. Army, Baker Company, 32nd Infantry Regiment, 7th Infantry Division. Interviewed April 19, 2022, Byrdstown, Tennessee. Born 1932. Died 2024.

> *I was looking, and a grenade came down. I saw it roll down. It was a potato masher. They called a masher; it had a handle. Anyway, it went off and hit me right in the eye, right there and there and there. Anyways, the first thing I thought of was my mother, I don't know why.*

Hill 255, named for its elevation—also known as Pork Chop Hill, saw some of the most vicious fighting of the Korean War. One of my interests in this well-chronicled conflict was how these hills got their names. This one was easy: From the air the terrain looked exactly like a pork chop. While it served no strategic or political value, both the Chinese and United Nations knew neither side would give it up, especially with peace talks happening just a few miles away. The leverage the Chinese believed they'd have if they held Pork Chop Hill, which they felt might influence the peace talks in their favor, was weak at best. The site was valueless, yet both the United Nations and the Chinese would send forces to Pork Chop Hill to fight and die.

I was able to interview two veterans who were involved in that devastating last battle, which took place July 6–11, 1953: Orville L. Dean of Falls City, Nebraska, and Forrest Mullins of Byrdstown Tennessee. A few weeks before my first major East Coast trip, Debbie Cross messaged me on Facebook, writing that her father, Corporal Forrest Mullins, was wounded on Pork Chop Hill. She wrote that she'd ask whether he'd be interested in meeting with me. After receiving word from Debbie that he was all for it, I called Forrest and was delighted to hear a most friendly voice with a very strong Southern accent, asking me about my mission, which I explained in detail. Forrest went on to briefly describe his first and only combat experience and his current medical condition. I told him about my mission, and he agreed to a meeting.

> *I was wounded by a potato masher, a hand grenade if you know what those look like, on July 7th, 1953, when I was on Pork Chop hill. I go to Nashville once a week for dialysis, but keep in touch and we'll figure it out.*

16. Forrest Mullins, U.S. Army: Pork Chop Hill

Forrest was the second to last stop on this trip, which was graciously funded by River Valley Express Trucking. My last two interviews were in northwestern Tennessee, and I was eager to see more of this beautiful state. To get to Forrest's house I had a pleasant drive through an ethereal apple and peach orchard and was warmly greeted at the front door by Debbie, who escorted me inside to meet her father. I set up my recording equipment, hooked the mic up to the old veteran's shirt, and Forrest took it from there.

Forrest Mullins in his U.S. Army portrait.

See, when I got over there, I had a buddy who was with me from over here. Course we went to Nashville, and from Nashville to South Carolina to what they called Tank Hill. But anyway, we were on a troop train all the way from South Carolina to California. We had our own car with a kitchen and everything. And this boy, John Cole, was with me when I got hurt in Korea. So many of us are dead and gone that I was with.

Familiar with Pork Chop Hill from previous interviews, I referenced the movie featuring Gregory Peck that Forrest said depicted the second battle, and that Forrest had fought in the last—his one and only combat experience. With tensions extremely high as peace talks were coming close to an agreement, both sides threw everything they had into Pork Chop Hill, making it one of the bloodiest combat ordeals of the war.

After arriving at the port of Pusan, Forrest was put on a troop train to Seoul, from which where he got his first look at the ravages of war.

We left there one evening and got in this train and it went all night. I remember going through Seoul, Korea, and off the train tracks we could see all the bridges blown out in the river. We passed by Seoul and went to the front where they sent us to our outfit—company, or whatever. This boy and I, they put us in trenches where we was gonna stay. And they was shooting at us. Bullets was flying over our heads, and I guess that's the way to welcome us.

Forrest's assignment was on the MLR (main line of resistance), within sight of Pork Chop Hill.

There was trenches all over those mountains you know, and every so often you would see a bunker. It had sandbags up on top, if certain things would hit it, you wouldn't get hurt. We slept in those on piles of como wire, which was used to for communications. But anyways, we had a little place in front of the bunker and every night someone had to watch for the enemy. We would stay two hours, and the next guy would go out and watch, and it worked out okay.

I asked Forrest if he was exposed to Chinese propaganda, which I'd heard was especially prevalent in and around Panmunjom, where the peace talks were being held—only a few miles from his position.

We heard them while I was up on the line—like Tokyo Rose. We had tanks sitting around the mountains there and they (the tanks) would fire on them every time they broadcasted. That's called harassing fire to let them know we was still there. They were on this mountain, and we were on this mountain, and there would be nobody's land, you know. They would send out patrols, and we had two boys in my outfit, and they would volunteer to go, and they would bring back some of them to prove they went over there. There would be six of us and sometimes we would go out in front of the line and lay and wait, and that's what you call a listening post.

"Scary" is how Forrest described being at a listening post, trying to stay dry from the rain, waiting … and waiting … and waiting.

You sit there, and some of the boys, well we had these ponchos, and I didn't smoke. But anyways, they would hide under their ponchos and smoke cigarettes. But it's scary. You lay out there and envy my buddies up there in the bunkers sleeping. We never did see or hear anything, and I went out a few times. One of the Black boys was out there one night with me for the first time. Anyways, frogs would start to holler, and he would say "What is that? What is that?" I guess he was scared, but I was too.

Forrest recalled being on the line for a month or two. Once a week, a chaplain would visit—not always on Sunday—to hold Mass. Forrest remembered the men gathering around wherever the Padre set up, some sitting on top of their bunkers, and all listening to the gospel: peaceful interludes, with the ungodly realities of war always just around the corner.

One night our lieutenant said, "Men, get out of your bunkers and get in your trenches, there's a battalion of chinks out there somewhere, and we don't know where or if they're gonna come through here or not." A battalion is about like a thousand men. Anyways, my hair stood straight up. They never did hit us, but one night the Turks and Ethiopians were attached to us, and they had a firefight down in the valley in front of us. You would see white clouds of smoke and I knew they was using white phosphorus. But we never got hit while online and I could see Old Baldy and, let's see, there was another, oh, T-Bone Hill. But you hear more about Pork Chop because it was a lot of men. My buddy stayed up there after I was wounded and said they stayed for about three to four days and almost all of them got wounded. Had I not got wounded when I did, I'd say I'd have been killed.

At the last battle for Pork Chop Hill, Forrest was in reserve below the MLR in what he referred to as a blocking—a reserve unit on standby should the embattled company on the line require reinforcements. About fifteen or twenty of his fellow soldiers were sitting in a tent the night before, talking about, among other things, what kinds of cars they'd buy when they got home. He recalled an uneasy feeling as they turned in for the night, and it taking forever for him to fall asleep. At daybreak, the alarm rang out and everyone was ordered to fall out and hop aboard trucks, which would be heading up the MLR towards Pork Chop, where they transferred to APCs (armored personnel carriers). Then came the drive up the hill to where their brothers were fighting off hordes of Chinese.

Well, our time came. Three, four, or five of us got in that APC. There were two men sitting in there, one was driving, and one was on the .50-caliber machine gun on top. It was kind of sitting sideways when we got in, and there was blood running into the corner. Anyway, we went up, the whole time the fella is wheeling around that .50-caliber machine gun shooting and they was shooting at us. But anyway, they backed it in, and it was a place that looked like a coal mine. They backed that thing up, and we ran out into a trench. There was a Chinese soldier there wanting us to help him, but our lieutenant threw a smoke grenade, and we went on up.

Forrest sat forward and began motioning with his hands and arms trying to describe how the trenches were arranged and explaining how they occupied the trenches in preparation for the coming attacks. At the time, the hill was held by A Company, 17th Regiment. The enemy, the PVA (People's Volunteer Army), attacked in full force, with the American and UN forces overwhelmingly outnumbered. Various sources and speculation point to about 6,800 Chinese storming Pork Chop between July 6 and July 11. Reports of hand-to-hand combat with the Chinese who were pouring into and over the trenches came from A Company. This was not the news Forrest and his buddies wanted to hear, especially during the heavy monsoon rains that fell during those first three days of the last battle. It was a furious and life-wasting time for all the combatants, both UN and Chinese, despite little reason for taking or protecting this godforsaken hill. But the orders for all were to fight or die. Reports from *Stars and Stripes* cited over 250,000 artillery and mortar rounds fired from both sides during this engagement, a staggering number of ordnances for just a few days. Accompanying the downpour of shells was intense Chinese small-arms and automatic rifle fire raining down on the GIs below.

I was up in the trench; it was full of men, and they were up over us. The Chinese were up over us, calling us "sons of bitches" in our own language. They put me with this boy from North Carolina and we went out towards you and then this way and squatted down. The lieutenant sent two or three boys up with a flame-thrower. Well, they came up by us and went around us going up there. Not far from us they lit that thing and burn them outta there. See, the enemy had a lot of those trenches taken over the night before we got up there. Now, they didn't know how to operate this thing, and flames came back towards us, so we got up and jumped back to a trench which was full of men. Well, I looked back up and heard something land in front of me. I was looking and a grenade came down. I saw it roll down. It was a potato masher. They called it a masher; it had a handle. Anyway, it went off and hit me right in the eye, right there and there and there. The one boy, and he was hurt, his cheeks were bleeding, but I don't think he was hurt too bad. I never did see him after that. First thing I thought it didn't really hurt at that time; I grabbed this eye to see and knew it was put out. Anyways, the first thing I thought of was my mother, I don't know why.

Forrest pointed to left arm, his left cheek, his right thigh, and just below his neck on his chest, and described where the shrapnel from the grenade had peppered his body, with one massive piece taking out his right eye. His lieutenant ordered a few GIs to "get that boy who has his eye hurt and get him below." Forrest was taken to an aid station down the hill, where his face was bandaged. He said he was glad they bandaged his eye so he could not see the other wounded men being carried in. On his way out of the aid station to be evacuated, he ran into his friend.

I passed my buddy going back down to that place to wait for that APC. Anyways I passed my buddy, and I told him, boy they put my eye out. And he said, "No they didn't, no they didn't." Course when he got home, he told me he knew it was out, but he wouldn't tell me. But anyways they loaded me in that APC and the Chinese were just hitting that thing. All you could hear was ka-pow, ka-pow, ka-pow, as they fired on it.

After being transferred to and treated at a nearby M.A.S.H. unit, he was shipped to a hospital in Tokyo, where he learned that a ceasefire was to be signed on July 27—twenty-one days after he was wounded, with all hostilities ending in Korea. The first thought for many veterans like Forrest who fought in the last days of the war was, it just didn't seem to make sense that their leaders would send them to fight and die for nothing. However, Forrest reassured himself like so many others:

It wasn't for nothing after seeing how South Korea flourished since.

Forrest would now begin his journey to recovery, and to home.

Anyway, I was in the hospital when I heard there was going to be an armistice signed on July twenty-seventh. I stayed there for about two weeks and got on a big four-motor plane there in Tokyo airport and they had some litter patients, but I was able to walk around. In Tokyo I was able to walk around some, and we had Ethiopian soldiers there, wounded, and they would wait on us and light cigarettes for you. We got out two hours over the ocean when a motor went out and they radioed back, and we went back to get on another.

From Tokyo, Forrest flew to Hawaii and spent two nights at the Tripler Army Hospital, where he told me with a smile that he particularly enjoyed seeing the women tending the wounded soldiers. He also had the pleasure of time in

Forrest Mullins presenting Ryan Walkowski with a pocketknife after his interview.

and around Honolulu, a tropical paradise for this country boy from the hills of Tennessee.

From the island of Oahu, Forrest flew to Travis Air Force Base in California, and then on to Fort Sam Houston, Texas, where optical technicians fashioned a glass eye.

Caught a train to Nashville, Tennessee, and then took a bus to Uphill, Tennessee, where my dad, mother, and wife met me there. I was back home, thank goodness.

Forrest was in Korea for only three months before he was wounded on Pork Chop Hill. The interview concluded with him mentioning that he knew Sergeant Alvin York, the famed World War I Medal of Honor recipient. Alvin York had captured 133 Germans during that "Great War." There was even an award-winning film starring Gary Cooper that featured York's exploits. York had lived just down the road, so Forrest knew him well, even attending the hero's funeral in 1964.

Further proof of the urgency of documenting Korean War veterans, a dying breed mostly in their nineties, was the sad news, while formatting this chapter, of Forrest suffering a stroke and opting to stop dialysis treatments. The next message from his daughter Debbie, a few days later, was that the old soldier had passed away. It was sorrowful knowing this gallant Tennessean and patriotic American would not be around to see this finished product, but I understood his decision to go out on his terms. As General MacArthur said in his famed farewell speech, "Old soldiers never die, they just fade away."

Forrest Mullins proudly wearing his Korean War veteran's hat.

Rest in peace, Forrest Mullins. You earned it.

CHAPTER 17

Frank English, USMC
No Racism in a Foxhole

Corporal, U.S. Marine Corps, How Company, 3rd Battalion, 1st Marine Regiment, 1st Marine Division. Interviewed August 21, 2023, Guilderland, New York. Born 1935.

Five Chinese soldiers came walking up, carrying litters, and I turned and said, "Hey Sarge, we got something going on here." Well, he went down to talk to them, and they expressed they wanted to retrieve their dead, which of course we allowed. One came walking up to me motioning with his hand for a cigarette. We sat there and talked for about twenty minutes.

I'd seen a post on a Facebook Korean War page from Juanita Aikens-English, seeking Korean War veterans who might have served with her husband Frank in H Company, 3rd Battalion, 1st Marines. She was looking for men who were at the battles for Boulder City or Hill 111 in July 1953.

I responded, stating that I knew Marines from other companies who'd fought in those campaigns, and added that I'd like to interview her husband. Juanita graciously invited me to visit whenever my travels took me to their neighborhood. Important to note is that the Korean War was the first hostility in which the American military was desegregated, thanks to President Harry Truman, who ordered this long-overdue change in 1948. It was important that I document what Frank was willing to share. I didn't know it would turn into such an amazingly emotional and insightful interview.

Frank was born in Jacksonville, Florida, May 17, 1935. When he was five, his family migrated to the primarily Black New York City community of Harlem, where he lived until he was seventeen. Like a few other veterans I've documented, Frank lied to get into the Military.

After my seventeenth birthday I enlisted in the Corps. Lied about my age. When the day came for me to ship out to boot camp, my grandmother asked me, "Where do you think you're going?" And I told her, "Well, I joined the Marine Corps." All she had to say was, "Okay, okay. Be safe."

Frank completed boot camp at Parris Island, South Carolina, in 1952, and was sent for advanced infantry training to Camp Pendleton, California, where he would become a Browning automatic rifleman. Next was advanced cold-weather training in northern California. In December 1952, Frank received orders deploying him to Korea. After almost two weeks on a troopship, he arrived two days after Christmas.

We left out of the Naval Station in San Francisco, and it wasn't just Marines, it was Army, Navy, Air Force. We ended up stopping at Yokohama, Japan, to drop off some Air Force guys. We had an overnight liberty; it was a thrill being seventeen years old and here I am in Japan. Up to that point, it was the furthest I've been since Florida as a kid. But anyway, the next day we continued to Korea. When I first got to Korea, I was put in the 1st Combat Service Group. We would keep the flow of ammunition and ordnance going to the Marines on the front line. It was about March 1953, and that's when I found out I was going to How Company, 3rd Battalion, 1st Marines. I was assigned to 2nd Platoon, 1st Squad, and I was in a fire team as a BAR man.

It had taken a full day on trucks to make it to Munsan-ni, where How Company was on the MLR, because every bridge had to be inspected due to guerrilla activity still plaguing the area. Not even provided with live ammunition, Frank and the replacements for How Company were in a convoy that stopped a few miles from the MLR, with everyone debarking to await further orders.

We weren't far from a battery of 155-howitzers, and we didn't know it at the time. We were about eight or nine trucks. And they had a firing mission, and we didn't know they were even by us. I had not heard a shot fired in anger yet, but when they cut loose, that's when it really settled in where I was.

Later, at a Regimental Command Post, Frank experienced his first incoming fire from the Chinese. This attack came when the Marines were sacked out in their tents.

That was the first night we got incoming. I was laying in my rack one night and heard BOOM! It was incoming. It was frightening as hell. Everyone got up and ran outside and dove in ditches and wherever you could find cover. The next morning, they put us in APCs—armored personnel carriers—and started to go up to How Company. The driver turned around and said, "Keep your heads down because we're coming up to 76 Alley." It was named 76 Alley and come to find out the Chinese overlooked the road with a 76-mm field gun. We were never fired on, and when we got to where we were going, that's when I found I was going to 2nd Platoon.

The first few nights on the line, replacements were not sent out on patrol. Called FNGs (fucking new guys), they had to first become familiar with the geography and modus operandi of their position—the trenches, areas of egress, where patrols would go out and reenter.

They placed us with somebody who had been there a while. I didn't go on patrols for almost a week. They let us get familiar with the area and terrain. I was out on a listening post one night with a guy, and that was my first introduction to Korea.

I asked, "Did you think, what the hell did I get myself into?" With a stern look, he said, "Hell yeah," and we shared a good laugh.

Training is one thing; you're shooting at targets, and they don't shoot back. There's no incoming. There's simulated explosions, and they shoot machines guns over your head. This is different, this is different, you know. It's very scary to say the least, it's kinda like, well I'm here and I can't go nowhere. But at the same time, I can't say this isn't what I signed up for, because I knew what I was getting myself into. But when you're there, it's a whole different experience.

Frank went on to describe his time in Korea as lucky, because by the time he got there, the line had been drawn, and it was more like trench warfare—a war of patrols and raids. The Marines go out and raid the Chinese, and the Chinese come out and raid the Marines. I knew right away he was describing what had since become the Outpost War—each outpost typically manned by a platoon of forty to fifty Marines and two Navy corpsmen. These small but well-equipped units were doing what Marines didn't do traditionally—playing defense. Often, overwhelming Chinese forces would make nightly attacks, with waves of hundreds and sometimes thousands of enemy soldiers, only to be repelled by the Marines.

It was kind of like hit and runs, but the big fights would come at us in mass at battles like Reno, Carson City, up in the Nevada complex, you know. East and West Berlin, there was a lot of outposts along the MLR, and I remember on one outpost there were only eighty-one of us and we got hit and overrun. So it was that kind of back and forth.

Asked how long they would typically stay on the line, Frank recalled anywhere between five and six weeks straight. For readers to get a true picture of what men in combat go through, this meant up to a month and a half with no shower or toilet facilities, wearing the same clothes and living off C-rations that were often dated back to 1942. It was living—no, more like existing—huddled in bunkers, unprotected trenches, and foxholes, with rain, snow, mud, and sleet. Each night was spent wondering if you're going to be hit by the enemy, and if you'll live to see the next sunrise.

We had bunkers we could go in that had pot-belly stoves, so you could heat up what little water you could spare in your steel pot and wash at least the vital areas. Under your arms, between your legs, around your ears and your head. Otherwise, you didn't shower at all until you got below the MLR to the portable shower units.

After coming off the line, Frank recalled being put in reserve for a few weeks, knowing not only that he'd be sent back, but also when. He laughed while explaining that a steak-and-eggs meal meant you were going right back above the MLR. Touching on C-rations, which have gotten missed reviews, Frank said they weren't that bad. You just had to know which to choose. Franks and beans you could eat almost daily if you had to, so he didn't think that was bad. The only C-ration he didn't like were the beef patties.

The macaroni and cheese were good, the spaghetti and meat balls were good, but the beef patties were terrible. Spam and hash were good. But you know, you had to know what to look for. Sometimes you could scrounge a cookie or something. It was

Frank English (left) with a fellow Marine who is wearing Frank's glasses as a joke. This is a great example of "the good times" during war.

only in reserve you would get a decent hot meal. But when you were on the line, you made the best of it. You're not going to starve, and guys would get packages from home and share them. It wasn't like the big wars in the Pacific where they would run out of food. We had plenty of food all the time.

Asking Frank to describe the Chinese mass attacks, he related the same accounts as most every other Korean combat veteran.

They did mass attacks at night, twelve hundred to two thousand guys, bugles and banging on pots and pans, screaming and hollering. Another funny thing they did, if you wanna put it that way, is they would charge under their own artillery. We would be hunkered down taking cover while they shelled us, and they would try to make it through their own barrage. When they would lift the barrage and we would get into our positions, they would be right on top of us already.

Frank explained that on clear nights you could see them forming further down the hill. Then, flares and bugles would signal the attack—a huge mass of screaming soldiers streaming toward the Marine position, even blasting these sounds over their loudspeakers in attempts to instill fear among the Marines.

17. Frank English, USMC: No Racism in a Foxhole

Frank English (sitting, far left), eating C rations with fellow Marines at minus twenty degrees in the vicinity of the Berlin Complex.

It was a scary sight to see. You could look down the hill and see them, and someone would call in mortars and artillery. Another person would yell and scream out, "Here they come!" Our best was to keep them out of the trenches if we could, you know. And they came in mass, depending on how they felt. When they hit us on Hill 111 it was about thirty-five hundred Chinese that hit our company.

Frank's major encounter was at Boulder City. Not that he didn't serve and fight in other embattled locations on the MLR, but his most intense engagements occurred at the Boulder City complex. The only way the Chinese could beat the Marines was with sheer numbers, and their most effective tactic was sending in swarms of troops. A safe assessment would be that at any given outpost, the Marines would be outnumbered five to one, if not by more. This brought up the question, "How many Marines were typically on the line?"

In the Marine Corps, there's typically three squads of thirteen men each, making up a platoon, and three platoons making up a company. So, George Company would be on Hill 119 and How Company—my company—would be on the Boulder City Complex. Supporting those platoons you got a 60mm mortar section and a machine gun section. So our companies, give or take, would have roughly a hundred Marines and they would hit us with anywhere from twelve hundred to three thousand men a night.

He detailed that Communist firepower was on-point and effective, and that the Chinese would come in faster than the Marines could kill them, often making it into the trenches. Almost every Korean War online veteran I've met and documented has been in hand-to-hand combat. We're talking up close and personal. When the Chinese would break the lines, the Marines used shovels and K-Bar knives. Some also carried a sidearm. Hand-to-hand is hard to explain; in the simplest of terms, it's one on one, you or him. Add in that many of the Chinese were younger than Frank, who was only seventeen. It was in Korea that he turned eighteen.

They would get in the trenches with us and right away you buddy up, you never want to fight by yourself. You want to be near somebody. We would buddy up and there was always someone to take charge, and we always managed to get by. The funny thing with me was I had a BAR, so I didn't have a bayonet. I managed to wrangle a .45 sidearm, which I wasn't supposed to have, but who is gonna take it away from me? But anytime we got overrun, I was with someone, so I always had a way to defend myself.

Frank backed up and explained that he was assigned the BAR in basic training, when every fourth Marine in a lineup would be chosen to carry the twenty-two-pound automatic rifle. The drill instructor would walk down the line of troops and say, "M1, M1, M1, BAR." For every fire team, at least back then, there would be three riflemen and a BAR man. Frank watched down the line, anxiously counting, and figured he won't have to carry that heavy weapon. He was wrong; he'd miscounted.

So, I'm sitting there counting how many guys there are to me and thought, well, looks like I won't have to carry this heavy thing. I counted wrong, but he pointed right at me and said, "BAR." All I would have had to do was switch places with the guy next to me, but I didn't. But that's how they did things back then, and that's how I got the BAR.

He went on to further explain that, unlike the M1 rifle, which automatically ejected spent clips, he had to manually reload, plus carry a basic load of ten twenty-round magazines. In a firefight, his two hundred rounds of ammo, plus the extra rounds his assistant carried, were usually spent rather quickly. Even though I'm almost sixty years younger than Frank, I know the firepower of a BAR and the different weapons used in Korea. As an avid gun enthusiast, I told Frank that I'd been to a few machine gun shoots where I got to fire the BAR, a Thompson submachine gun, grease gun, and of course the famous M1 Garand, of which I own several.

In our fireteam bunker, we had enough ammunition—we used the same ammunition as the M1s, black tip, armor-piercing .30 caliber. But that's how I wound up with that weapon, it's a lot of firepower you're carrying with that BAR.

Frank soberly confessed to living with survivor's guilt: thirteen months in Korea without a scratch, except for a minor hit by a ricochet. This was a common theme throughout my journey; it was so sorrowful to see tears rolling down combat veterans' cheeks while they were telling deeply emotional stories that were burned into their seventeen- to twenty-one-year-old minds, horrifying happenings thousands of miles from home, fighting alongside young men they'd just met who quickly became their brothers.

Ya know, I look back and do feel bad about that, I went through all that and never got a scratch outside the regular bumps, bruises, and barbed wire. You dive into a hole during incoming, or you get cut doing this or that. There was a guy in my company, and I honor him every year. I didn't know him personally, but he was killed two days before the cease fire. And I remember him because he was laying across the trench tangled in the barb wire, and we had to go back and forth by him all day long before he was retrieved. In 1993 or 1994 when they dedicated the Korean War Memorial in Washington, they gave printouts of men who died there. His name was Ramone Costello, and he was killed in action July 25, 1953, just two days before the cease fire. I said to my wife, "You know, I went through all that, the incoming, the patrols, the raids, and the mass Chinese attacks."

I asked Frank about his patrols.

Most were designed to probe the area and make contact with the enemy, just to harass and let them know that we're still here. Also, to set up ambushes to capture Chinese for intelligence purposes. Sometimes the ambushes backfired, resulting in fierce dark-of-night firefights. The biggest patrol I was on was a twelve-man patrol. I used to always make a joke and say, "Why we going out looking for them? We know they're out there." And Sarge would say, "Shut up, English!" And he tells me we're going looking for Chinese and I'd tell him, well we know where they're at. They're right over there, and I would point. We would go lay out in the rice paddies and just look around and harass them like they harassed us.

On these patrols that had become nightly routines, Frank's mind often imagined things that weren't real. Like, in the dark, everything was a Chinese soldier.

The mind is the first thing to play against you when you're expecting something to happen. I don't know if any other combat veterans said this before, but it seems like when you're on patrol and you're walking along, you want something to happen. You want something to focus your mind on. Are they out here? Do they see us coming? Do they hear us? You're out there sloshing around in the snow with your Mickey Mouse boots and parka on, clanging around. It's not exactly stealth. So, you wonder … do they see us, what are they waiting for?

Frank went on to mention certain times his mind raced fast and furious, such as on the listening outposts in front of the line. Or when it was only him and a few other Marines sitting and waiting and listening to absolutely nothing.

I've seen elephants, man, I seen giraffes. I would nudge the guy next to me and say, "Is something moving out there? I think there's something out there." You know, you look long enough, and a bush becomes an entire platoon of Chinese. When you're really unsure, you call back for the 105's to send a flare up and you look down as it goes off in the sky and there's nothing there. So, your mind can play tricks on you.

Once when he positive he'd seen movement, a fire team went out to make contact, but returned empty-handed when they found nothing but Frank's imagination.

There was one incident that, uh, when you went on your patrols the barbed wire crossed, and we called that the gate. When we went on patrols, we never came back the same way, even though we had the password. Well, one night we were on fifty percent alert after getting hit a few hours before. I was with this guy, and I can't think of his name now, but he said, "English, there is something out there moving." I could see a body, but I thought he was dead. I told him, no man, he ain't moving. He was sure of it, so I asked what do you wanna do? So, we called in for a flare. We put our heads down and after it went off, we looked up to see him halfway under the barbed wire fence. So, we opened him up and a fire team was sent out and they found a satchel charge on him. He was probably going for one of the machine gun bunkers.

No doubt the infiltrator was crawling toward a machine gun bunker, to eliminate the crossfire cover the marines had set up to protect Hill 111. This is the one time Frank recalled being thankful they reacted to what they first thought was their minds playing tricks. When I asked Frank his opinion of the enemy, he gave me the same answer I received from every veteran featured in this book.

Outside the mass attacks and disregard for their own life, they were good soldiers, man. And I'm sure they listened to their officers just like we did to ours. The mass attacks were just a waste of life, but they did them every night. They would come in three or four waves screaming, "Marine you die! Marine, you die!" Any that turned around would be killed by their own officers. I never witnessed it, but I heard that enough.

In detail, Frank described the human wave tactics used against the Marines in his sector of the MLR. In the first wave, the Chinese appeared to be paired up, with one soldier armed with a weapon that the other would recover when the owner was taken out. The second wave seemed to have had no weapons at all, retrieving whatever they could pick up from dead or wounded comrades. The third wave was usually armed only with hand grenades.

They would have loudspeakers set up across the valley and first they would begin with the bugle marching music. Then they would bang on pots and pans and begin screaming as they came across the valley. Then they would pop flares, and you see the mass attack waves and to me it looked like each wave had a purpose, you know.

Some of the guys would just have satchel charges, some would just have hand grenades, anyone with a rifle would be followed by someone who didn't have one. And they just keep coming, keep coming, and then after it was all over, we would let them come get their wounded and dead. But sometimes they did leave them.

I could tell from the look in Frank's eyes, this kind of assault had to be a terrifying battlefield nightmare. I dared to ask, "What were your exact thoughts and feelings?"

It's eerie, man, especially the first time I heard it. It was like, what the hell is that? It's demonic, it doesn't belong here. You know there's going to be shooting, but you think what in the hell is that here for? All the screaming and yelling with the noises. Ironically, I never heard of any of this in training, and next thing you know here you are and here they come, and you got flares flying up and machine gun fire with 105 and 155 artillery coming in. You'd see them coming en masse, and you'd engage right away and start knocking 'em down.

From Frank's expression, it seemed to be the right time to change the subject. I asked what life was like below the line. He said they'd get some hot meals, showers, a change of clothes, and beer that was only distributed while in reserve. However, Frank was not much of a drinker at the time and would often trade his beer ration—usually Schlitz or Pabst, which he described as watered down when he did go for a sip.

I think it was privates, private first class, and corporals, we would get three cases of beer. Sergeants and up got, I forgot how many, but then we started getting Japanese beer. But Sigmund Rhee, the South Korean president at the time, had a three-four-dollar tax on it because the Koreans didn't like the Japanese. But when it came to beer rations, guys would run around to the others that didn't drink and buy their beer off them. I didn't drink too much at the time. A guy came around and would say, "Hey, English, you getting your beer ration?" and I'd tell him, yeah. And I'd get three bucks or so for each case of beer off the other guys.

The money, in military scrip, Frank would turn in to keep it on the books, to be used later on R&R in Japan. Our conversation turned back to the attacks, which Frank reiterated was something he just couldn't get used to, especially since most of the combat was during the night.

If anyone ever told you they got used to it, I don't believe the man, 'cause I never did. The pots and pans with the screaming, I never got used to it. It scared the hell outta me, man. It was every time they attacked, every time. You know it's coming, but it's scary, and it's like you're giving away that you're coming. They would play music on loudspeakers in the valley and then hit us with propaganda.

The Chinese continuously broadcasted propaganda to UN forces, with the main message "Why are you here fighting a war that doesn't matter to you?," often adding that loved ones at home miss the men and they should drop their weapons and return home. One usual theme specifically aimed at Black Marines was the race issue: "Why are you fighting for a country that makes you a second-class citizen when you return home?" I'd had never heard this until this interview, and asked Frank, "How did that make you feel? Because at the time they were right."

> They would play some slow romantic song and ask, "Don't you want to be with your loved one?" And they would even get on the racial tier. They would say, "And those United Nations soldiers who are Black, you're just going to go home and ride on the back of the bus and drink separate," and things like that. But to me that didn't bother me one single bit because they weren't telling me nothing I didn't already know. I had too much else on my mind to care and honestly it was the truth, I already know it.

"They weren't telling me nothing I didn't already know" was Frank's very honest statement. He knew he faced bigotry issues at home, but that didn't matter in Korea, where he was a Marine serving with other Marines from all over the country, including the South. I asked, "Did you experience racism in Korea?"

> There's no racism in a foxhole, no racism in a foxhole. I bunkered with Southern boys and even went on R&R in Japan with Southerners, and we had a great time. One time I was washing up in the trenches with my steel pot and when I was about to toss the water a Southern boy told me, "Don't throw that water away. I need to clean up too." He used the same water as me and it was dirty, but that didn't matter. There was never any racism in Korea that I saw, no flying of the Confederate flag on top of a bunker or APC. My Vietnam buddies later told me it was quite out and out in Vietnam with the flying of flags and such. But I never seen that in Korea.

On July 23, the Chinese Communists mounted full-strength offensives across the entire Jamestown line, hitting the 1st Marine Division especially hard attempting to gain last-minute victories before the armistice (ceasefire) would go into effect at 10 a.m. on July 27. The Boulder City Complex, as well as all the other outposts along the line, saw vicious fighting that rivaled the historic battles of both World War I and World War II. Once again, Frank and his fellow Marines faced waves of Chinese that just kept coming and coming. Frank, like the many other Korean combatants I've interviewed, told me the same thing, "We'd cut Chinese down like grass." The fighting was so fierce that the Chinese would overwhelm most of the outposts, engaging the defending marines in vicious hand-to-hand combat. I've recorded many similar stories, always getting goosebumps as my interviewees described the way the Chinese kept coming through the shower of machine gun fire and artillery air bursts. Frank relayed one story about this that had tears welling up in his eyes, but bravely held back. After a moment of silence, this account:

> I really felt like I was going to die, there was no way I was going to survive this. They hit George Company and the night of the twenty-fifth they hit us. They weren't getting anywhere with George Company because they put up a good fight. Our saving grace was we were getting artillery fire from the New Zealanders, and we had some British tanks up by us too. I'd never seen so much incoming and outgoing; it was like

you could walk on the stuff, man. They really started coming and we managed to keep them out of the trenches for a while, we managed to keep 'em out of the trenches. But then a few got in with us. And we were able to dispatch them, and we were able to plug up that area, but they just kept coming.

During this part of the interview, Frank paused to catch his breath. I never expect a combat veteran to tell me things they'd prefer to keep private, but Frank was okay with being open, once he pulled himself together.

The enemy did exactly what Frank described: They just kept pouring into the trenches. Dispatching Chinese at point blank range with his .45 caliber 1911 pistol, Frank thought the worst was over, but the Chinese never stopped. Though this was all happening at night, there was no darkness. With all the tracers, flares, incoming, outgoing, and Willy Pete grenades, it was like daylight. And then there was the deafening noise, of machine guns and rifle fire and explosions, mixed with the screams and crying from people being hit. The scariest thing for Frank—and every Marine—is that the Chinese never stopped or faltered. They'd run through the hail of bullets and shell fragments, overwhelming the Marines with sheer numbers. Even through all this chaos, the Marines never gave up … holding their ground, even if it was by a thread.

Frank English during his interview with Ryan Walkowski.

Item company came up and helped us, I think it was Item Company. The Chinese finally withdrew on the evening of the twenty-sixth and then they shelled the hell out of us. The next day on the twenty-seventh we heard they were signing the ceasefire at ten a.m. but wouldn't go into effect until ten that night I think it was. They sent out a few daytime patrols, but I wasn't on any of them, and the ceasefire was on a Monday. I'll never forget it. Once the patrols came back in, we started getting shelled again and I can't remember how long it lasted. Word got around to us they were just trying to shoot off their ordnance and the 11th Marines did the same.

The ceasefire went into effect precisely at 10:00 p.m., Monday, July 27, 1953, ending all hostilities that had been plaguing both sides since June 25, 1950. At this historic moment the troops heard a bugle call and watched the Chinese withdraw, but in a way that contradicted their fierce fighting spirit. As the enemy was checking out, over their loudspeakers down in the valley—once used to torment the Americans, came a female voice now congratulating the Marines. Frank and How Company, and nearby units, were being complimented for their fighting spirit and given due respect. It all seemed so bizarre, to go from killing each other in any way possible, to no longer fighting and offering praise. All within just a few minutes.

Everything stopped. At ten o'clock it was like that was it, everything stopped, man. Both sides started shooting flares, star clusters, and star shells. Red, blue, green, and different colors lit up the entire MLR as far as you could see. It was during all that, that the Chinese again began broadcasting over loudspeakers congratulating the United Nations and the 1st Marine Division.

Frank English camped at Panmunjom, North Korea, after the ceasefire in July 1953.

The following morning, both sides were given seventy-two hours to break down the bunkers, fill the trenches, and pull back a mile and a half. As stated in the chapter featuring Paul Marsa, this would create the demilitarized zone as we know it today.

We were tearing down bunkers when a buddy said, "English look at this." Here came about five Chinese soldiers carrying litters. I turned and told the Sarge we got something going on here. Well, he went down to talk to them, and they expressed they wanted to retrieve their dead, which, of course, we allowed. One came walking up to me motioning with his hand for a cigarette. The guy spoke damn good English. We had a conversation for about ten or fifteen minutes. We talked about our families and being able to go home, and I remember him telling me, "Now I get to go home." They didn't have no rotation like we did, they were there from start to finish. I said to myself that this is weird, this is weird man, 'cause just twenty-four hours ago he would have killed me, or I would have killed him. It was weird, I'll never forget it, man.

Completing his tour of duty in Korea in 1954, Frank returned home.

Talking with Frank was extremely casual and laid back; he almost made me feel like I'd known him my entire life. Before I left this gallant Marine, he shared pictures he'd taken in Korea, as well as showing me a full two-page spread from *Life Magazine* of Marines coming off the Boulder City Complex, and there was Frank—right smack dab in the middle of the photo toting his BAR. We sat and continued chatting, with Frank admitting to a struggle with alcohol after the war that lasted for years, his way of coping with his nightmare. He talked about his career as a firefighter, from which he voluntarily retired when he felt, because of his age, "no longer capable of doing the job."

Frank English and Ryan Walkowski after Frank's interview and signing Ryan's Korean War veteran's flag.

Frank and his wife treated me like I was their neighbor, even generously donating a few dollars to help keep alive my mission of Remembering Korea, the Forgotten War. After seeing pictures of his children, all of whom are members of our nation's military services, we shook hands, and I was down the road for my next adventure.

You know Ryan, I told you things I never told anyone before, even my wife and children. Especially about the struggles with alcohol. The Marine Corps changed me for the better and looking back, I have no regrets. My wife and I thank you for your efforts for the Korean veterans.

CHAPTER 18

John Breske, USMC
The Hall of Famer

Private First Class, U.S. Marine Corps, Easy Company, 2nd Battalion, 1st Marine Regiment Reinforced, 1st Marine Division. Interviewed March 14, 2022, Elderon, Wisconsin. Born 1931.

The captain, I said to him to give me about three guys, and we'll take a stretcher, and we'll go out there just about dusk. So, we cut a hole through the barb wire, concertina wire. And uh, we, I'd say it was damn near dusk. When I got to the hole where that guy was set up, it was hard to tell but he was set up for us. He was a Korean who must have figured we could see him, so anyway I shot him. We looked around a little bit and got into it again and got out of there. Never did find that guy.

The toughest part of my two-year journey documenting Korean War veterans was choosing which interviews to be featured in this book. I hated the thought of not including everyone I interviewed. Regrettable as the task was, the culling had to be done. Then there was selecting the interview that'd be the closing chapter. This, as you'll see, was a no-brainer.

It was U.S. Marine John Breske, from the small town of Elderon, Wisconsin, just fifteen minutes from where I live. Elderon is like a second hometown for me, with one of my best friends living there, and the great taverns where we'd raise hell, most notably Mark's Bar.

When I learned from my friend Kyle Wilkowski that there was a local who'd fought in Korea, I knew I had to track him down and hoped he'd share his story. I recognized the last name, because John's brother was Wisconsin Senator Roger Breske. I also knew that the Breskes played baseball for years against my Grandpa Resch's BABA team on all the diamonds in the area.

I was on a job in Arkansas—as an electrician—and from there, I punched in Breske's number. John answered and said he was willing to talk about his time in Korea. I'd be home the next week, so we agreed to meet.

I know next week I got an appointment Tuesday at the VA, but just give me a call.

To this day, I still get nervous pulling into a veteran's driveway—I'm asking these old-timers to recall some unpleasant memories, but once I'm set up it becomes second nature. That's how it was with John. We talked about his baseball days, and I mentioned that my grandpa was Jerome "Jiggs" Resch. John knew right away who he was and told a few stories about their ballplaying days.

We set up at John's kitchen table, where he started by talking about going down from Marathon County to Milwaukee with about forty other draftees. At the induction center, almost all the young men were assigned to the Marine Corps, due to the high casualties the 1st Marine Division had suffered in the early days of the Korean War.

A man came out and pointed out who went where, and that's how I got into the Marines. Next thing you know I'm in San Diego for basic training. The first week or so was a little tough, but once you get with it, it's no problem. None of the stuff bothered me. As far as the training and whatever they made us do, I handled it. No problem.

At the time, even when basic was close to being completed, John had no clue about being shipped to Korea. With all the scuttlebutt going around about things heating up along the MLR (main line of resistance), the recruits made fairly good guesses about their next duty station. Word was out that one of every seventeen or eighteen Marines would be sent to the front.

I had a good idea that I'd be in infantry. I mean, when I got to Korea, I just knew I was going to the front. There was very good chance of it. The rest are put into reserves or whatever.

Like many of the placements replenishing the 1st Marine Division, John came through Inchon, where he boarded a train for a fifty-mile trip, and then was trucked directly to the MLR. He recalled the devastation he saw along the way: He couldn't help but notice the rivers, streams, and even the harbor, being the dirtiest he'd ever seen.

Going from the beautiful blue waters off San Diego to the muddy filth-ridden waters of Korea was just the beginning of grim sights and grimmer experiences. When assigned to their new units, grizzled, battle-experienced Marines who'd been in country would bring the rookies up to speed.

They gave us about ten days or so of orientation and got us familiar with the area and that's when they placed us into our units. I was assigned to Easy Company and that's where I stayed the whole time. I'd say I spent eighty percent of my time in Korea on the front lines in combat.

John described Korea just as the other veterans I interviewed did: bombed out with the terrain in absolute ruin. There was little to no vegetation on the bombed-out front lines, with refugees everywhere begging for food.

Towards the end of the war, there was Boulder City, ASCOM City, the Vegas cities, Bunker Hill, there were a lot of casualties there. Everybody knew where Bunker Hill was. It wasn't much of a hill, but there were a lot of casualties. A lot of people got banged up or killed on that hill. I was on just about all of them. We moved around, never were in the same place. You'd stay in the area thirty days, that was probably tops in the area, and we'd go to the next hill or outpost.

In each of these historic battles, John experienced fierce fighting against seasoned Chinese regulars fanatically dedicated to annihilating the 1st Marine Division. John was on constant night patrols, probing no man's land, hoping to make contact with the Chinese and gather information on enemy strengths and positions. They were always looking for anything that would help the Marines on the frontline strengthen their defenses for when the Reds would strike.

We did a lot of patrols. If you'd get to an outpost then you'd patrol probably into no-man's-land, probably a mile, a mile and a half. A squad of Marines would sneak around to see if you could find out something. We did a lot of that. Otherwise, we would be improving our positions, Ah, you know, digging in a little better. Making it a little more comfortable for everybody, you know. Over there, it was pretty much the same routine.

Interviewee John Breske posing with his M1 rifle before shipping off to Korea, Camp Pendleton, 1952.

I was amazed at how candid he was, and how sharp his mind and memory were, able to recall many details. Stating that he accepted each situation for what it was—war—he went on to confess that although he had killed people, he had no regrets because it's you or them. John also admitted that he did feel bad and that no one should have to take another person's life, but it's just the way it was. And that's why he's approaching his ninety-third year. Much as in Chapter 1, featuring Stewart Sizemore, John said, "It's kill or be killed."

With constant personnel changes—men wounded in action or rotating home—John mentioned that about only four or five of the same Marines survived during his entire time with the platoon. I could see in John's eyes that even at ninety-two years of age, he was reliving these experiences like they happened yesterday.

> *Well, you took a few casualties every day like, guys getting hit with shrapnel and some of that. A lot of patrols you'd go on we'd never fire a shot or anything; it was quiet, real quiet, but, ah, then you'd have where you got a lot of casualties, probably fifty percent of the platoon. Sometimes the squad that went out on patrol, something would happen to somebody. I had a couple of good friends that were MIAs that were just missing. You don't know what happened, so much going on and all of a sudden this guy wasn't there any more. You always brought back your dead or whatever, but it doesn't always happen. It's not that you don't try, but, ah, it's just sometimes it just doesn't work. I tried to follow up on some of the guys that were MIAs and never did really find out what happened.*

This old veteran remembered going back time and time again, as part of a Marine fire team, to locate the dead or missing. They weren't always lucky. Often, missing Marines had become prisoners of war, a grueling fate that Charles Ross (Chapter 2) endured for thirty-four months. During this phase of the war, there were mostly hit-and-run style ambushes that took place at night, making those experiences that much more eerie and terrifying.

During one of these many after-sunset patrols, John earned our nation's third highest honor—the Silver Star. Here's the story.

Typically, on a mission, there'd be a point-man leading the team, scouting for any sort of ambush. The job of the Marines at the tail end—where John was positioned—was to protect against sneak attacks. Should there be contact, the rear guard's mission was to provide covering fire so the rest of the unit could fall back with any wounded. Front and rear: the most critical and dangerous positions, especially on nighttime missions.

John explained that sometimes they had to watch for choppers coming in to pick them up, since helicopters were now fully incorporated into combat, making extraction a lot easier when things got hot and heavy. On the night of February 10, 1953, John was holding down the rear, when the ambush that the team was attempting to set up was compromised by a Chinese patrol that had been lying in wait. This night, this time, the Americans were outnumbered by a superior Chinese force that inflicted heavy casualties. During all the craziness, chaos, and confusion of a vicious firefight, John administered first aid to the wounded, then rushed forward, establishing a firing position to ensure that his teammates could fully withdraw with the injured. Falling back continuously and reestablishing better firing positions, John continued to cover his fellow Marines with accurate and damaging protective fire, dispatching Chinese with single shots. John did this until they were all safely out of harm's way.

How long was this entire ordeal? John said that in the heat of combat you don't keep track of time, but that it felt like quite a while. The exact details surrounding the experience were a blur due to the rush of adrenaline, the urge to survive and keep his buddies alive. Upon reaching the MLR, they realized they were missing one Marine, so John volunteered to go back out at dusk with a small fire team and a stretcher to look for the missing man.

> *We pulled back probably a couple hundred yards, then got ourselves organized and went back again. And like I said, we didn't find our people there. They were taken prisoner, I'm sure. The captain, I said to him to give me about three guys, and we'll take a stretcher, and we'll go out there just about dusk. So, we cut a hole through the barb wire, concertina wire. And uh, we, I'd say it was damn near dusk. When I got to the hole where that guy was set up, it was hard to tell but he was set up for us. He was a Korean who must have figured we could see him, so anyway I shot him. We looked around a little bit and got into it again and got out of there. Never did find that guy.*

It was this highly professional and selfless act that led to John receiving the Silver Star for Valor.

The interview turned to a lighter note when John explained that while on the front line or manning outposts, the guys often received what he described as "special care packages" from home that contained bottles of forbidden liquor sealed in lead containers or boxes. The Marines would pop the cork and make the best out of living in grimy trenches and dusty bunkers at those desolate battle outposts. After getting a nice buzz, John and his buddies would toss the empty bottles out of their trenches and foxholes, and the bottles were often found by their superiors, but no actions were taken. Sometimes morale, in those inhumane circumstances and conditions, was more important than discipline.

It was during this moment that John shared his praise for every Marine's saving grace, the Navy corpsmen.

> *You could have a whole company going on patrol, but most of the time we went with probably ten, twelve guys and usually you always had a corpsman with you. You had one corpsman per platoon. So that'd be like three firing squads, that'd be one, two, three, four, five, six, seven, eight, nine, like ah, nine or ten squads and you would have one corpsman, and he was assigned that. So, it was pretty good, we were damn glad to have them. They saved a lot of Marines, including me.*

In many of my previous interviews, veterans mentioned they'd often switch weapons. John confirmed this. He would change from the trusted M1 Garand to a lighter weight M2 carbine, or rapid-fire weapons like the Thompson submachine gun and BAR (Browning automatic rifle), and even shotguns. Browning shotguns were weapons extremely familiar to John, a grouse and pheasant hunter since he was a kid. When given the option of being armed with a Browning shotgun, John—the outdoorsman—was right at home.

> *That gun was very much a part of me. I didn't mind at all carrying that, especially at night, with the buckshot that was given to us because of the spread of the shot. You could rely on it and ah, you know, you got that spread, what, it was about nine*

pellets per shell. So, when you shot that into the dark, it was good fire power. When the chinks would charge us in waves, they were easy targets for me. Everyone thinks Chinese people are little and that's not true because we were up against Chinese Marines, and they were all six foot two to six foot five. You could fire off five shots in a hell of a hurry with that shotgun and that came in handy.

John added that he preferred the M2 carbine over the M1 Garand, only because it was lighter, explaining that toting the heavier M1 tended to make one lax and not on guard. I've received mixed reviews on the M2 carbine, often hearing it would jam and foul up, but John never experienced these malfunctions. The advantages with the M2, as John described, were its high rate of fire and its bantam weight, allowing him to stay on his toes. However, he did say the knock-down power and accuracy of the M1 Garand were nice, but not for close-in combat, especially hand-to-hand, which John said he'd experienced too many times. The conversation again led back to going on patrols when I asked, "How long did the patrols last?"

Sometimes you'd start right after dark and wouldn't come back till it was daylight again. But then most of them were three-to-four-hour deals. All depends how cold it was. If it was really cold, you could only set one up for probably a few hours at the most before moving to another spot. Then you had to come out of that, because you couldn't last that long. We were well camouflaged, you know, we had white clothes in wintertime.

Once it was daylight, John and his squad, after spending twelve to thirteen hours in no-man's-land, would sneak back to their line, go through a debriefing, find chow, and crawl into their sleeping bags for some well-deserved sack time, But too often, *Stars and Stripes* reporters showed up to interview the returning Marines, cutting into their much-needed rest.

You were glad you got back. I mean you made it again, you know. You were always questioning what was happening to your close friends. Because sometimes not everyone would come back. Then you'd have your little rehearsal in the morning, what went on that night before with the 2nd Lieutenant, before you went in front of the higher-ups, and Stars and Stripes.

When I asked what other nations and units were fighting alongside the Marines in his area, John said it was often Turks and Canadians. Also thrown in the mix were the 25th and 24th U.S. Army Divisions. Commenting on the Turks, John explained they were a rough bunch of warriors. As for the Canadians, John mentioned that they were a good source for anything you needed. Once back in reserve, John and other Marines and GIs often traded American cigarettes for booze. The liquor offered by the Canadians was usually vodka and gin, not the first choice for the Americans, but it did the job.

They always had some booze, them guys did. Which we were trading them for, probably our cigarettes or something like that. I never smoked, so we always had a lot of cigarettes there. When we got back, they all gave us cigarettes when we were there; that's the only reason I kept them, though. The only reason I used them was for bartering with them or to buy something else. So, Canadians were, I think they had it a little better than we did. What I figured out about them Turks is they smelled damn strong. They never took a bath, you know, they'd clean up, but they were a dirty bunch of guys. They were supposed to be a rough bunch, but they got pushed around too, just like everybody else. There were Turk casualties, and they lost ground too and took it back. So, I'd say the Turks were no better a unit than anybody else.

The common bill of fare for John and his brother Marines when on the outposts or above the MLR on the frontline was C-rations or A-rations. Occasionally, and it was a rare commodity, they'd get their hands on some eggs, which he'd boil or cook with the Spam that was sent from home in care packages. For Christmas and Thanksgiving, a full spread of the traditional holiday menu was distributed throughout Korea. It was often unheated, but at least John and his buddies got to enjoy a decent-tasting meal. For John, when on the front lines, it was beans and franks, a meal a guy could eat every day if he had to. Occasionally, chocolate bars and hot chocolate, along with coffee, would make it up to the trenches for the battered Marines. John also described that these activities—eating, sleeping, and cleaning up the best you could—all happened during the day, mainly in the mornings.

> We got back to reserves, then we'd have, they'd have some of these portable setups, you know, where we could get hot food. But when you're on the front there was very little, only C-rations, you know.

John was almost continuously on the front line, facing enemy assaults that mostly occurred at night, with the usual blaring bugles, chimes, whistles, and screaming enemy soldiers, the strategy designed to demoralize, confuse, and scare the Marines. Instead, John and E Company would meet the Chinese with a devastating toll of weapons, with the most feared being Willy Peter—white phosphorus grenades—and mortar shells. White phosphorus is deadly and effective. Once the grenade explodes, it sends up a cloud of smoke with particles that cover the area like a blanket. White phosphorus ignites on contact with air. It burns fiercely and sets fire to cloth, fuel, ammunition, and other combustibles. The moment WP touches a human body it causes severe burns and is extremely difficult to extinguish.

John was the second Marine to talk about "Box Me In" support: calling in artillery to shell your own position because you're being overrun. Then there's no choice but to hunker down, take cover, and pray. This time, the call was put out to the 11th Marines below the MLR, to smother their position with all the Willy Peter on hand.

> Well, you try and lay as flat as you can. That's about the biggest thing, otherwise you might take a round. When mortars and artillery are coming, and they had a lot of duds, and of course you don't know which side it is. Things were coming down there making a ssshhh sound. Like that's going and all of sudden it thumps, and when it does that, it doesn't go off, well, you're pretty god damn happy. But we'd

fight them off and get out of our bunkers and holes and start fighting again. I had several of them close to me that went thump and nothin' happened. They didn't go off. I remember that plain as day.

Even though John got lucky with occasional duds, plenty of ordnance did go off.

Actually, you could be pretty close to a round that would hit, and if you'd have your helmet towards it or if you'd be lying nice and flat, you'd be okay, you'd probably get a hell of a concussion, but you get lucky that way.

This hero's battle experiences lasted right up to the last minutes of the war, when he witnessed the ceasefire going into effect. There's a saying, "A million-dollar wound is the one that sends you home." John was hit twice on July 27, 1953, the last day of the war.

Although his memory is sharp as a tack, he told me that it's hard to remember in which of the battles these events took place; it's just a constant feeling of wanting to survive, mixed with always being on the move. On patrol the morning of July 27, John and his squad walked into an ambush that was zeroed in by Chinese mortars. While taking cover, he received shrapnel wounds. Getting out of the firefight and back to their line, John and his squad braced for the coming attacks as the Chinese made one final push to gain ground for a victory.

I don't think I've seen any darkness then through the last three days. It was just, the sky was just completely lit up, everything going off like fireworks. It was like a fireworks show. And I can tell you, I don't need no damn Fourth of July celebration. I seen enough fireworks in the last three days of Korea. It was really hot. A lot of artillery and mortars and there was a lot, lot of casualties taken in the last two days. 'Cause I was hit with shrapnel about probably nine to nine-thirty in the morning the day it ended. I got bandaged up and there were so many more casualties yet.

The fighting lasted until the very last minute, and the moment the ceasefire went into effect, you could almost hear a pin drop. John was wounded again about an hour before it ended and was evacuated to an aid station below the MLR. It seemed both sides gave it everything they had until the very last minute, as mentioned in a few previous chapters.

However, John never experienced the shaking of hands and trading between Marines and Chinese. Hearing this perspective of the war again made me feel like it was just a waste of life for nothing; they knew it was over, yet still fought to the very end. And for what? I'm sure at the time, all the troops on the ground from both sides didn't know. The casualty rates in the last days of the war were absolutely staggering; an accurate figure doesn't exist. John was the first veteran to tell me he saw the soldier who shot him.

I was shot at from the back of me, more or less. I was looking this way, then this guy came in the back and shot me. That's when I went, WOO! That really hurt, hurt me a lot. Otherwise, all the other ones I could handle. I think a problem when you get hit, I can see why people go into shock and ah, the shock comes from loss of blood.

I think you lose too much, and you get a little weak. And I know I was getting weak when I was laying back there. I was, I was a little dizzy or whatever. I knew I was probably gonna have a little problem with shock and tried to talk myself out of it or whatever.

Moments after John was hit, a fellow Marine dispatched the Chinese soldier who had almost killed him. Luckily for John, he was evacuated immediately by a Navy corpsman and taken below the MLR for treatment.

When they shut it down, you know. Then everybody just went and picked up their dead, the guys told me. And ah, they even talked to one or other. You know, it was kind of weird hearing that. I was damn glad it was over. Just like a baseball game or a football game, or anything else. Everybody kind of shook hands and was glad it was over with. I didn't see that. I was evacuated before that.

When he was wounded, John thought he'd lost his arm, but checking himself after getting the cobwebs cleared, he saw he was in one piece. By the time he reached the aid station, the ceasefire had been called, and the war was over with everyone celebrating, including the doctors and medical staff. It seemed everyone was having a good time except John, who was still dealing with the pain of his wound. He was lying on his cot when a doctor approached.

"Get him ready," he says ... and he laid down right alongside of me and took a little nap. He woke up and I knew he was drinking. Then he got up and he operated on my arm and that's it. I had no problems. He did a good job, the guy did a good job, even if he had a few drinks. It didn't bother me any.

We both shared a good laugh: a wounded Marine, expecting to be operated on and taken care of, and the doctor taking a drunken nap right next to him on his cot.

They finally removed the bullet and other pieces of shrapnel, cleaned and redressed his wounds, and that was it. John explained it was a big deal if the cloth of your dungaree was pushed in by the bullet or shrapnel because of the potential outbreak of hemorrhagic fever that affects all the organs and slowly shuts the body down preventing normal function, and you'd die a slow painful death.

I think they were worried about hemorrhagic fever at that time. 'Cause, any time you get hit with shrapnel, that shrapnel pushes the clothes in, you know your dungarees. There was so many rats around there and that's what was carrying that hemorrhagic fever. So, I think they were worried about you getting that hemorrhagic fever from the dirty clothes. The shrapnel and bullets itself were clean, 'cause it was hot. So no problem there, where that cloth that was pushed into the wound could give it to you. We lost a lot of men from that.

After his transfer to the USS *Haven*, a Navy hospital ship, he boarded a plane to Japan for further recovery. Finally home in Wisconsin, he discovered his lifelong love for the Green Bay Packers football team. As a passionate fan, he began renting and running buses to Lambeau Field for every home game, starting this venture

John Breske with Ryan Walkowski at a Green Bay Packers game after taking Breske's Packers bus.

in the early 1960s. John also opened a barber shop that he operated for many years, even cutting my dad's hair while he was growing up. But few ever knew he was a brave Marine who served so gallantly during the Korean War ... the Forgotten War.

I was fortunate enough to snag a last-minute seat on one of his buses, catching a ride to Lambeau Field with my friend Dylan. Although the Packers didn't win against the Buccaneers, it was an awesome experience to ride with John and attend a game with this ninety-two-year-old combat Marine veteran. Before the game the bus parked at the Green Bay Resch Center, and John rolled the red carpet, offering coolers of drinks and trays of food. A conversation quickly sparked between us. People not knowing who I was, which is fine, told me I was talking to a Hall of Famer. I told them, "I know that, but I'm also talking to a Marine who served his country in Korea and is a featured veteran in my upcoming book."

John Breske and Ryan Walkowski enjoying those last two ice-cold Busch Light beers from the Elderon Fourth of July parade, 2024.

I went to my first Packers game when I came home from Korea. I was wounded, and I was in a hospital in San Francisco. And uh, I went to church Sunday morning and after church I went to a Wisconsin tavern they had there, and someone came through and said the Packers are playing in town today. So about ten of us went to the game. That was at Kezar Stadium. And uh, we got in free because we had our uniforms on. I would say there were probably ten thousand people at that game, and that was in 1953. I've been going ever since.

In 2023, John was nominated for the Green Bay Packers Fan Hall of Fame. Some very deserving nominees were also on the slate, but this old Marine—recipient of the Silver Star and a Purple Heart, and dedicated Packers fan—beat them all.

I see John from time to time at Mark's Bar in Elderon and a few other spots, when he ventures out with his wife. I'm always happy and proud to buy them drinks. One thing for sure, I have every intention of riding John Breske's bus to a lot more games.

Final note: On July 4, 2024, at John's hometown holiday parade, I rode with him in my 1946 Willys, a Jeep which I made up to look like it served in the Korean War. I was representing both the local VFW Post and one of Elderon's favorite local establishments—Mark's Bar. The Post Commander and I surprised John with the invitation, and he was thrilled. He said that his last Jeep ride was in Korea. Along the way, Katelyn, my girlfriend at the time, was handing out candy to the kids and dishing out ice-cold Busch Light beer to the adults from the back of the Jeep (provided graciously by Mark's Bar owner Tara). At the end of the parade, she saved two cans of beer, which John and I enjoyed together, a perfect ending to this journey.

Conclusion

The End of One Journey ... the Beginning of the Next

Ryan Walkowski

If someone told me one day I'd be a published author, I'd have laughed and left them standing there talking to themselves. A writer? Not this blue-collar kid from northern Wisconsin. I never dreamed I'd be traveling the country interviewing a dying breed of forgotten warriors, but I did, with almost three years of sleepless nights on the road, catching naps at truck stops because I couldn't afford a motel, and too many days away from home that have cost me heartache and heartbreak. My determination and zeal documenting Korean War veterans has, in most cases, been more fervent than some of my relationships, which suffered because of my passion for and obsession with this project. I've seen cities and towns I never thought I'd visit, just to capture a moment of history with a grizzled soldier, sailor, and Marine. Countless miles have been put on my vehicle—not to mention all those flights to destinations unknown for brief visits that often felt like home, thanks to my interviewees' hospitality and graciousness. During this time I lost my mother, one of my biggest advocates, and it really tears at me knowing she'll never see the finished product. There's the same regret, with too many of the veterans I've documented no longer with us. But that's life, isn't it?

I hadn't done a lot of things right in life, but documenting and honoring these veterans had to be done and was the right thing to do. I'm proud to have helped tell their stories. In a sense, writing has become my therapy, and I owe this newfound relief to featured veteran and author Ed Gruber, now ninety-six years young. Ed didn't have to help me along this exciting and fulfilling road, but he did. For his patience and for his mentoring—he called it a "labor of love"—I will forever be grateful.

Do I now know as much as the historians? Of course not, but I do know that hearing history firsthand from the men who made that history is an education money can't buy. And the best part is that our readers get to also share these significant memories.

It was remarkable and surreal, and sometimes sorrowful, when combat veterans opened up their memory banks and their hearts, especially when bringing up wartime events bottled up for more than seventy years. For reasons unknown, and I may never know why, they trusted me enough to tell me things they never told their own families. I will never understand what our veterans went through, but maybe, just maybe, these interviews helped bring some peace of mind to even a few.

Important to note is that every dollar donated was used strictly for travel expenses. All proceeds from book sales will go toward a video documentary, and toward a Korean War memorial that's already in the planning stages, to be placed at the new Elderon VFW Post 8068, where the Commander has guaranteed a sanctified and prominent site. I don't know how to sufficiently give back to the veterans in this book who have given me so much, but every one of their names, along with those not featured that I have documented, will be on that memorial.

Finally, my journey to honor America's wartime veterans is not over. While I continue to document Korean War veterans, I have moved to other historic eras as well. I don't see myself ever stopping.

To all my readers, thank you for joining me on this amazing journey. God bless our veterans. God bless our military. God bless America.

War Statistics
The Korean War
June 25, 1950–July 27, 1953

American Casualties
33,651 Killed
103,284 Wounded
8,271 Missing

Index

Across the Blue Pacific 87

Bloody Ridge 68, 80
Boulder City 185
Bunker Hill 128, 129, 130, 143, 145, 146, 151

Chorwon Valley 118
Chosin Resevoir, 40, 41, 43, 47, 57, 59, 95

FNG 22, 182

Heartbreak Ridge 68, 70, 71, 81, 83
Hill 104 104, 105
Hope, Bob 89, 90

Inchon 15, 24, 33, 38, 42, 51, 52
Iron Triangle 118

Jamestown Line 148

Kapaun, Father Emil 34

Mize, Ola 115, 116
MLR (main line of resistance) 116, 127, 139, 158, 167, 171, 176, 177, 183, 185, 188, 198, 202
Munsan-ni 95, 96

Naktong River 12, 13, 14, 15

Operation Little Switch 32
Operation Pole Charge 107
Osan 7, 8
Out Post Dagmar 168
Out Post Esther 168

Panmunjom 94
Pearl Harbor 89, 90
Pork Chop Hill 174, 175, 176, 177
Punch Bowl 68
Pyongtaek 9

Red Cloud, Mitchell, Jr. 17

7th Fleet 84

Taejon 9, 10, 11, 12
Task Force Smith 7
Toktong Pass 56, 59

Unsan 25, 34

Wayne, John 88

Yalu River 15

www.ingramcontent.com/pod-product-compliance
Lightning Source LLC
Chambersburg PA
CBHW060343010526
44117CB00017B/2940